BE — A DISCIPLE'S JOURNEY

To Cerys

BE

— A DISCIPLE'S JOURNEY

Simon Edwards

RELEASING LEADERSHIP

First published in Great Britain in 2013
by
RELEASING LEADERSHIP
79, Church Road, Combe Down, Bath BA2 5JQ

ISBN 978-0-9576038-0-6

Printed in Great Britain
by Imprint Digital, Exeter

Contents

Almighty God, whose Son Jesus Christ, the Lord of all life, came not to be served but to serve, help us to be masters of ourselves that we may be servants of others and teach us to Serve to Lead, through the same Jesus Christ, Our Lord, Amen.

The Collect of the Royal Military Academy, Sandhurst

As the body without the spirit is dead, so faith without deeds is dead.

James 2:26, NIV

1

A Culture of Fear?

"I can now go straight because for the first time in my life someone believes in me." *A prisoner*

To be or not to be?

It was 11.11 a.m. on 11 November 2004 – Remembrance Day. We stood in silence in a soulless room in the heart of Bristol Prison, quietly reflecting on the sacrifice that had given us the freedom to be there at that moment, though we all knew that some of us had the freedom to leave and some of us didn't. We were an extraordinary mix: a former Army Officer, the chairman of a top headhunting company, a jeweller, a senior officer from the Probation Service, and various prison staff. We were there to mark the graduation of the first seven prisoners to have completed the *Beyond* programme, a transitional mentoring initiative for those leaving prison under the auspices of *Believe*, a charity I had set up two years earlier. Here was an extraordinary array of backgrounds brought together in a relationship, which would have a profound effect on everyone present. For me, the act of Remembrance in a prison brought together my old life and the new life I was being called to, the fruition of which is still a work in progress.

I attended my first Discharge Board in Bristol Prison in April 2002. I witnessed ten prisoners who were due for release – in varying degrees of hopelessness. Eight were drug addicts, seven had nowhere to live on release. How they all got there was not at this stage apparent. What struck me at the time was that each was a unique human being with endless potential. I recalled the occasion when I first met this group of prisoners. Their life stories had many common threads – individual lives that hadn't had a chance since the moment they were conceived. This is not to excuse their behaviour, but to seek to understand it.

Tough on crime; tough on the causes of crime became the mantra of New Labour, a phrase used by Tony Blair to signal a new approach to law and order. Interestingly, in his autobiography, Tony Blair gives the credit for it to Gordon Brown. But it remains a mantra as society continues to insist on being tough on crime without either understanding or addressing the causes of crime. During the riots in the summer of 2011, the voices of revenge were far more vociferous than those which sought out the reasons why. I had the following letter published in *The Times* immediately after the riots:

When the moral outrage has subsided and the tough talk dissipates as the news agenda moves on to the next crisis, there is a need to understand. We can no longer paper over the cracks of a subset of our society, many of whom are represented by the 20% of 16 -24 year olds who are not only unemployed, but unemployable. They have been let down by dysfunctional families and an education system that has become so focused on getting 50% of young people to university that it overlooked the rest. They do not feel as though they have a stake in the society that now condemns them. The only role models in their lives are gang leaders and drug dealers. There is nothing to look forward to and little hope that there ever will be. Young men, who made up the majority of the rioters, have been particularly let down. They yearn for respect and have been encouraged by society that this is earned by what you possess rather than who you are. They need a positive outlet for their energy and a cause greater than themselves. One of the main motivations for the rioters was the sheer excitement of it all. The final paragraph of the letter, which wasn't published, went on to say:

The world is now looking at the UK as the host of the Olympics with understandable concern. We have shown that we are capable of investing over £10bn in an event for the world's elite. It is time to invest in those that are not the elite to allow them to fulfil their potential too. The Olympic motto is 'Live as One'. If we fail to understand the lessons from these riots and address the root causes behind them we will continue to live in a divided society.

We talk about equality being a human right, but we don't live it. How does a young man naively placing a post on the internet inciting people to riot (when he thought he was just messing around) compare with an MP and government minister knowingly defrauding the taxpayer of £56k? Yet one is imprisoned for four years and the other is suspended from the House of Commons for seven days. Why was it that the authorities pursued the rioters with such vigour, when those who used their positions to manipulate the interest rates in banks in the City of London were not? Who created the greater damage? How do we expect young people to respect the rule of law when they see travesties like this every day? Yet in discovering why it was that thousands of young people, mainly men, exploded onto the streets of our cities, mindlessly looting and destroying, we can find something profound about ourselves and the world that we have created.

An only life can take so long to climb clear of its wrong beginnings and may never. *Philip Larkin*

I began to understand this through the lives of people like a 21-year old called Tom, one of that first group in Bristol prison. His life story typified that of many I have worked with. He never knew his father. His mother had a series of lovers, one of whom decided it would be good sport to rape the 5-year old Tom with some of his mates. A BBC Panorama documentary in 2004 reported the case of a circuit judge in Plymouth who, when trying the case of a serial sex offender, realised that he recognised most of the witnesses. *I can't talk about individual cases. But when I looked up to the gallery that day I recognised a lot of faces that had been before me again and again and again....* It dawned on him that they had all been up in front of him for some crime or other, and usually fairly often. Of the seventeen men who gave evidence against the defendant, every single one was known to the police. Apart from one minor offence for shoplifting, none of them had offended before they were abused.

The clear conclusion was that there was a direct link between the sexual abuse and the criminal behaviour. Abuse of this sort places particular shame on the victim, who would rather live with the guilt than report it. That carefree innocence of childhood is brutally ripped away as a desperate reality of life kicks in. Unconditional freedom freezes in a bottomless lake of childhood fear. Fear of others who are different, fear of not wearing the right clothes, fear of not being in the right group, fear of failure and, worst of all, a fear of taking responsibility. It eats away inside leading to very low self-esteem and disengagement from social interaction including education. Tom was no different and ended up being excluded from school at the age of fourteen as his teachers could no longer deal with him.

Drug dealers love excluded kids, since they are looking for an escape from the grim reality of their lives while also seeking a way of maintaining a livelihood. Tom was no exception and he was soon hooked on cannabis. In order to maintain the habit he started stealing just to survive. For brief moments life was bearable. He soon ended up in prison and was introduced to heroin there, which further dulled the pain. Interestingly, when he entered prison his drug of choice, as it is for many, was cannabis. But like all prisoners he found himself subject to random drug testing and discovered that while cannabis stays within the blood stream for twenty-eight days, heroin or crack cocaine only last twenty-four hours. It's a no-brainer. His addiction drove his crime for many years and he became what is termed a prolific offender, one who re-offends within a short time of release, usually just to feed his habit. One of the most pressing reforms needed in our judicial system is to tackle this root cause of crime by making proper drug rehabilitation available for those in prison. Some might argue that a decriminalisation of drugs is the only solution. It seems counter-intuitive to keep one of the largest industries in the world entirely in the hands of criminals. Prohibition didn't work in the US in the 1930s and isn't working now.

What struck me at the time was that Tom, like the others, was a unique human being with endless potential. Society was quite happy to see that potential rot and pay the price for it. But could I? I have always been very struck by the words of Jimmy Reid, the Glaswegian trade union leader who talked of walking through the tenements of his city:

Behind every one of these windows is somebody who might be a horse-jumping champion, a Formula One racing champion, a yachtsman of great degree, but he'll never know because he'll never step on a yacht or Formula

One car – he'll never get the chance.

There is approximately 20% of the population, often generationally unemployed, usually unemployable, for whom this is true. The words 'aspiration' and 'opportunity' do not generally feature in their vocabulary. My reflections at the time were, with the benefit of hindsight, poignant. Am I able to walk away from this? Is it just too difficult? Most of them are there because their life outside is without hope – no home, no job, no family. At least there in prison they have a roof over their heads and three square meals a day. It costs more than twice the annual fees of Eton to keep each one in prison, but without the benefit.

Am I to lay down my career, risk the future of my wife and children? But how, now I have seen this, can I walk away? It is a huge challenge, yet if I, with all my shortcomings, walk away, who will pick up the baton?

Churchill famously said that the treatment of crime and criminals is one of the unfailing tests of the civilisation of any country. For me this was the start of a voyage of discovery, both through experience and internal reflection, to try to understand how we measure up today. It is a journey about human behaviour and why we are the way we are. It has taken me from schools to prisons, from boardrooms to the Arabian desert, from the challenges of entrepreneurship to the human casualties of modern warfare. Yet it is a universal journey where I discovered that we are all, to some extent, locked into prisons of our own making – prisons primarily determined by fear:

> Love is what we are born with.
> Fear is what we learn here. *Anon.*

Justice can get lost somewhere between the twin towers of deterrence and revenge. Prisons exist principally because of the public fear of those inside them: currently approximately 88000 souls. For centuries, an 'out of sight, out of mind' approach has allowed us to sleep easily in our beds at night, in the knowledge that these beastly criminals are locked up behind bars. Revenge, however it is dressed up, still seems to be the prime motivator. But, I wonder, would you sleep so easily if you met some of these poor souls, people like Tom, for whom life as it should be – could be– is still unknown territory. For those who enjoy statistics (I am not a great fan since they are used to justify anything you want to hear), 70% are suffering from some sort of mental health problem, 50% are under the influence of drugs either illegal or prescribed (such as methadone [the heroin substitute]), and more than 50% have learning or literacy difficulties. More than 60% re-offend within two years; for young offenders the figure is 80%. Many have nowhere to live when they are released and most are unemployable. Is this a way to run a prison system in the 21st century? Are you able to sleep easy at night knowing that our own justice system is content to preside over such injustice? As Tom's story illustrates, until we understand the root causes, we will never end the cycle of re-offending. As long as fear determines our response, the potential of people like Tom will never be realised.

Fear defines the story that underpins our culture. It is a fear of other people. It is a fear of not having enough, a fear that we are not quite as good as the next person. It is a fear of not having as much as the next man. The pursuit of executive pay is driven not by the level of remuneration, but by peer comparison: the fear that someone might have a better package than you. It is a fear of being different – so we spend fortunes on creating conformity, overlooking the simple fact that, as human beings, we are the same. It is a fear of the unknown – the uncertainty of tomorrow. It is a fear that stems from the breakdown in normal relationship. It is the fear of failure. It is a fear of taking responsibility. We seem to invest more and more in the avoidance of failure and the responsibility for it. It has led to numerous high profile cases such as the Mid Staffordshire NHS Trust scandal. The author of the report, Robert Francis QC, says this:

> I heard so many stories of shocking care. These patients were not simply numbers they were husbands, wives, sons, daughters, fathers, mothers, grandparents. They were people who entered Stafford Hospital and rightly expected to be well cared for and treated. Instead, many suffered horrific experiences that will haunt them and their loved ones for the rest of their lives.
>
> The Inquiry found that a chronic shortage of staff, particularly nursing staff, was largely responsible for the substandard care. Morale at the Trust was low, and while many staff did their best in difficult circumstances, others showed a disturbing lack of compassion towards their patients. Staff who spoke out felt ignored and there is strong evidence that many were deterred from doing so through fear and bullying.

We are so afraid to get things wrong that we have consigned even the most human of functions as nursing to processes, which soon become more important than the patients. This is what happened in the Mid Staffordshire NHS Trust. Basic human compassion went out of the window as managers became obsessed by ticking boxes. What is needed across the caring professions is less qualification and more human kindness. Like the canary down the mine, these are wake-up calls to us all. Is this the culture that we want to pass on to our grandchildren?

There is nothing wrong with failure. Every human achievement has been preceded by years of failure, yet we so often hear the puerile phrase *failure is not an option*. Well sorry to disappoint, but it is not only an option, it is essential, and every child should be allowed to fail from time to time. *There's no success like failure* said Bob Dylan. There is little to learn from success, but in the pit of failure there is bountiful learning. It takes courage to take the risk of going there, but this is where we discover how we can become all that we could be. That can be a frightening prospect!

Instead, we have created the culture of a machine where we are all individual cogs in an engine that fears scarcity and demands uniformity, control, order and predictability driven to greater efficiencies, and relentless economic growth, an engine we drive harder and harder. We demand that the engine starts each day with the predictability of a reliable car. We see it in our financial systems, we see it in education through the relentless pursuit of targets, we see it in politics where there is a fear of tackling the really important issues, we see it in our criminal justice system which continues to operate, as we have seen, from the perspective of the least attractive of human responses – revenge. We see it in our child protection and as we have noted, we now see it in our hospitals. And all for what?

When we individually and collectively ran out of money to feed the consumerist monster, we drove reluctant mothers out to work; when there weren't enough days in the week to shop, we started shopping on Sundays; when that wasn't enough, we encouraged debt so that people could continue to buy whilst putting off payment to another day. Then, in 2008, the bubble burst and the reality of what we had created became apparent. We continue to invest billions in this engine, trying to create certainty in an inherently uncertain world in denial of what has already taken place. Miraculously, we can find another £100 billion to bail out a national economy for a day to keep the markets at bay: an expensive plaster for an ever-gaping wound. In his sermon at the service to mark the Diamond Jubilee of the Queen, the Archbishop of Canterbury, Dr Rowan Williams, referred to the ludicrousness of greed. Greed is not only about the acquisition of wealth, it is about trying to hang on to what you have when reality makes this impossible. Surely it is time to recognise that maintaining this failing economic machine, servicing invisible markets, is no longer worth the human cost.

We have bought into the culture that generates dissatisfaction in order to generate growth – *"because you're worth it"*, in the language of the advertiser. We are inundated with images on a daily basis telling us that we are not good enough, but if we buy this new dress or this new aftershave our world will be transformed. So we go out and buy it with money we don't have, feel guilty half an hour later, and our world doesn't change ... until the next advertisement persuades us to go out and buy again. We have forgotten the human factor. We are seeing the warning signs of a system that is deeply flawed, failing, and will collapse. People are squeezed between process and profit. There is now too big a gap between the world we have created and the way it should work, and the world is fighting back. The industrial model upon which our current institutions were founded was based on controlling the masses. No longer could we deal with human beings as individuals. The building blocks of human society, the family and the community have been eroded as we have sought to control, failing to understand the complex web of interdependent relationships in which people were all connected to each other and aware of our shared environment. We have sub-contracted personal responsibility to hierarchies where we have trusted those at the pinnacle to have the greater knowledge and therefore the better ability to lead. But hierarchies create childish behaviour, reducing individual responsibility and confidence. When *something must be done*, it is always someone else who must do it, never us.

We are creating a perfect storm of diminishing resources, growing food prices, global terrorism, rapid environmental changes, corruption, disease and famine, combined with a breakdown in the world economies, social injustice, and a moral vacuum in our politics, law enforcement and journalism. It is a world that conspires to feed the most primitive aspect of the human condition – survival motivated by fear, ambition, self-interest, and a sense that since 'everyone' behaves like this it must be OK. There is a separation between what is legal and what is moral that demeans both. And if we try to protest we soon discover that power and wealth doesn't like to be criticised. Furthermore, the institutions that have allowed themselves to be driven by the lowest human values will discover that their very existence is threatened as people become aware of their behaviour. The banks are beginning to realise, reluctantly, that their continued existence relies upon them having an ethical framework, a set of values that determines the behaviour of those they employ.

How little personal responsibility there is in our leaders these days. When something goes wrong they so often find someone else lower down the food chain to take the blame, failing to understand that, as leaders, they are responsible for the governance and the culture that determines the behaviour of those for whom they are responsible.

We human beings are about to snap like an elastic band under pressure. Public discourse is full of righteous anger as we collectively realise that the hierarchies we have paid homage to for so long no longer serve us. So much has become corrupted. We live in a world where the 'seven deadly sins' are tangible, where greed and envy are underpinned by lust and coated in a layer of pride and an anger that recognises that our souls are out of kilter with the world we have created. And we are too lazy to do anything about it.

Because another great fear is of change. Change is unpredictable, uncertain and unmanageable. We stand before an abyss of change so profound that life as we have lived it will never be the same. We face stark choices. We can continue to live in denial and believe that a culture of relentless economic growth whatever the human and environmental cost is the only game in town. We can continue to throw money that we don't have to service the debt that threatens to bankrupt nations. We can wait for the messy changes to our world that now seem inevitable, over which we have no control – or, individually and collectively, we *become* the change.

So the challenge for the future lies within each of us. We should no longer look to institutions and government to solve all our big problems. Many solutions lie within. Countless books have been written about happiness, and the coalition government in the UK has placed 'well-being' on the political agenda. But the truth is that happiness and well-being are elusive, and are often transient when found. I believe that both are only achieved when we have discovered who we are, our purpose in God's plan, and our place in the world. Then we can live a life of complete authenticity, truth and creativity, working to our strengths effortlessly, and use this knowledge to make a tangible, worthwhile difference.

My life has been happy because I never had any uncertainty about the meaning of the word 'good', the meaning of the word 'true', the meaning of the word 'beautiful' and the meaning of words like 'original' and 'new'.

Jacob Bronowski

We live in a largely unhappy world, a world in crisis. The world we took for granted has demonstrated its frailty. The world has lost its way. There is a crisis of leadership in a world that is facing a level of complexity combined with challenges that threaten its continued survival. The concept of leadership being defined through meritocracy in pursuit of wealth and power has been so undermined in recent years as to make it redundant as far as the needs and aspirations of the twenty-first century are concerned. Leadership is underpinned by human behaviour, and in the post-modern world of relative morality, anything goes. The ends are seen as justifying the means. So we have witnessed the behaviour of our politicians lining their pockets, the bankers who have presided over the collapse of the world economy while pursuing their own self-interested greed. Money trumps everything. It is often said that markets are amoral, and at one level this is true. But the markets are run by human beings, who are capable of acting within a moral framework. It used to be said in the City of London that a gentleman's word was his bond. Trust was essential. But the banking crises since 2008 are indicative of a system that has become separated from the moral values that used to underpin it. We have created technology that is able to generate hundreds of billions of pounds of transactions in one investment bank in a single day. Those who run banks have often had insufficient oversight of these systems or of those operating them. The banks now find it difficult to lend money since they have no framework beyond the process within which they can assess the suitability of those to whom they lend. There is no personal relationship. In the days when everyone had a personal bank manager, a relationship was possible. The manager knew the individual and their circumstances and was able to assess their suitability for a loan. We understood that relationship was foundational to human interaction. 'The computer says no' has become a mantra of our age – an acceptance that we no longer value the human element in our transactions.

We have seen journalists descend into criminal activity in order to get a good story. We have seen a failure of leadership in the church as it hovers on the fence of human morality. At its best it seems to be more concerned with the smaller issues of order and procedure than confronting the mighty challenges of an unchristlike world. The pace of change demands a new level of leadership. The current emperor of leadership has been without clothes now for so long that he has becomme a shivering wreck.

I include the following text to offer an alternative perspective. It is taken from a speech by Paul Hawken, environmental entrepreneur and founder of Wiser Earth:

When asked if I am pessimistic or optimistic about the future, my answer is always the same: If you look at the science about what is happening on earth and aren't pessimistic, you don't understand data. But if you meet the people who are working to restore this earth and the lives of the poor, and you aren't optimistic, you haven't got a pulse. What I see everywhere in the world are ordinary people willing to confront despair, power, and incalculable odds in order to restore some semblance of grace, justice, and beauty to this world. The poet Adrienne Rich wrote, "So much has been destroyed I have cast my lot with those who, age after age, perversely, with no extraordinary power, reconstitute the world." There could be no better description. Humanity is coalescing. It is reconstituting the world, and the action is taking place in schoolrooms, farms, jungles, villages, campuses, companies, refugee camps, deserts, fisheries, and slums.

You join a multitude of caring people. No one knows how many groups and organisations are working on the most salient issues of our day: climate change, poverty, deforestation, peace, water, hunger, conservation, human rights, and more. This is the largest movement the world has ever seen.

Rather than control, it seeks connection. Rather than dominance, it strives to disperse concentrations of power. It works behind the scenes and gets the job done. Large as it is, no one knows the true size of this movement. It provides hope, support, and meaning to billions of people in the world. Its clout resides in idea, not in force.

This is the elusive Big Society and it is happening, but it is happening from the bottom up. Politicians, by their very nature, have a minimal role to play. Until they learn to let go of power and the means to support it, they will be stuck in the old paradigm. Leadership is no longer about power and money, it is about the common good. We need to have the confidence to embrace a new approach where we take the lead, where we become the change. And the only way of finding out is making that act of faith, taking that first step into uncertainty where we can begin to reveal the certainty of our being. We remember those who have died to give us freedom – the freedom to choose between the prison of fear and the liberation of being. It is a choice between the worst and the best of the human condition and never has the world depended more on our making the right choice and taking a lead.

This movement across the world is real, but it is not exclusively Christian. Indeed the vast majority of it isn't, since Christians have not been equipped for mission. Yet in many ways the church has been doing the Big Society for two thousand years. All the great social reforms – abolition of slavery, education, hospitals, prison rehabilitation – have been initiated by Christians. If all those Christians who quietly work away each day with the homeless, the outcasts, the lonely and the poor withdrew their free labour, the government would be unable to cope. Yet Christians have just forgotten to tell people or provide living examples in a way that make a tangible impact on the world today. I was talking to a group of wounded soldiers about the challenges of disengaged youth. One of them said, *They don't stand a chance these days. The only role models they have are celebrities who are only celebrities because they are celebrities, and overpaid, poorly behaved, footballers. Isn't it about time for the good people to step up?*

What is immediately provoked by this statement is: so define 'good' people! This tempts us to step straight into judgement, and potentially that 'holier than thou' mindset that allows some people to think they are better than others. The truth is that we are all sinners, and the first challenge is to acknowledge this. We all have the potential to choose good or evil, and wherever we look in the world, the darker side of human nature, the propensity to sin, is seen in the raw. Because I am a Christian I know that Christ died to save me from the penalty of sin, but sin confronts me every moment of my life. I should be aware of my own sin, but that does not mean I should be going around judging others. My experience has been that the grace of God (a free gift, seen supremely in the sacrifice of Jesus for my sake) allows me to know both that I can repent and be forgiven, and that he then wants to unlock all the potential in what he has given me, and goes on giving me. I love this about my faith – I am then entrusted with this gift of real life.

There needs to be a shift from the hierarchical, people imposing power and control on other people and always seeking someone else to take responsibility, to being released in freedom, marked by right relationships with others – taking responsibility under the Lordship of Christ, whom we are serving. In the thought of St Augustine, true freedom is the freedom to pursue what is good in life.

Change means risk, and risk means the possibility of failure and judgment. Christ sets us free to take the risk of failure. We are free to attempt to do the right thing, in the knowledge that even if we mess up, we live under the grace of God that allows us to be forgiven and wipe the slate clean. Every time we mess up, we learn. Every time we learn, we get closer to God and can become instruments of good in the world.

Those brought up in other religions also need that freedom of which I am speaking. Many are bound by a rigidity and a fear of making mistakes that goes with a legalistic system of outward conformity.

Of course we need to live within an appropriate framework of laws in society – laws which should be just, to encourage what is good and to restrain the worst manifestations of wickedness and vice that endanger others. Anarchy would not be freedom, so we need laws in order to exist as the fallen human beings we are. Our Judeo-Christian heritage has shaped the law of our land. But it is hardly surprising that Christianity gets such a poor press when its exponents spend proportionately more time judging than loving. Judgment offers certainty: there are rules, which we either obey – good, or disobey – bad. Everyone knows where they are!

Christianity set the early believers free from the outward observances of many of the regulations in the law of Moses. In that sense, faith set people free from that particular law. But what we could call 'licence' is not the way either. We have been given free will, but with that comes the responsibility – as was expressed for me in the Sandhurst Collect – to master ourselves. It is only when we become aware of our shortcomings that we are able to work on them. Self-discipline is a New Testament precept. We recall that, in a particular situation, Christ said that one who was without sin could cast the first stone at a sinner caught in the act. There weren't any takers in that incident, and we are reminded not to have a harsh, judgemental attitude toward others who have fallen.

Christianity is interesting and subtle. It acknowledges the sin up front, but offers us the means to overcome it – God's grace, love, opportunities for repentance, assurance of forgiveness, a living relationship with a living Lord.

It always amuses me, and it is a beautiful irony that others might like to share, that those who rush to judgment are sometimes reflecting something within themselves. I may be judging the arrogance of others because, at one level, I am aware of, and fear, my own arrogance. I may judge the greed in others, because I am aware of and fear the greed in myself. I may judge the anger in others because I am aware, and fear, the anger in myself.

This is something of what this book is about – the ability to acknowledge the gift of the awareness of sin as marking a route to finding something better. This is an encouragement to step up and start to make an impact on the world. It is not a 'religious' thing – though it is based on the example of Christ, simply because there is no better foundation. His life, death and resurrection reminds us of why we exist. Following him as his disciples, we discover the full potential we have been given and we may bring hope to an increasingly hopeless world. When we talk of our 'faith' it is not some theoretical construct, and we know we cannot 'earn' our way to eternity. Only a relationship with the living God enables us to make sense of the world and the life we have been given.

Religion is the institution that man erects around faith

and because it comes from man it must be fallible. Faith is what we are given from God. It is pure.

The Conscience of the King

This book is not designed to knock anyone. My observation of working extensively in the Middle East is that there are those who have been brought up in a variety of traditions who show love for others. But there is so much that may be 'religious' which reflects the fallen nature of man.

So what really is *true* religion?

Religion that God our Father accepts as pure and faultless is this: to look after orphans and widows in their distress and to keep oneself from being polluted by the world.

James 1:27, NIV

In the UK, church attendance and the associated activities of organised religion are in decline. So from where will an alternative leadership emerge, and what will it look like? I believe it will be defined by the needs of our world today – *the orphans and widows in their distress* – and the many similar cries of humanity in its distress. In order to be effective as Christians we also have to work on the other part of the verse from James, *keeping oneself from being polluted by the world*. The essence of the *Disciple's Journey* is being set on course for an interior journey that will bear fruit. What the world needs now is a return to proper *relationship*.

As we face the prospect of becoming financially poorer, we have to find other ways of becoming richer. Serving others really is enriching in so many ways. When I set out on my own journey (twelve years ago) I had no idea how things would pan out, but in some way, from beyond me, I was being driven forward – even when every fibre of my being wanted to stop. God was moving, and calling me. It seems to me that he has been getting a lot of bad press recently. There are those who argue against the whole concept of God. But 'God' is not a mere theory, he is the Creator, and he is personal and living.

Many prefer to talk about 'the church', confusing the buildings that are part of the beautiful architectural heritage of our country with the reality – the church is made up of people. The term 'church' provides for some a convenient hiding place from the raw spiritual humanity that the word 'faith' evokes. At best the 'church' in the false sense of the word has just slowly withered into tense, musty, 'unignorable silence' as beautifully described by Philip Larkin:

> Once I am sure there's nothing going on
> I step inside, letting the door thud shut.
> Another church: matting, seats, and stone,
> And little books; sprawlings of flowers, cut
> For Sunday, brownish now; some brass and stuff
> Up at the holy end; the small neat organ;
> And a tense, musty, unignorable silence,
> Brewed God knows how long. Hatless, I take off
> My cycle-clips in awkward reverence.
>
> Move forward, run my hand around the font.
> From where I stand, the roof looks almost new -
> Cleaned, or restored? Someone would know: I don't.
> Mounting the lectern, I peruse a few
> Hectoring large-scale verses, and pronounce
> 'Here endeth' much more loudly than I'd meant.
> The echoes snigger briefly. Back at the door
> I sign the book, donate an Irish sixpence,
> Reflect the place was not worth stopping for.
>
> Yet stop I did: in fact I often do,

A CULTURE OF FEAR?

And always end much at a loss like this,
Wondering what to look for; wondering, too,
When churches will fall completely out of use
What we shall turn them into, if we shall keep
A few cathedrals chronically on show,
Their parchment, plate and pyx in locked cases,
And let the rest rent-free to rain and sheep.
Shall we avoid them as unlucky places?

Or, after dark, will dubious women come
To make their children touch a particular stone;
Pick simples for a cancer; or on some
Advised night see walking a dead one?
Power of some sort will go on
In games, in riddles, seemingly at random;
But superstition, like belief, must die,
And what remains when disbelief has gone?
Grass, weedy pavement, brambles, buttress, sky,

A shape less recognisable each week,
A purpose more obscure. I wonder who
Will be the last, the very last, to seek
This place for what it was; one of the crew
That tap and jot and know what rood-lofts were?
Some ruin-bibber, randy for antique,
Or Christmas-addict, counting on a whiff
Of gown-and-bands and organ-pipes and myrrh?
Or will he be my representative,

Bored, uninformed, knowing the ghostly silt
Dispersed, yet tending to this cross of ground
Through suburb scrub because it held unspilt
So long and equably what since is found
Only in separation - marriage, and birth,

And death, and thoughts of these - for which was built
This special shell? For, though I've no idea
What this accoutred frowsty barn is worth,
It pleases me to stand in silence here;

A serious house on serious earth it is,
In whose blent air all our compulsions meet,
Are recognised, and robed as destinies.
And that much never can be obsolete,
Since someone will forever be surprising
A hunger in himself to be more serious,
And gravitating with it to this ground,
Which, he once heard, was proper to grow wise in,
If only that so many dead lie round.

At worst it has ceased to be a place *where all our compulsions meet, are recognised and robed as destinies.* We have become so obsessed by church as a place, physical space, buildings. It is not that the building is unimportant. Some of the most beautiful and inspiring places are churches and cathedrals. They are where people gather. But we focus on the buildings at the expense of the people. How many incoming clergy believe that their legacy will be the reordered church, the pews ripped out, the sound system installed? How much easier it is to reorder a building than the highly complex and contradictory being that is man. Man is driven by compulsions often too scary to confront. Is the vicar really trying to save souls or raise enough money for the underfloor heating so that the poor souls who come to listen to him on a Sunday won't get cold? We waste our energy and our money on the wrong things. It is easier to invest in what we can touch than it is to invest in people. People are unpredictable, and because we know the local drug addicted offender will just go out and buy more drugs, we spend the money on a new altar cloth; and nothing changes. But it is through people coming together in deep relationship and conversation that change comes about. It is through service to each other. But do churches really encourage this? The irony, and the joy of the English language, is that the clue is in the same word that we use for the gathering of people in church – Sunday Service. Sadly, though, 'service' is not what it is truly about: *Pastors pastor, congregations congregate, nothing changes.*

The *Disciple's Journey* serves to reveal our individual compulsions, recognising and affirming them so that they may be robed as our God-given destiny to the world. Then slowly, over time, we can be released into the leadership that the world is yearning for. As I write this I can hear the reader saying *I am not a leader; that is for other people.* It is true that we can only be good leaders if we are also good followers. That simple request "Follow me", however, is an invitation to step into leadership, at what ever level that might be; it starts within each of us accepting responsibility for ourselves. And in that abrogation of personal responsibility an underlying problem in the world today is exposed. Let me illustrate how one person can make an impact by having the courage to accept responsibility, to lead beyond authority and boundaries.

Neil was the Deputy Head of a secondary school. Within his school, as with all schools, there were young people who struggled to engage with their education. They were either more vocationally orientated or they were struggling with the issues of an upbringing already described in Tom's story, which underpin many young lives. As he got to know these young people and sought to understand the challenges that they were facing, he realised that a strategy that excludes young people from school is fatally flawed. By so doing schools not only push them further away from society, but also the interventions that might help build a future. The safe approach for Neil was to stay put and to do what he could to ameliorate the system. But Neil felt increasingly challenged to step out of his safe, secure, well-paid comfort zone and to do something innovative to address the needs of these young people facing exclusion. He discussed it with his wife and together they decided to take a risk and step beyond their authority to set up a new venture, Urban Pursuit, which would provide exciting opportunities for young people at risk in Bristol to discover themselves through urban adventurous activities.

It is hard to walk away from a secure job, a good career and, most importantly, a monthly pay packet. Unless you have felt compelled by faith to do it, it is difficult for any rational individual who has not taken that risk to understand. But Neil is a modern day disciple and he knew that Urban Pursuit was a fulfilment of his calling. Unlike other less courageous souls he could not walk away from it. I have witnessed the pain of that sacrifice: living on a constant financial knife-edge not knowing whether you will have enough to cover the bills at the end of the month: the huge pressure it puts on our closest relationships as the 'hunter gatherer' in us men fails to bring home the means to survive; the loneliness (there are not many kindred spirits in this); the silent incredulity of those who watch, maybe silently judge, but don't help. I believe that there are people within every church who are gifted at making money. Would it be radical to suggest that their part may be to support people like Neil rather than hoard it away in 'barns'? It is tough to step out but, in so doing, Neil is changing lives and, more importantly, he is shifting the paradigm by which we engage those young people who are slipping between the cracks of our society. People like Neil drive real change by leading beyond boundaries.

Throughout the Western world people are facing up to some profound questions about the future societies we want to live in. Anti-capitalists are filling the headlines without really having a vision for the future. They know what they don't like, but haven't been able to articulate an alternative. Rioters take to the streets to express an inarticulate anger that is otherwise hidden by boredom. A new generation prepares to pick up the mantle of responsibility, only to discover that for many of them there is no job. And the vast majority continues to behave in denial of the reality that confronts them, encouraged by politicians who won't accept that the game is up. Power and money remain a heady combination and there is no leader yet who is ready to let go of either. Safer to borrow more money that doesn't exist to patch up the world economy, pushing back the problem to those that have been persuaded to start their lives in debt in order to get a degree.

The world waits, as the Arab world waited for the spark that ignited the Arab Spring. That spark came from one man who was fed up with the petty rules and regulations of an undemocratic, authoritarian regime, where just selling oranges had become so difficult. Enough. And so he turned himself into a human sacrifice, setting fire to his body in an act of final desperation. He would have had no idea how a single act would continue to reverberate around the Arab world from Tunisia to Bahrain, from Syria to Egypt, for years to come. Needless to say, we certainly do not commend suicide, but we are reminded that a single act can have big consequences.

We all have the potential to do an immense amount of good (or evil). We can see how the very worst aspects of our human nature have informed our behaviour and our intentions in the world in which we live today. Yet there is a paradox. We berate the greed of bankers without seeing the mote of envy in our eyes as we do so. We display mock horror at our journalists for bringing the stories that we want to read to our breakfast tables each day. We despise our politicians, especially when they abuse the privileges we would love to have and exercise the power we are afraid to take for ourselves. Democracy is a great way of abrogating personal responsibility, so we shouldn't be surprised when the few take advantage of the fact. What we get from our politicians is a direct reflection of ourselves.

So, if we want a different world, the change must start within each of us. We must reconnect with the living God and *his* purposes. We must discover what makes human beings special, and develop outstanding leadership which is godly and wise.

As we shall see in the chapters that follow, I have observed remarkable qualities in some of the least likely people in the least likely places: the geeky girl no-one wanted to talk to, the humiliated Palestinian, the prolific offender trying to turn his life around, and many others. But the fruit of my journey has been the discovery (or gift) of qualities I didn't know I had. I am not special or unique, simply a human being in search of a better world for my children to live in. All I did was decide to respond to the call on my life, and then to embark on the journey describe here. It is the deepest of human quests, not searching for material wealth, but that 'pearl' which is available to all of us. In the Way that is the *Disciple's Journey* we can find all that is needed to allow us to live full and fulfilled lives.

2

What the World Needs Now....

A question: does Christianity still have a relevance to the world we live in? For years I went along with the nicey niceness of it all as I sat on its sidelines part attracted to the comfort it brought but equally repelled by the way it expressed itself in its self indulgent, exclusive and often judgemental way. In our post modern world Christianity seems increasingly irrelevant to the majority of the world's ever increasing population. I, like many others, felt vaguely embarrassed in describing myself as a Christian. Not for me the fish on the back of the car or the exuberant, often frightening certainty of the recent graduate of an Alpha course. Not for me the faith of the evangelist or the missionary. And then one day I stepped into it; or more accurately it called me in a way that I couldn't ignore. This is the result, as I discovered that not only was Christianity extremely relevant to the world, but there is an urgency for others to step fully into it too. If this serves to inspire others to do, as the early disciples did, to step away from all that was known to them, into a world where their existence as human beings was fully realized, then I have fulfilled my purpose in putting pen to paper (or inadequate fingers to key board, if you want to be pedantic).

A small caveat to insert at this stage. I have noticed how many of those who come to faith, believe that they have discovered the absolute truth of life. In history, and to this day, this attitude has allowed people to behave in ways that contradict everything that we can learn from the life of Christ. It has been used to justify everything from the Inquisition to the intolerance of others so prevalent and alienating in the church today. In pursuing the truth it is wise to keep the words of the great Protestant ethicist, Reinhold Niebuhr at the forefront of the mind, *The truth, as revealed in the Christian revelation, includes the recognition that it is neither possible for man to know the truth fully, nor to avoid the error of pretending that he does.*

So if I give the impression at any stage that the *Disciple's Journey* reveals the truth of life, remember these words even if I may seem to forget. In searching for the truth, perhaps the greatest challenge facing our world today is that of understanding what it is to be a human being and, as a human being, what it is to be part of society. We will not understand what it is to be a human being by sitting at home reading a book nor will we discover the secret by pursuing worldly ambitions or wealth. We will only begin to unravel the mystery of life at the point that we are prepared to lose everything and follow the promptings of our soul. To follow you can't stand still. It requires action. It begins with personal leadership through which we deny those often very attractive sinful aspects of ourselves in order to step into the glory of new life. The first and paramount responsibility of anyone who aspires to discipleship is to lead and manage self: one's own integrity, character, ethics, knowledge, wisdom, temperament, words and acts. It is a complex, never ending, incredibly difficult, often avoided task, requiring the individual to step out of their comfort zone with great humility and become salt and light to the world. In taking the first step into discipleship we begin the tough journey of confronting those aspects of our nature that do not serve us as leaders: pride, greed, envy, anger, laziness, gluttony and lust and begin to reveal the virtues listed in Colossians 3:12 – mercy, kindness (compassion), humility, gentleness and peace, forgiveness and above all love. And by revealing all of these in ourselves we bring hope; not only hope through the way we are subsequently, but hope to others who may be encouraged by us to do the same.

Despite economic growth and increasing wealth, as I highlighted in Chapter 1, the world is facing greater challenges of poverty and social justice than at any stage in human history. This is a simple reflection of the less attractive aspects of man and the leadership structures that he has created. For example, the model of autocratic, hierarchical leadership is necessary in times of crisis and it could be argued that this allowed us to win the Second World War, but, as we are seeing in the Arab Spring, people across the world are looking for something more inclusive. The imposition of authority may well produce conformity but it does not encourage individual virtue. It creates a paradigm where most people will be who we tell them they are.

All the problems in the world are underpinned by human behaviour, so often governed by fear. That fear stems from the doubt that even Christians feel, or from an absence of a relationship with a God who is longing to reveal his purpose for us individually and collectively. If fear can be defeated, human possibility can be unlocked. Through fear's antidote, love, we can discover that we are stronger than we think we are. As we overcome challenges we reveal the eternal values that allow us to become stronger still. We discover that the power of Christian community is limitless and allows us to find courage we did not know we had.

As beacons of hope and optimism we can defeat fear and darkness. To be effective in this we need the Holy Spirit to fill and empower us. He is more potent than we can imagine, and can transform our lives and the lives of others.

In his sermon when installed as Archbishop of York, John Sentamu invited Christians to reach out to the demonized and dehumanized, the Muslims, the Sikhs, the Hindu, the agnostic and the atheist. Love does not judge. We must be prepared to take a risk. *Compassion is not defined by giving a poor person a coin, but setting out to change the system that created poverty. We must step outside our comfort zones to create a healthy spiritual economy. Nothing is created through inertia. Jesus taught us through his example that we must risk everything – our well-being, our reputation, our riches – in order to make a difference to the world.*

There are many fine words written and many great intentions articulated, but nothing much changes. Every day Christians pray for peace, for an end to injustice and famine, for a better world. But prayer without action is only fulfilling half the deal. God can work with us to achieve all that we pray for, but we have to do something too. Words without actions are just words and the world is not short of words. *The road to hell is paved with good intentions.* The reason is that we are not equipped for the battle. As a soldier, I was trained to act, to be disciplined, to think strategically in service to something greater than I was. As Christians we must do the same.

Henry David Thoreau said:

There are thousands who are in opinion opposed to slavery and war who yet do nothing to put an end to them. There are nine hundred and ninety-nine patrons of virtue to every virtuous man.

It is true that for every one thousand ideas only one per cent is ever realized. We all witnessed the church's failure to respond to the Occupy movement outside St Paul's Cathedral in the heart of the City of London in 2011. It was an opportunity to reach out to the marginalized and provide an alternative vision for the world after the failures of the capitalist system became apparent with the credit crunch. It was an opportunity to highlight the fact that when economies fail it is always the poorest that suffer most. It was an opportunity to stand up for social justice and an alternative economic model for which all could flourish. But their hesitation spoke volumes of the modern church pulled between the opposite forces of God and mammon. The fear of upsetting mammon was too great and the church lost another chance to be fiercely relevant to the world.

Globally, 98% of Christians are neither envisioned nor equipped for mission in 95% of their waking lives, but imagine if they were.

London Institute of Contemporary Christianity

Imagine Christians discovering their unique God given gifts and talents and thereby their purpose and were empowered to use this knowledge to make a tangible difference to the world. I often think that evangelism is missing the point. If we have to go out into the world to tell people about Christ, we are failing to be Christ-like witnesses in the world. Be a beacon of Christ's love to your neighbour and you might just find that your neighbour is drawn to you without the unintended manipulation that can often be felt by those in the hands of the enthusiastic evangelist.

If the gospel is to challenge the public life of our society, if Christians are to occupy the "high ground" which they vacated in the noon-time of "modernity", it will not be by forming a Christian political party, or by aggressive propaganda campaigns. Once again it has to be said that there can be no going back to the "Constantinian" era. It will only be by movements that begin with the local congregation in which the reality of the new creation is present, known, and experienced, and from which men and women will go into every sector of public life to claim it for Christ, to unmask the illusions which have remained hidden and to expose all areas of public life to the illumination of the gospel. But that will only happen as and when local congregations renounce an introverted concern for their own life, and recognize that they exist for the sake of those who are not members, as sign, instrument, and foretaste of God's redeeming grace for the whole life of society.

Lesslie Newbigin

I love the words of St Francis of Assisi, *Preach the gospel always, and when absolutely necessary, use words*. Suffering does not happen because God doesn't care. Suffering occurs when we fail to fulfil the needs of our fellow human beings by being a bridge between them and God, a reflection of Christ. This book sets out to help us be the reflection of Christ that draws people in. It will describe some of the challenges we face based on the stories of some of those I have met since embarking on my own *Disciple's Journey*. These stories highlight the need for the transformational change in our world on a scale achieved by those early disciples, who recognised that the resurrection was our cue to begin to live the life of the kingdom on earth.

Then I saw a new heaven and a new earth, for the first heaven and the first earth had passed away, and there was no longer any sea. I saw the Holy City, the new Jerusalem, coming down out of heaven from God, prepared as a bride beautifully dressed for her husband. And I heard a loud voice from the throne saying, "Now the dwelling of God is with men, and he will live with them. They will be his people, and God himself will be with them and be their God. He will wipe every tear from their eyes. There will be no more death or mourning or crying or pain, for the old order of things has passed away."

Revelation 21:1–4, NIV

Why me? You will be asking yourself. Change and progress happen because people look around the world and see what needs to be done. Why not you? The future belongs to those who have the courage to ask these questions and the faith to take the first step. What are we waiting for? Individually and collectively we have been given the power to make a start. There was a wonderfully unassuming exhibit in the Sensations exhibition at the Royal Academy in 1997. It was a straight line of various photographs of individual people finished in different styles. In the centre of the photographs was a small slightly yellowing newspaper advert simply seeking those who believed they looked like God to submit an image of themselves to a certain address. Some found this blasphemous, but within it I found a profound message. We are made in the image of God. When the Holy Spirit (who is God) is at work in us and we are serving others, we are serving God.

Whoever claims to love God yet hates a brother or sister is a liar. For whoever does not love their brother and sister, whom they have seen, cannot love God, whom they have not seen.

1 John 4:20, NIV

The preoccupation with 'self' is an absolute obstacle to human happiness and fulfilment because human happiness and fulfilment can only be attained through genuine love. Therefore we need to discover the power of service within ourselves, understanding our unique contribution to the world, so that we can work collaboratively with others. As Gandhi said, *the best way to find yourself is to lose yourself in the service of others*. This is my experience, but it is not easy to make the shift from the self-centred, narcissistic and individualistic culture that shapes our world. It is hard for all of us as beautifully described in this poem by Alexander Pope.

> Know then thyself, presume not God to scan;
> The proper study of mankind is Man.
> Placed on this isthmus of a middle state,
> A being darkly wise and rudely great:
> With too much knowledge for the Sceptic side,
> With too much weakness for the Stoic's pride,
> He hangs between; in doubt to act or rest,
> In doubt to deem himself a God or Beast,
> In doubt his mind or body to prefer;
> Born but to die, and reasoning but to err;
> Alike in ignorance, his reason such
> Whether he thinks too little or too much:
> Chaos of thought and passion, all confused;
> Still by himself abused, or disabused;
> Created half to rise and half to fall;
> Great lord of all things, yet a prey to all;
> Sole judge of truth, in endless error hurled:
> The glory, jest, and riddle of the world!

This book is a story of that very human tension and a record of my journey in search of answers to questions I didn't even know I was asking when I set out. It is an attempt to answer the eternal question famously articulated by Hamlet, "To be or not to be". Not only is it the question, it is the question we should be asking of ourselves day by day. In seeking the answer it is impossible to remain where we are.

The essence of the *Disciple's Journey* is Christ made relevant to the world we live in. Lord Harries of Pentregarth wrote recently *It is widely recognized that for the majority of people today Christianity has become a foreign language and what goes on is church strikes them as strange, even alien. This is especially true of young people.* The world sees Christians go to church every week, worship in a way that seems exclusive and slightly weird and nothing changes. The message of Christ is lost in a world that is no longer listening, because while dancing on the pinhead of human sexuality, there is a cacophony of silence with regard to the issues that really matter in people's lives. When people feel that the world they knew is shifting they begin to search for something better. This is where the world is now: astride an axis of change from the rational world that has created the power to destroy itself to a world that is based on the principles Christ taught us 2000 years ago. In a world of risk adversity and fear we seek its antidote, love. In a world of love, compassion and trust we are able to take the risks that allow us to be all that we were born to be, in the knowledge that when we stumble we won't be alone to face the consequences.

Therefore I urge you brothers, in view of God's mercy, to offer your bodies as a living sacrifice, holy and pleasing to God – this is your spiritual act of worship. Do not conform any longer to the pattern of this world but be transformed by the renewing of your mind. Then you will be able to test and approve what God's will is – his pleasing and perfect will.

Romans 12:1–2

This is the invitation to be the change in the world. We have been accustomed in the world we live in for change to be driven from the top. When something needs to be done we generally look to elected politicians to provide the solutions. The Big Society isn't working as a concept since it exposes this paradox. Society is all of us and therefore must be driven from the bottom upwards. It cannot be imposed. It will come with a shift in human consciousness, the root of which is the Latin word 'conscire', which means 'to know with (God)'. When we become more conscious we think with the heart of God through the example of his son Jesus Christ, but only when our souls are open and ready to listen. Through the grace of Jesus Christ, life presents a series of opportunities for learning, which increase our consciousness and draw us closer to God. However the paradox is that we need to be conscious of this. In a rational and often comfortable world, we miss the opportunities to learn and grow because we live in a state of unconsciousness. The *Disciple's Journey* maps out the shift from unconsciousness to consciousness as a start point of growth that leads to service. I believe that the paradigm shift that the world is facing will emerge from the most unlikely source. Jesus gave us a clue in his own ministry *I have not come to call the righteous, but sinners* (Luke 5:32). While we are all sinners, having worked with the more obvious sinners over the last twelve years, criminals, drug addicts, the disengaged, I retain the hope that change will come through them fulfilling the verse in the Beatitudes, *The meek shall inherit the earth*. That is where the potential lies.

When I started to write this book, it was designed to fill another hole on the growing bookshelves for books on personal development, which has become a major industry during the last twenty years. As the book unfolded, I began to realise that this was a denial of my faith. Indeed I began to realise that the growth in the personal development industry was a reflection of a world that had largely abandoned my Christian faith. It would be disingenuous to write an ersatz version that wasn't underpinned by my faith, which has, after all inspired the book and my own journey contained within. I have also felt squeamish about the overused word 'journey', but in describing something as dynamic and all encompassing as living is, it is difficult to find a satisfactory alternative. I am also conscious that in using the analogy of the journey I am creating a narrative, a story that attempts to bring my faith alive. I am no theologian, nor indeed am I an authority on the Bible, so forgive me for any gaping holes in my understanding. By creating a narrative for my own story, I am hoping that others will be able to do the same. Indeed the fundamental lesson of the *Disciple's Journey* is that our story is universally the same. This book would not have been possible without my taking that first step. I hope it proves to be an encouragement to you to do the same.

There is also an important caveat to all that follows which is best described by that great theologian Stanley Hauerwas in his autobiographical book *Hannah's Child*. In describing his own encounter with the power of narrative he quotes a passage from George Eliot in her book Adam Bede: *Our deeds determine us as much as we determine our deeds; and until we know what has been or will be the peculiar combination of outward and inward facts, which constitute a man's critical actions, we will be better not to think wise about his character.* Stanley Hauerwas goes on to say, *I certainly don't want to think myself wise about my own character for as George Eliot observes, 'there is a terrible coercion in our deeds which may turn the honest man into a deceiver, and then reconcile him to the change.' What so often makes us liars is not what we do but the justifications we offer for what we do. Our justifications become the way in which we try to defeat the contingencies of our lives by telling ourselves consoling stories that suggest we have done as well as was possible.*

It is for the reader to decide whether this book is simply a justification for my deeds or, more importantly, my lack of deeds when required. I wish I could say that I have done as well as possible, but I know this not to be true. In wasting the potential in myself, I am passionate that others don't do the same. In my defence it is only when I consciously stepped into the narrative of my own life that I was able to see this. In writing this book I am encouraging the reader to step into the narrative of their own lives and by so doing becoming more conscious of their capabilities and those aspects of their being that block their potential. But stepping into your narrative, and thereby the essence of your being, requires a lot of faith and faith requires courage.

Faith is a gift. If we ask for it we receive and this requires humility. It is open to all and available in many different flavours. For those of us with faith we understand this; we often take it for granted and find it difficult to hold our own in an argument with militant secularists for whom the value of our being is weighed by the level of our intellect. This creates an arrogance that militates against the humility required to seek faith and a sterile belief that life is purely a function to be lived out with no ultimate purpose beyond the material. Fully *being* involves discovering *purpose*, though not as an end in itself. The Lord's Prayer contains the line *Your kingdom come* an invitation for us to begin to create it here on earth through living out our purpose within the kingdom in harmony with others. We are brought up to believe that heaven is something to be earned through good behaviour during our life on earth, but what if we had the gift of creating the kingdom on earth here and now? It is a liberating thought maybe out of sync with our traditional understanding of religion, which at best, we have seen as a uniting force for the individual and collective good earning its right into eternity, and at worst a highly authoritarian, fundamentalist, intolerant entity driven by the need to control human behaviour.

This is the biggest challenge for Christians of our generation. As the Anglican Communion struggles to articulate a united vision in a way that resonates to those both of faith and with no faith, the words of Matthew Arnold resonate rather sadly.

The sea is calm to-night.
The tide is full, the moon lies fair
Upon the straits; on the French coast the light
Gleams and is gone; the cliffs of England stand,
Glimmering and vast, out in the tranquil bay.
Come to the window, sweet is the night-air!
Only, from the long line of spray
Where the sea meets the moon-blanch'd land,
Listen! you hear the grating roar
Of pebbles which the waves draw back, and fling
At their return, up the high strand,
Begin, and cease, and then again begin,
With tremulous cadence slow, and bring
The eternal note of sadness in.

Sophocles long ago
Heard it on the Aegean, and it brought
Into his mind the turbid ebb and flow
Of human misery; we
Find also in the sound a thought,
Hearing it by this distant northern sea.

The Sea of Faith
Was once, too, at the full, and round earth's shore
Lay like the folds of a bright girdle furl'd.
But now I only hear Its melancholy, long, withdrawing
roar,
Retreating, to the breath
Of the night-wind, down the vast edges drear
And naked shingles of the world.

Ah, love, let us be true
To one another! for the world, which seems
To lie before us like a land of dreams,
So various, so beautiful, so new,
Hath really neither joy, nor love, nor light,
Nor certitude, nor peace, nor help for pain;
And we are here as on a darkling plain
Swept with confused alarms of struggle and flight,
Where ignorant armies clash by night.

Dover Beach by Matthew Arnold

These verses seem to paint a grim picture of where post-modernism has left us with *the turbid ebb and flow of human misery* that I will bring alive in the next chapter. Our faith, once so full, retreats to the naked shingles of the world. But the hope must lie in the opening lines of the verse that follows: *Ah love, let us be true to one another! for the world that lies before us* (surely the kingdom) *like a land of dreams, so various so beautiful so new* currently has no light, no love, no joy since we, as Christians, are doing little to reflect light, love and joy to the world we live in. I would argue that as an Anglican communion we are *swept with confused alarms of struggle and fight, where ignorant armies clash by night*. Is that the Church tearing itself apart, often driven by the ignorance of the opposing point of view?

But go back to that opening line *Ah love, let us be true to one another!* This surely is the key – being true to each other in the being that we are – the people that we have been created to be. We all hide behind our various masks, fearful of exposing our individual insecurities and to avoid the most profound truths of our own existence. By being true to our own calling we can have the confidence to collaborate easily with others in a way that can make an impact on the world – creating the cascade of grace that Tom Wright talks about.

Surely this is a new way of expressing our faith in a way that makes Christ relevant to the needs of the world today? I am optimistic that as a generation we are (or can be) midwives to a new expression of Christ that will be manifest in the young generation. But as with all change, we have to leave the familiar behind – never easy. It is a transition that many will refuse. We must embrace uncertainty since it is only by having the courage to face up to it that we allow the possibility of the vacuum of silence being filled. By so doing we can be filled with the excitement and expectation of what is to come, not fear at what we are losing or fear that nothing awaits us but silence. I believe that we are being called back to the simplicity of a faith that is based on love, truth and the hope that is generated when a small number of people begin to take action. A *Disciple's Journey* has been designed to address this.

This has been a personal story of how taking a risk, facing up to fear and remaining faithful to the love that Christ has taught us, we can enhance our consciousness and be released into leadership that draws in others and allows us to be the change in the world. We no longer need to play it safe. We can embrace uncertainty with every step and overcome our perpetual enemy, fear. In the next chapter I want to illustrate how *the turbid flow of human misery* affects lives, through the eyes of various people I have encountered on my own journey, and to describe how they used their own misery to find something within that allowed them to step into leadership and make a difference. By so doing they inspire others to look around them to see where they can play their part in stemming the relentless tide. These are just snapshots of a few lives that have made an impact on me. They maybe just isolated examples of human misery; they maybe a reflection of many lives trying to survive in the complex world we have created.

3

The Turbid Flow of Human Misery

Emma was a very shy, awkward girl – overweight, with lank, listless hair, and the butt of her fellow pupils' humour. Her lack of confidence was evident through an absence of social engagement and limited eye contact. She was a deeply unhappy teenager wondering what it was all about. She hid her fear and sorrow behind a mask of invisibility.

Emma was one of many young people who had concluded at a young age that life was hope-less and felt condemned to live out a life of quiet desperation just to survive. That was the overwhelming witness of her community. She attended a very large comprehensive school on one of the biggest council estates in Leeds. The catchment area was 100% social housing. A large percentage were eligible for free school meals. It was a school that was enlightened for its time, wanting to help pupils find the best in themselves in order to create the inner motivation for their education, but with classroom sizes this was an uphill struggle. Like many 'bog standard comprehensives' it struggled to maintain the balance between the very best and the very worst while keeping the vast majority who get lost in the middle, motivated and performing.

Much is made of self-esteem as it relates to physical appearance. Our media's obsession with creating reality television programmes focusing on bodily appearance is symptomatic of a very sick society. As with many things in our society we are barking up the wrong tree. Feeling unhappy about physical appearance is a symptom not the root cause, which is about a lack of inner confidence. Did you know that the 'beauty' industry is worth $274 billion worldwide? Imagine if we spent that money on improving internal beauty. I had designed a programme for schools to help young people of the age of 14 – 16 to unlock their inner confidence, communicate more effectively and to find themselves by innovating ways of serving their communities. This programme was targeted at 'the majority in the middle' group with a view to inspiring them to be the best while preventing them from becoming the worst. A key to finding yourself is unlocking that inner creativity we all have but which gets suppressed in that underlying agenda to conform.

In asking the group of sixteen pupils, who thought they were creative, no one put their hand up. During the second session of the programme, the group was invited to create an idea for a project that would either be of benefit to the school or to their community. Each had to present their idea. At the end of the presentations the group then had a ballot to choose the idea that they would take forward to implementation, a simple introduction to democracy.

Emma stepped forward very reluctantly and started to speak. One of the hardest things in life is to articulate a dream or an idea, since the expectation is that everyone will laugh at you. Emma had been laughed at enough not to care. Although her delivery was hesitant, she talked of her idea to create a space within the school for her year group. With a large school population, there was nowhere to hang out during breaks. For the first time in her life she experienced applause, an acknowledgement not only of her existence, but that her existence had value. To receive this from her peers who hitherto had ignored her at best was empowering and even more so when they voted. She inspired the group sufficiently for them to choose her idea.

She had never had the opportunity before to initiate or lead. Not many young people do. An observation of schools is that they tend to pick the same confident pupils to take the leading roles. I believe that everyone has the capacity to lead, but this needs to be unlocked. Schools just don't have time, so go for the solution of least resistance. Emma turned out to be a natural leader and organiser. As with many leaders she was able to think laterally. There was no spare room within the school to establish the space for her year group, so she approached every mobile home and office company in the Leeds area until she found one that was prepared to deliver an old mobile office to the school and set it up. Emma organised a team of decorators and the job was done. She went from zero to hero overnight. She discovered many qualities that had lain dormant within her until the opportunity came along to unleash them. Imagine if every child had the opportunity to find their unique skills and talents? This should be the first duty of a school, not academic excellence, since it is inclusive and everyone has a chance to shine. It develops aspiration, motivation and hope, releasing young people into their full potential.

It is always notable in schools that those who are told they are good do well; those who are put down don't. There is rarely an approach which allows all to be valued for what they have.

If education is about growth, it is also true that only the person who has experienced love will be capable of growing. In his recent book *How Children Succeed*, the American writer Paul Tough discovered that it wasn't intelligence, skill or natural ability that created success. The answer did not lie in the intellect at all. It was something more profound built around character traits such as self-discipline, courage, gratitude, optimism and, most importantly, what Tough describes as grit. Grit, or resilience, is the determination to keep going whatever setbacks we encounter. It stems from an inner confidence wrought out of a strong connection with the soul. It is the ability to overcome failure, grief, betrayal and any other challenge that life throws at us. This is the journey of faith, the *Disciple's Journey*, beautifully described by Rabbi Jonathan Sacks,

I learned to embrace failure instead of fearing it. Why? Because at some point on my religious journey I discovered that more than we have faith in God, God has faith in us. He lifts us every time we fall. He forgives us every time we fail. He believes in us more than we believe in ourselves. He mends our broken hearts. I never cease to be moved by the words of Isaiah: "Even youths grow tired and weary and the young may stumble and fall, but those who hope in the Lord renew their strength. They soar on wings like eagles, they run and don't grow weary, they walk and don't grow faint." The greatest source of grit I know, the force that allows us to overcome every failure every setback. every defeat, and keep going and growing is faith in God's faith in us. It is a faith that will fuel the race.

Emma found grit and through this created new hope for her life.

Sadly it is not just education that can make a difference. When you have nothing and are constantly worrying about how to pay the rent, feed the children or heat the house, it diminishes us as human beings. It is easy to see how poverty eats away at confidence and self-esteem. It is not just the financial poverty, although clearly this is important, it is the poverty of aspiration. With aspiration comes the hope of something better. Much has been written about generational unemployment and lives lived on benefits. It is easier for those who are better off with more advantage to condemn and blame. But without aspiration there is no hope. Life seems hope-less. Griffith University in Australia has done a study on hope and made some interesting discoveries, none of which come as a surprise. Hope is a part of a complex coping process. It is not confined to a single life domain. People need to see that there is a pot of gold at the end of the rainbow; not just money but good things in life.

Hopeful thought reflects the belief that one can find pathways to desired goals and become motivated to use those pathways...and serves to drive the emotions and well-being of people." (*Snyder, Rand & Sigmon, 2002*)

Interestingly it talks about pathways intimating movement and a journey. We first have to find the pathways and then use them. I would not want to confuse hope with passivity. A constant theme of this book is the need to be proactive. Hope only stems from action; as long as we are doing something to create forward momentum we will create hope. When we do nothing we may soon lose hope.

One of the big challenges of this generation worldwide is youth unemployment. In the UK it is stuck at 21%, condemning over a million 16 – 24 year olds to worklessness: lives without purpose and without hope. Nearly one million young people with no future to look forward to, while being bombarded with images of what life should be like. No wonder their lives are disorientated and lacking in meaning. It is surprising that there isn't more social unrest, although an underlying anger occasionally breaks through as with the UK riots of the summer of 2011. This is a generation that has been let down by the culture we live in. They are expected to conform to a world that has nothing to offer them. Working with young people I sometimes feel a bit of a fraud: opening up something within them that the world can't utilise. It can be a bit like rescuing them from the sea and plopping them back on the deck of the Titanic.

In the war on poverty we need to start with this generation. I am optimistic since I see endless potential. Furthermore I see within young people the creativity and energy to start addressing some of the issues they face. What is needed is an umbrella of encouragement, and support from adults to empower them. Change has to start within education. The industrial model has served its purpose and is now letting down those it is supposed to serve. And yes education is service, something that many academics have forgotten. The servants are the teachers not the other way round. The word education comes from the Latin word 'educare', which means to draw out. It assumes that as human beings we have within us an unlimited capacity to learn and that the role of the teacher is to draw that out. Instead of which we have created a system based on an academic model, which immediately disadvantages the non-academic. The 11 plus was used to segregate the academic from the non-academic and stream their schooling accordingly. The non-academic were condemned to lives of failure since this was how they were judged at a crucial stage in their development. The arrival of the comprehensive system just dumbed down the whole process. It is no coincidence that there has been an increase in Attention Deficit Disorders (ADHD) as more and more young people felt disconnected from their education. The cure was Ritalin or exclusion, itself often, as stated earlier, another route to drugs. The key to education is unlocking individual talent. And herein lies the problem.

Now it is interesting that most adults have no idea of their true talents. They bump along through life unfulfilled doing what they think is right rather than what they are passionate about. Yet a few love what they do and live life to the full. They have that inner confidence. What makes the difference? Being good at something is not a good enough reason for doing it, especially when you are constantly striving to fulfil the expectations of others. We are human beings not human doings. The key is being you and finding that one thing where your natural talent meets your passion. The noted educational academic Sir Ken Robinson calls it your element. I call it your own perfectly shaped jigsaw piece, where talent and passion combine. Life is simply about discovering the shape of your piece and then seeking out those pieces with which it fits. It is essential for human fulfilment and the pursuit of that elusive word happiness. It is also essential in terms of finding personal authenticity, integrity and a moral compass that allows us to respond to the challenges of life in the right way. It is vital for the health of wider society. If people are disconnected from themselves they are more likely to be disconnected from other people and cause problems to themselves and others. So confidence is not the shallow kind often displayed by those who lack it. It is a deep inner confidence that comes from being comfortable in our own skin. We know it when we see it.

The irony is that it doesn't always exist, in an authentic way, where you would expect it. I once ran a workshop, which brought together some Chief Executives from FTSE 100 companies and a group of young homeless people. In pairs the Chief Executives were invited to share the secret of success; the homeless were invited to share their dream. Geoff ran a national telecommunications company; Leroy was homeless and unemployed. Leroy was articulate and confident as he shared his dream to open his own radio station. Geoff talked of hard work and perseverance, but there was a sadness to him. I asked him what that was and he admitted that his life was too busy to dream; he had no vision for his own life beyond the material success that his role brought him. It is something that I have noticed in many 'successful' people.

David was only 50. He was the life and soul of any party and lit up every room he came into. He had the easy charm of the Irish, drawing in everyone he met. What none of his friends realised at the time was the misery that underpinned his leadership. He was an astute businessman, building up a very successful financial advising company. Latterly he provided financial advice for soldiers returning from Afghanistan, something he did quietly and without charge. He dispensed his wealth as easily as his bonhomie, discreetly helping those in need. When a local charity was wound up, two of the trustees were left personally liable for an overdraft. After three years of painful struggle with the bank, David stepped in and negotiated a settlement, which he then paid.

As he wrote the cheque he never revealed that he had been betrayed by one of his directors, who had embezzled a large sum of money from the company. He never revealed the pain this caused him as he tried to recover an impossible situation. The fear of losing everything was overwhelming. His first priority was to protect his family, his wife and his ten year old daughter. He had created a comfortable life for them and he didn't want to pull it from under them. Pride is one of our greatest enemies. When we mess up, or, as in this case, are messed up by others, we feel that we have to find the solution alone. How can we trust others when we have been betrayed? Who else can get us out of the hole we have dug for ourselves? Only me. And when 'I' is not enough, we try and hide ourselves behind a thick wall of pride, fighting off those compassionate enough to attempt to scale our defences. It's OK I'll sort it. But embroiled in our self-sufficiency we tumble deeper into the pit of despair. We lose connection with who we are. Our souls become a distant echo of our reality. And we feel there is no way out.

On an early grey November morning, David found his way out. He could no longer fight the battle; the fear was too much. He was found by the son of the owner of a lock up in which he used to store company papers. He had attached a hose to the exhaust pipe of his car and went to sleep with a copy of the Bible next to him. He had renewed his faith in the last two years of his life but even this had not been enough. He clearly felt that he done the best for those closest to him. His pride had convinced him that his continued presence would hurt those he loved most. After all he had let them down. He had lost his fortune and could no longer support them in the manner that they had become used to. His fear of losing his material wealth won in the end. But in his suffering he found compassion and during his last few years he quietly made a difference to many people's lives.

Mid-life crisis comes in a number of guises and the seeds of it invariably lie in those early years when true self is suppressed to meet the needs of a world to which we are conditioned to conform. To 'succeed' in material or career terms requires drive and a level of ruthlessness, which creates the focus perceived to be essential for achievement. This focus is found at the expense of all other aspects of life. For some this single-mindedness is in pursuit of an ambition or career chosen by them. Their determination to succeed can leave a wake of broken relationships, ignored children and a lack of friendships behind them. I have met many late middle-aged men who have 'succeeded' in worldly terms, yet arrived at the top of the tree to discover that there is nothing there. Those in pursuit of power discover that absolute power is elusive; those in pursuit of money discover that wealth has an emptiness to it and that however much they have, they always want a little bit more. Another friend who reached the summit of his ambition looked back down the mountain and saw how much he had lost along the way. He gets to mid life with an acute sense that this wasn't how it was meant to be. And it seems too late to reverse things. Sadly, so many slip into depression, addictions and unhappiness. Marriages break up, children suffer, the safe career evaporates and life, in any true sense, comes to an end. In a few tragic cases this is literally true as suicide is seen as the only way out of the personal hell that has been created.

The seeds of this hell often find fruit in the life that is spent pursuing the ambitions of others. Ben was one of those young men who some would describe as golden. He was a great sportsman and gained a First at Oxford. He was, to the frustration of his male friends 'a babe magnet'. He excelled at Sandhurst and passed out into a good regiment. Marriage followed and two sons. It all seemed perfect. Then Ben decided to leave the army. He could have done anything but he decided to become a banker. At first he did very well and was soon promoted. It looked as though he would slip effortlessly up the ranks of the bank.

No one noticed the drinking. The army had a very heavy drinking culture and the City was no different. Drinking was part of the game. There is a fine line between heavy drinking and alcoholism. When Ben crossed that line no one really noticed but a sudden nervous breakdown signalled the tension between the pretence and the reality of his life. He took time off work to recover. Three months stretched to six. Then it became clear that a return to work was unlikely. Watching the descent into alcoholism is like watching a car crash in slow motion. The end is inevitable but as a bystander there is always the hope that you might be able to prevent it. But you can't. Ben and I spent evenings when he would precociously drink water, while disappearing to get something, go to the loo, help in the kitchen; the excuses were manifold and inventive.

The psychiatrist peeled back the onion skin of his life to try and reveal the root cause. There were many. Two highly successful professional parents did what all parents of their background did when Ben was a child. They sent him away to school. In its practice the school had changed little since Victorian times. It was brutal disconnection from the age of innocence that preceded it. Corporal punishment was meted out with an abandon that seems extraordinary today. Male teachers mysteriously disappeared overnight before the word 'paedophile' was ever articulated. Bullying was ignored by those who could have stopped it. He did not know that he was being prepared for public school used to condition generations of young men for service in the colonies. He was toughened up, learned to conform, to be self-sufficient. So often that essence of self that defines us uniquely and allows us to fulfil our potential is abandoned before there is consciousness of its existence.

And then there was the expectation. Two highly successful parents could not have anything less than a highly successful son. It was not ill intended; far from it, the intent was loving. So often there is no praise for those who achieve their potential: it is expected of them. Yet we all need praise like flowers need water. It is said that if we are not praising young people we are wounding them. Maybe his parents were proud of him, but they never told him. I am sure that they loved him but they never showed it: the hug, even a pat on the shoulder or the simple words 'I love you'. The simplest, but sadly neglected, actions that help make people whole, confident, at ease with themselves. But the pressure to meet expectations not only in terms of the 'right career' but success within it became overwhelming. As children (and adults), we want to please our parents. But if in so doing we separate ourselves from our truth, we sow the seeds for an unhappy future. Ben did everything to please his parents and paid for it with his life.

In order to try and snap him out of his alcoholism he was persuaded to join Alcoholics Anonymous. For a time he tried really hard but to no avail. He left home and spent his last years in a dingy council flat with nothing much more to furnish it than empty bottles. He was just 43 when he died. At his funeral some members of his Alcoholic Anonymous group slipped silently into the back of the church. They told stories of his unconditional support and love to them: simple acts of kindness that had allowed them to survive for another day; inspiration to transform their own lives. In his nemesis he had found his truth: in service to others he revealed his purpose. In doing so he had become a leader and changed the lives of many.

Ben's story is one of many in our culture and there are many more Bens to come, paying the price for living inauthentic lives. So busy doing he forgot that he was a human being. He had a privileged background and was able to make an impact in many ways in his shortened life.

Joe was the sort of guy you would want on your side in a fight. Well built and lean, missing a few teeth after a confrontation with a fist on some long forgotten Saturday night out on the lash. Joe was angry. He was another of the catalogue of unwanted children that I have encountered on the margins of society. The fruit of unbridled lust that had no care for the consequences of the casual encounter that met the physical needs of two lost souls. Joe's mother didn't know what to do with him when, nine months later, he was born, as her parents hadn't had a clue to do with her. No one to blame; just the reality in a society that has confused sex with love. So Joe ended up negotiating a childhood that started in foster homes and ended up in care – the dumping ground for unwanted children. Just dwell on that word for a moment – unwanted. What would you feel like if you were unwanted; no family but the superficial relationships that drifted in and out, always with the expectation that one of them would be that person who wanted you. It does not take long for that sense of unwantedness to extend to society. Yet we all need to belong; it is a basic human need – those three 'A's, attention, affirmation and affection. Just imagine as you read this what it would be like to be unwanted with no one to turn to.

After Joe came out of care he drifted before joining the Army, needing the many facets that come from institutional living – most of all that sense of belonging and being wanted. By becoming part of something greater than himself, he began to discover the good qualities within himself that allowed him to be an invaluable member of his team. He became an infantry soldier and ended up serving in Northern Ireland as the peace process was beginning. The province continued to be a place of conflict and the Army still had an active role to play. Joe was on patrol on when a bomb went off close to where he was standing, the fulfilment of his worst nightmares. He was unhurt but he witnessed some horrific injuries and played a key part in attending to one of the victims. Nothing prepares us as human beings for the brutality that we are capable of inflicting on each other. The carnage that we see so frequently on TV and in films is far worse in reality and the images are burnt upon the consciousness of the bystander. As a soldier you are expected to just get on with it while deep down wondering whether the next bullet or bomb will have your name on it. There is no time to reflect, just move onto the next task. It is the only way that an army can continue to be effective. Black humour hides the internal scars and often the impact doesn't hit home for years. Joe had only signed up for four years so it was not long after his tour in Northern Ireland that he was discharged.

For those who have experienced dysfunctional childhoods, the services provide structure, discipline, camaraderie, a sense of purpose, a cause greater than ourselves, teamwork as well as three meals a day and a roof over the head at night. For many their experience sets them up for life; for others like Joe though the transition into civilian life is frightening. Joe had already experienced the harsh reality of leaving care at the age of 16. For whatever its shortcomings care had provided for his basic needs. He dreaded being on his own again. The Army is not great at resettling soldiers who have served for a short time. There is little support.

It is now well documented that Post Traumatic Stress Disorder (PTSD) presents itself on average thirteen years after the event that provoked it. So it was well after Joe left the Army when he was overwhelmed by depression. His life fell apart. He lost his job and he ended up on the streets, his pride preventing him from seeking out help. Eventually he sought medical assistance. Inevitably those responsible for his healing had no idea of what Joe had been through, nor how it affected him, nor how to treat him. So they did what they could to suppress the pain through drugs. Yet what Joe really needed was someone he could trust to listen to his story and by doing so unlock the pain within.

But he was lucky. He met a girl. He got married to the first person he truly loved. Becky was also the first person he ever trusted. They settled down and planned to have the family that Joe had never had. Years went by and there were no children. Then early in 2011 Becky became pregnant. In September she went into labour 11 weeks early and a baby girl was born. Adele was immediately put in an incubator and for weeks Joe and Becky spent all their time at the hospital wondering whether Adele would survive. Joe spoke to the hospital staff about his post-traumatic stress disorder (PTSD). He felt increasingly anxious about his ability to cope with a sickly baby. When he was able to pick Adele up, this anxiety was transmitted to her and she became distressed. All the time Joe was under the microscope as the hospital staff observed his relationship with Adele. It is bad enough being under constant surveillance at the best of times. When you have PTSD it can raise levels of anxiousness to unbearable levels and this was the case with Joe. The hospital staff were sufficiently concerned to call in Social Services and Joe and Becky were exposed to the humiliation of having every aspect of their lives taken apart and examined; such are the draconian powers we have given to those responsible for child protection. Rightly the child's needs are seen as paramount, but this can be at the expense of the needs of the parents. If you have children just put yourself into the shoes of Joe and Becky. Understand how threatened you would feel. I remember as a young parent, living in Cyprus at the time, we were woken early in the morning by our newly born daughter crying incessantly. We thought she would settle if we took her for a drive in the car. So off we set along the coastal road from Episkopi to Paphos. The crying did not subside. And then it hit us: she was hungry. We might seem to be incredibly unintelligent, but the fact is that as a parent you learn on the job. We had no mothers around to guide us. Joe had never had a mother.

There was talk of sending them to a Parental Assessment Centre. Joe, seeing which way the wind was blowing, decided to volunteer for it before they were pressed to do it. The Parental Assessment Centre ran a 12 week course at a residential centre in the Midlands. Joe, Becky and Adele found themselves under the microscope again as they completed different elements of a very intensive programme. No one tried to understand Joe's PTSD because none of the staff had had any awareness training; so it was better just to ignore it and put Joe's behavioral issues down to poor attitudes. They endured a week until, in the second week, a young social worker ordered Joe to complete a session on the use of play dough. It was an integral part of the process and could not be missed. Not seeing the relevance of play dough to a 3 month old baby, he refused. When he was challenged on this he understandably, if inappropriately, lost his temper and said things that he would later regret. The social worker immediately reported his behaviour to her bosses. Without warning, Joe and Becky were thrown off the programme and Adele was placed into foster care two weeks before her first Christmas. Joe and Becky had no idea where she was and access to her was denied.

As you read this, I wonder if, as I did, a more appropriate scenario could have played out. What if, at an early stage, someone in the system had bothered to understand Joe and his PTSD? What if someone had offered Joe and Becky a proper relationship? What if Joe and Becky had been treated like human beings? What if people didn't rush to judgment? What if we lived in a world that wasn't so underpinned by fear that we had to rely on process for everything? The truth is that wherever there is need, we invest so much in the infrastructure and the process to protect bosses from blame and litigation when things (as they will) go wrong, that there is little left to spend on the beneficiary at the end of it all. What if we cared? Before the welfare state, people cared for each other in their communities. If there was a problem people rallied around. We still reminisce about the blitz spirit, when, at our darkest hour, we supported each other. The irony was that at that same time Beveridge was designing what we now call the welfare state. Its objectives were noble and have done a great deal to end poverty, but it has been at the expense of individual and collective responsibility. Whenever something 'needs to be done', we look to the state to create a solution. What if we reformed the welfare state, turning it upside down so that it worked from the bottom up rather than from the top down – surely the intent behind the Big Society?

Let us just imagine how Joe's life might have played out if we truly embraced the power of relationships to nurture and heal. Overlooking the controversial fact that he was born without any relationship beyond the biological, how could society have eased his path into mature adulthood? The first point, which is now being addressed by the Government, is to make adoption easier. If Joe had been placed into adoption when he was born, many of the subsequent problems might have been avoided. He would have been brought up by loving trusted parents within a supportive and nurturing framework. The attitudes and behaviours that prevented him living in long-term foster care resulting in him being placed in care might have been very different. Had there been some form of transitional support from care he might have avoided the heartache of abandonment. Only the Army began to fulfil some of his basic human needs and provide the self-respect, discipline and camaraderie that had been lacking from his life before. His transition to civilian life could have been easier with support especially with a greater understanding of PTSD. He was lucky eventually that he had the support of a girl who loved him. But it is the most recent situation that reflects so badly on the society that we have created. Because of high profile cases like Baby P we have, rightly, taken the matter of child protection seriously. Social workers are trained to look for early signs of abuse. Joe's underlying effects of PTSD would have set off alarm bells. But this is where it all went wrong. In all matters we should seek to understand before we act. But this takes time, as relationships need to be established. And time equals money. It is easier and cheaper to create a checklist of generic factors that would indicate high risk to the child and once a threshold has been crossed act regardless of individual circumstance. The fear that exists within our society does not serve the public good and certainly hasn't served Joe.

And, finally, Tracy. Tracy arrived at the homelessness charity I chair in Bristol, Bristol Foundation Housing. Like many residents who end up with us, her behaviour often reflected the wretchedness of her life. One day she 'kicked off' at a time when the CEO, Justin, was visiting. He was told that there was no alternative but to evict her: to move her wretchedness on for someone else to take responsibility for it. But Justin decided to talk to her, to build a relationship, to seek to understand. No one had ever bothered to ask her what her story was, but in a painful hour it all spilled out. Tracy was 25. She had lived in 500 homes during her life, a life that had started with rejection. From foster homes, to care, from care to hostels no one had actually cared. The only attention she received was abusive. She lost herself in alcohol, drugs and sex, the fruit of which had been six stillborn children. Finally she gave birth to a child, who was immediately taken from her and placed in adoption since she was not deemed to be a fit mother. She told Justin that one of her stillborn children had been placed in a pauper's grave. She had sought it out and found it covered in weeds with no markings – another lost and unidentified soul like her. Having listened to her story, Justin gently told her that he would buy a gravestone for that child and organise a ceremony to mark his life. She wept and within a moment her whole attitude was transformed; her body language reflected for the first time the love that she had received. She now lives as a model resident, her room always tidy with the self-respect that a simple act of kindness and compassion instilled. What Justin demonstrated was a leadership that transmitted the simple love that Tracy had never felt before.

The tide of human misery still flows around us but we are both blind to it and, more importantly, fail to see the potential that comes from the challenges we all face in life. What of those many people who face a lifetime of disappointment and even suffering? Surely we should be giving them the opportunity to discover their purpose, the experiences that will help shape their destiny – and give them hope. We live in a rapidly changing world and it will be Emma's generation who hold the key to its future. There are Emmas, Bens, Davids, Tracys and Joes in every parish. Are we aware of them? What could we be doing to create the relationships that might just prevent this tide of misery? They need disciples like Neil, the Deputy Head, modern leaders who see a need and take the risk of trying to meet it in big and small ways. Our faith is best expressed through social justice. It allows the Disciple to bridge the gap between the teaching of the church and practical action which makes that teaching relevant to the wider world. After trying to understand discipleship and describing the journey, I will endeavour to propose how contemporary Christians might respond by becoming agents of change and how those who are perceived as 'problems' can be fulfilled in service to others in the world.

4

The Disciple

Truth is the doorway we must walk through in order to be free. Pope Benedict XVI

The first question to answer is: what is a disciple? Jesus defines this clearly in John 8:31–2 when he says: *"If you hold to my teaching, you are really my disciples. Then you will know the truth, and the truth will set you free" (NIV).* Stephen Cherry describes it well in the excellent book *Barefoot Disciple* (from which I will unashamedly quote frequently):

> The disciples are not them [the twelve disciples] or at least not exclusively them, but us, all of us who are trying, and who have tried down the ages, to follow the way of Jesus. Based on the Latin word 'discipulus', which means 'pupil' or 'student', the words 'disciple' and 'discipleship' carry the often hidden message that the quest for authentic, positive, Christian living involves learning. Discipleship learning is neither academic nor functional. God's curriculum, if we can think of it that way, is less about learning new things and more about becoming new people. It is not about ensuring that people are being informed so much as transformed.

And we don't learn new things or become new people by standing still. It is easy to go to church, pick up a book or join a study group, but this was not Jesus' way. Many Christians choose to follow the well-worn paths of others. *Do not go where the path may lead, go instead where there is no path and leave a trail.* (Ralph Waldo Emerson) This is the way of the true Disciple; he will be seeking the path less travelled that is true to his calling. It is no coincidence that Jesus says, *I am the way the truth and the life* (John 14:6). The 'way' hints at a path or a journey and this was the way that Jesus taught his disciples by taking them on journeys. Many of the great biblical stories are told around a journey, whether on a large scale in the escape from Egypt, as Moses led the Israelites to the Promised Land, or the final walk of Jesus to Golgotha and the cross. In its early days Christianity was described as the 'way'.

Ultimately the *Disciple's Journey* provides a narrative which allows the Disciple options at every stage. In a world that demands certainty, the narrative creates the opportunity to explore possibility, through which truth can emerge. In a post Christian culture there exists a paradox. The younger generation are the first to have been broadly educated beyond the Judaeo/Christian foundations which used to underpin our society. Yet they are seeking meaning in a way that is spawning a range of New Age alternatives and an attraction to the Eastern religions. I offer the *Disciple's Journey* as a means of discovering that meaning and purpose to life through a Christian faith which I hope finds new relevance. It is an opportunity not only to ask 'Who am I?, but also, maybe more importantly, 'who am I not?'

This book attempts to describe the journey in pursuit of this quest. Interestingly, the clues are all around us but we just don't notice. I can recall as an officer cadet at the Royal Military Academy Sandhurst, reciting the words from the

Collect that starts this book:

> Almighty God, whose Son Jesus Christ, the Lord of all
> life, came not to be served but to serve, help us to be
> masters of ourselves that we may be servants of others
> and teach us to Serve to Lead, through the same Jesus
> Christ, Our Lord, Amen

But it was only years later that I really began to understand their power. The Collect from Sandhurst, deeply embedded in all who graduate from what is one of the world's foremost centres of leadership, provides the essence of the *Disciple's Journey*. It highlights the word 'service', reminding us that the short earthly ministry of Jesus Christ was about service to others. As aspirant disciples, the first step is to find the humility to become masters of ourselves so that we may be servants to others. By so doing we are able to become passionate leaders in a world that is crying out for Christ-like leadership – leadership that is in service to the common good. Equally, the famous invitation from Jesus to follow him are some of the most quoted words in the New Testament, but do we really understand their significance in our lives as Christians?

> Then Jesus said to his disciples, "If anyone would come
> after me, he must deny himself and take up his cross and
> follow me. For whoever wants to save his life will lose
> it, but whoever loses his life for me will find it. What
> good will it be for a man if he gains the whole world, yet
> forfeits his soul? Or what can a man give in exchange
> for his soul? For the Son of Man is going to come in his
> Father's glory with his angels, and then he will reward
> each person according to what he has done.
>
> *Matthew 16:24–27, NIV*

It is the toughest invitation you will ever receive. It is easily refused since the implications are too great for most of us to bear. The prospect of losing life is not one that we readily embrace in the material world we become so attached to. But the great thing is that the only life we lose is the one that isn't serving us, however attractive it might appear. Looking back, attachment to the material stultifies life without much real forward momentum, although achieving ambition or wealth may give the impression of progress. It is only when we take a conscious step away from our old life, the one that we are going to lose anyway, that the process of learning begins. I run mentoring programmes for young entrepreneurs in the Middle East. We learn by walking through the desert or wandering through olive groves. There is great power in walking and talking and this was Jesus' way of communicating his wisdom. It allows relationship to develop in a non-confrontational uninhibited way. Think of the walks you have enjoyed and the conversations you have had: often more real than those we have when sitting facing each other over a table. It is this journey not only in relationship with God, but with our fellow human beings, that lies before the Disciple

The concept of the journey underpins so much of the human story. Ultimately the *Disciple's Journey* is the summed up in the story of the three wise men as expressed in Jesus of Nazareth: The Infancy Narratives by Pope Benedict XVI in which he writes, *The key point is this: the wise men from the east are a new beginning. They represent the journeying of humanity towards Christ. They initiate a procession that continues throughout history. Not only do they represent the people who have found the way to Christ, they represent the inner aspiration of the human spirit, the dynamism of religious and human reason toward him.*

Stephen Cherry again: *True disciples are those who absorb*

Jesus' wisdom by becoming his travelling companions on the way. What happens to us on the road is a vital source of deep learning and real insight. The journey of discipleship involves crossing the boundaries of our personal comfort zone again and again. This is always going to be disconcerting and sometimes painful, but it seems to be the way in which God organises our apprenticeship in Christ. We are true disciples when we are doing our best to latch on to Jesus' way of life by being open to the adventures that God has given us. It is when we take three things together: learning from Scripture, learning from Christ's travelling companions and learning from our own experience on the journey, that we open ourselves to being constantly renewed.

Discipleship is an adventure: it is the adventure of our lives, but like all adventures it is full of challenge and takes courage to start. It is the experience of the adventure that allows us to learn and grow into our particular discipleship. Another great description of discipleship is contained in the book *Seven* by Richard Johnson *A Disciple of Jesus is someone who tries to live all their life in a Jesus way. A disciple is an active, intentional learner, a practitioner, a doer of the Word not just a student. A disciple is accountable to someone who knows them and helps them grow and live. A disciple is an apprentice.* A key component of the *Disciple's Journey* is experiential learning, personal growth and collaborative action. It allows us to develop self-knowledge and an understanding of and empathy for others. It encourages inner work, which is more about being than doing. Jesus is the supreme example and the Holy Spirit is the prime agent of personal transformation through which we can discern his calling on our lives. This can be a difficult and painful journey and thus easily avoided rather than embraced. But the key is accountability through a mentor who is there to support the process of growth.

Now the Lord is the Spirit, and where the Spirit of the Lord is, there is freedom. And we, who with unveiled faces all reflect the Lord's glory, are being transformed into his likeness with ever-increasing glory, which comes from the Lord, who is the Spirit.

2 Corinthians 3:17–18, NIV

Stanley Hauerwas in his book *Hannah's Child* offers another perspective. In the sermon he gave at his father's funeral he talked about his father's gentleness. *Jesus does not tell us that we should try to be poor in spirit, meek or peacemakers. He simply says that many of those who called into his kingdom will find themselves so constituted. We cannot try to be meek or gentle in order to become a disciple of this gentle Jesus, but in learning to be his disciple some of us will discover that we have been gentled. Jesus' gentleness is nowhere more apparent than in his submission to the cross and, even there, in his wish that no harm would come to his persecutors. But it is no less apparent in his willingness to be touched by the sick and troubled, to be with the social outcasts and powerless, and, in his time of agony, to share a meal with his disciples that has now become the feast of the new age.*

Because the *Disciple's Journey* is a journey of faith, it is only with each step that God reveals his heart and we discover the virtues that allow us to become the mirrors of Christ in the world. We can't set ourselves the target of becoming more humble or more gentle, but by having the courage to take the next step we allow these virtues to be revealed within us in a way that others can see, while we may not. It is one of the great paradoxes of our faith.

This is the key: the glory of God shines within each of us, but we have locked it into a prison of fear and doubt so that it can't be a light to the world. By stepping into the journey of faith, we begin the process of releasing the light from the prison. As a nation, through faith in something better and forgiveness, truth and reconciliation, South Africa demonstrated that if fear can be defeated, human possibility can be unlocked. Through fear's antidote, love, we can discover that we are stronger than we think we are. As we overcome challenges we become stronger still.

It is unsurprising that much of Jesus' ministry was highly critical of the Pharisees. They are a reflection of the world in which we live where the law reigns supreme. How often does one hear of an immoral act justified by the cry, *Well, it was legal*. This is a journey from the law, which defines right and wrong in the material world and in so doing limits our freedom to being all that God created us to be, to the Spirit which defines right and wrong in heavenly terms and allows us to fulfil God's calling on our lives. The law insists on straight lines to create certainty. Inevitably it is black and white for it demands clarity. And it needs judgement – you are either right or wrong. This was the approach of the Pharisees and sadly we see it too often in our church today when people are quick to judge the behaviour of others. This was not the way of Jesus and cannot be the way for his disciples. He rejected the approach of the Pharisees. His greatest commandment was that we should love our God with all our heart and our neighbour as ourselves. The law and the judgement that goes with it creates a fear that freezes and keeps people where they are. As the disciples of Jesus discovered, they had to give up the certainty of their lives, their jobs, their material wealth and security for the uncertainty of faith. It is a tough call, but as Jesus says we must be prepared to give up everything, particularly our attachment to the material world in which we live, in order to fully serve him.

Jesus looked at him and loved him. "One thing you lack," he said. "Go, sell everything you have and give to the poor, and you will have treasure in heaven. Then come, follow me"

Mark 10:21

There is something about travel. It seems so much easier to engage with complete strangers and get new perspectives on life and this is true for the Disciple too. One of the things about the work I do with mentoring is the speed at which a room full of strangers can open up in a way that, often, they have never done before, and would not do if the room were full of some of the closest people in their lives. Stephen Cherry talks about *the exposure to difference* as a stimulation to adult learning. Mentoring, more of which later, unashamedly addresses the attitudinal and behavioural challenges of becoming a Disciple – often those emotional challenges that we dare not talk to anyone about. It creates an environment where people are encouraged to discuss their innermost hopes and fears. As Stephen Cherry puts it, *This, I believe, is a relational, spiritual and formational process through which we discover we have more in common with strangers than we thought and that we are ourselves stranger than we ever dared imagine.*

Because discipleship is also a journey of learning, we discover that we only really learn through the challenges that life throws at us. When bad things happen to us our first reaction is *Why me?* and *If there is a God, how could he let this happen to me?* Bad things do happen, but that is where the gold is if you are seeking it. It is through the tough experiences of life that God is able to refine us and get us to be the disciples and leaders he wants us to be. Again you won't get it from a book. It is a relational, spiritual and formational process, which comes alive by having the courage and humility to step out of the comfort zone of your known world into the unknown territory of a future that God has planned for you. Indeed it is about becoming more like Jesus so that he can use you to play the role planned for you in the kingdom. The twelve disciples had Jesus as their mentor and through the Holy Spirit he remains one now, but we also need someone to walk alongside us as we embark on our own journey, which is why the role of the mentor is so important.

If the title of this book is 'Be', what better way to sum up the attitudes required of a Disciple than reminding ourselves of the Beatitudes (Be Attitudes) which beautifully summarise the kingdom that we all want to build, and how by being a true Disciple we can play our part in achieving it:

> Blessed are the poor in spirit,
> for theirs is the kingdom of heaven.
> Blessed are those who mourn,
> for they will be comforted.
> Blessed are the meek,
> for they will inherit the earth.
> Blessed are those who hunger and thirst for
> righteousness',
> for they will be filled.
> Blessed are the merciful,
> for they will be shown mercy.
> Blessed are the pure in heart,
> for they will see God.
> Blessed are the peacemakers,
> for they will be called sons of God.
> Blessed are those who are persecuted because of
> righteousness,
> for theirs is the kingdom of heaven.

Blessed are you when people insult you, persecute you and falsely say all kinds of evil against you because of me. Rejoice and be glad, because great is your reward in heaven, for in the same way they persecuted the prophets who were before you.

Matthew 5:3–12, NIV

* * *

Blessed are you for giving it a go.

5

The Disciple's Journey

As a prisoner for the Lord, then, I urge you to live a life worthy of the calling you have received. Be completely humble and gentle; be patient, bearing with one another in love. Make every effort to keep the unity of the Spirit through the bond of peace. There is one body and one Spirit, just as you were called to one hope when you were called; one Lord, one faith, one baptism; one God and Father of all, who is over all and through all and in all.

But to each one of us grace has been given as Christ apportioned it. This is why it says:

> "When he ascended on high,
> he took many captives
> and gave gifts to his people."

(What does "he ascended" mean except that he also descended to the lower, earthly regions? He who descended is the very one who ascended higher than all the heavens, in order to fill the whole universe.) So Christ himself gave the apostles, the prophets, the evangelists, the pastors and teachers, to equip his people for works of service, so that the body of Christ may be built up until we all reach unity in the faith and in the knowledge of the Son of God and become mature, attaining to the whole measure of the fullness of Christ.

Then we will no longer be infants, tossed back and forth by the waves, and blown here and there by every wind of teaching and by the cunning and craftiness of people in their deceitful scheming. Instead, speaking the truth in love, we will grow to become in every respect the mature body of him who is the head, that is, Christ. From him the whole body, joined and held together by every supporting ligament, grows and builds itself up in love, as each part does its work.

Ephesians 4:1–16, NIV

We all love stories whether delivered in books, film or theatre. Stories are how we make sense of our lives. In every great epic story there is a hero or heroine who struggles to fulfil a quest of some sort. The optimism of their dream quickly descends into the reality of the challenges and at some point all seems lost. But the hero or heroine perseveres and against all the odds wins through in a way that profoundly moves the reader/viewer. It moves us since this is the eternal story stirred within each of us to pursue our own story, our destiny to reveal the hero within. The *Disciple's Journey* maps out that story.

This passage from Ephesians sums up the essence of the *Disciple's Journey*. Within these sixteen verses are the secrets to fulfilling our individual God given destiny in life and in so doing fulfilling God's destiny for the world. We live in a world that craves meaning. What is the purpose of our lives? Why are we here? Why do we have a church? We seek the kingdom, but fail to realise that we have it within our grasp. It is interesting to note that St Paul begins the passage with the phrase *As a prisoner for the Lord*. There is not only the reality that he was writing from prison, but the inference that he had become a 'prisoner' of God's love which had released him into service to the world. As human beings the paradox is that we have to release ourselves from the prison of ourselves first before we can embrace the 'prison' of God's love. The *Disciple's Journey* is about releasing ourselves from the prison of fear and doubt to discern our calling, for you have been called by God. St Paul is writing to all the churches in Ephesus so we can assume that he is using the word 'you' in the plural. The letter was to believers but the call to believe is for everyone. God calls all of us since we have all been created uniquely for a specific purpose. That purpose is revealed individually but used collectively in order to live the kingdom life here and now. Our calling does not arrive in a registered envelope with a clear mission laid out before us, nor is it something we choose – it chooses us, but only when we take the first steps to reveal it.

Richard Rohr puts this well when he describes the two halves of life. The first half is about establishing identity and he calls this our 'container'. It is about discerning what I am and what I am not. You see it with young children in the playground. They explore each other to establish those things that hold them together and those that hold them apart. It can be a painful time as we realise that we are not all the same. Paradoxically as we identify our uniqueness and those parts of us that are different from others, we soon forget the many aspects which hold us together. This leads to a strong sense of individualism and self-sufficiency. The *Disciple's Journey* will help us to remember (re-member – reconnect). Discerning the call on our lives is a long process often full of trial and error, full of blind passages. It is a process of self-refinement, constantly ridding ourselves of those elements that don't serve us, allowing our fulfilled self to emerge. In our own self-sufficiency we believe that it is down to us. But it remains true that God never calls us to do what *we* can; he calls us to do what *he* enables us to do. And this requires humility: *Be humble and gentle, and be patient with each other making allowance for each other's faults through your love.* These virtues are a continual theme of the *Disciple's Journey.* While it does take a level of humility to start, the depth of understanding of humility does not reveal itself before a time of suffering. For the *Disciple's Journey* is a constant battle between the 'flesh' and the spirit. The flesh will constantly want the glory for itself and will be impatient to achieve it. It will be impatient of the faults of others, trampling their dreams in pursuit of its own. The flesh will pursue self-interest at the expense of others. Ring any bells in our current world?

St Paul makes it quite clear in the next passage that our own calling is only relevant in the context of the bigger picture. . *Always keep yourselves united in the Holy Spirit and bind yourself together with peace. We are all one body; we have the same spirit and we have been called to the most glorious future.* In other words, to paraphrase the words of some of our current politicians, *We are in this together.* We are one body with a glorious future, but only when the individual parts of the body wake up and realise what their function is. This is the greatest challenge of our church today. Those who profess to be followers of Christ have fallen asleep on the job, allowing themselves to revel in the Holy Spirit without asking the crucial question *So what?* Coming to Christ is only the first step. We rightly celebrate when people do and get so carried away with the party we forget the purpose. It's wonderful being part of the team, one body, but the body cannot function unless the individual parts know what their function is, and that glorious future is but a distant dream if the body as one, in love, cannot step into it.

There is only one Lord, one faith and one baptism and there is only one God and Father who is over us all, in us all and living through us all.

It is interesting to note that St Paul uses the word 'one'

four times in a single sentence: one Lord, one faith, one baptism and one God. That sense of unity is over believers. We experience him in relationship. And this is the challenge of our era, where the concept of God and salvation through Jesus Christ seems utterly irrelevant to the vast majority of people. Even many who call themselves Christian are unaware of what this really means. The Holy Spirit leads us and helps us to discover and live out the purpose of our lives, enabling us to be witnesses for Christ, working as parts of the whole body.

Then others can see and be drawn to the light of Christ. When we are living in Christ, and have been filled with the Holy Spirit – and go on being filled and led by him – we can be used as living examples, enabling others to begin to see something of the character of Jesus. This is where the link with the passage from James is so crucial.

What good is it, my brothers, if a man claims to have faith but has no deeds? Can such faith save him? Suppose a brother or a sister is without clothes and daily food. If one of you says to him, "Go, I wish you well; keep warm and well fed," but does nothing about his physical needs, what good is it? In the same way, faith by itself, if it is not accompanied by action, is dead.

But someone will say, "You have faith; I have deeds."

Show me your faith without deeds, and I will show you my faith by what I do. You believe that there is one God. Good! Even the demons believe that – and shudder.

James 2:14–19, NIV

This passage provides the connection between our inner being and how we act in the world. We do not manifest our faith by congregating in church buildings (though of course we should not give up meeting together.) Going to church may nourish and feed our inner being, but, in the same way that we eat food to live, the act of eating is not life itself. We make manifest our faith through our deeds in the world in a way that is relevant to the world and meets its needs.

So what does that mean to me? *But to each one of us grace has been given as Christ apportioned it. This is why it says: "When he ascended on high, he led captives in his train and gave gifts to men."* Each one has been favoured with gifts apportioned by Christ through the Holy Spirit as he ascended into heaven. Yet again there is that reference to captives, indicating that we are held prisoner in his love through which our gifts are revealed – but only when we follow his lead, again the essence of the *Disciple's Journey*. Following, by its nature, does not allow us to stand still. We have to step out with the knowledge of that grace, as Christ clearly manifested during his own short earthly ministry. As he did, so we are invited to do.

This leads us to reflect on the crucifixion of Jesus, a terrifying cruelty, voluntarily entered into by him to free us from sin. Understanding the pain we create for ourselves through sin, he endured our punishment upon the cross. What love, what leadership! This single historic act allows that even though I mess up I can still repent and find forgiveness – through his grace growing closer to him, so that I may truly serve the king in his kingdom.

Having been raised from the dead, Christ could take the highest place at the right hand of the Father. The Spirit was sent and the Holy Trinity was revealed.

When we find ourselves in dark places there are choices we have to make – we either wallow in self-pity or take the opportunity to rid ourselves of unhelpful things, and grow into the full discovery of who we are in Christ, and go on to live out the fullness of our calling – knowing that he, Jesus, has endured so much pain for us.

It was Christ who gave some to be apostles, some to be prophets, some to be evangelists, and some to be pastors and teachers, to prepare God's people for works of service, so that the body of Christ may be built up until we all reach unity in the faith and in the knowledge of the Son of God and become mature, attaining to the whole measure of the fullness of Christ.

In the passage from Ephesians 4 the five principal roles for followers of Christ are clearly laid out; apostles, prophets, evangelists, pastors and teachers along with their purpose. Let us look at the purpose first since this informs the roles. Each are to prepare God's people in the world for works of service to each other. This allows the essence of our faith to be made manifest while allowing us the opportunity to discover who we are and why we are here. But the works of service are only part of the journey; they are not the destination. The destination is the body of Christ built up until we reach a unity in faith attaining to the full measure of the fullness of Christ. United with him,in him, our faith will be so powerful, it will destroy the fear that pervades our culture and holds us all apart. What does that look like?

We get occasional glimpses of the possibilities that could be unlocked if Christians truly came together in service. When the British nation stood united against a common enemy during the Second World War, we collectively found an extraordinarily deep sense of unity in a shared purpose.

The five principal roles or functions described by Paul are to enable believers in Jesus to operate effectively in unity – under Jesus Christ, whose will is to draw people to himself. The roles and functions to be exercised in unity in Christ are different but complementary.

It has been argued that the Western church has become so focused on evangelism, pastoral work and teaching that it has failed to acknowledge the crucial roles of apostles and prophets. There are many reasons for this. On one hand in our self-effacing way we believe we are not worthy to be called apostles and prophets; on the other they are seen as principally male functions and in an emasculated church they have become less valued. But let us look at each of them in more detail, for we will see that the neglect of these two functions is at the root of the failing church.

The writings of Alan Hirsch offer an interpretation of the nature of these roles. In his book *The Forgotten Ways* he brings their character to life. Those who are 'sent out' on the Christian 'mission' may have something in common with entrepreneurs (though without the profit motive). They seek for new ways to make an impact in the world. They are constantly focused on the future, bridging generations, creating new ideas and developing new leaders. They are unconventional and often seen by those of a more conservative disposition as mavericks. They are unsettling individuals since they are, by nature unhappy with the status quo, and seek alternative means of communicating. They embrace uncertainty in a world that craves certainty. In a church that has tried to create certainty in its structures and its hierarchy, 'apostles' can be seen as a threat. They revisit the Bible and interpret in new ways. They are impossible to control and hate accountability since they see this as limiting their freedom. They are essential to the fulfilment of the kingdom since God will use them, as he has throughout the course of biblical history, to shake people out of their complacency and their certainties.

Prophets may discern God's will and often speak into the present. They protect his truth against the mores of the culture of the day. They keep us focused on the right path. They are complementary to the apostles. Evangelists use their enthusiasm to draw people to faith. Pastors are there to nurture and protect God's flock. They are the natural care-givers, healing and forgiving. Teachers help us to make sense of the Word. They are there to discern meaning and wisdom, and communicate it to the flock. St Paul placed no hierarchy on these functions and there are some who would say that the church has done pretty well without apostles and prophets. But maybe in focusing on the other three we might also be revealing the crisis of leadership in the church today.

By stepping into discipleship, we take the first step into discerning our function within the body of Christ. I will return to this theme again since it fundamental to a fulfilling life. Once we know why we are here, it gives us that inner confidence that allows us to fully 'be'. With this, as this passage from Ephesians goes on to say, *Then we will no longer be infants, tossed back and forth by the waves, and blow here and there by every wind of teaching and by the cunning and craftiness of men in their deceitful scheming.* This does not mean that we will become people of arrogant certainty, although the risk of this is always there. It means that we can live our lives knowing what our purpose is and how it fits into the bigger picture. While we are still searching, we are vulnerable to *being tossed back and forth by the waves … and to the cunning and craftiness of men.* Young people are particularly vulnerable during this stage, which is one reason why mentoring can be so helpful.

Instead, speaking the truth in love, we will in all things grow up into him who is the Head, that is, Christ. From him the whole body, joined and held together by every supporting ligament, grows and builds itself up in love, as each part does its work. This is the glorious alternative to being tossed back and forth by the waves. As we extend our journey of discipleship, we grow ever closer towards Christ, who as the ultimate leader, the Head, has prepared a unique and particular place for us within the body, the fulfilment of which is the kingdom of God. Notice the phrase that the body 'grows and builds itself up in love', as each part does its work. Each part requires careful nurturing within a loving environment. Just reflect on this within your own experience. Are the churches geared up to nurture congregations towards the fulfilment of their individual purpose? Do they even create a loving environment within which the individual parts of the body can identify themselves and grow? Or are we more likely to rush to judgement driven by fear and kill the very seed that is trying to burst into flower? Does the church reach out to help people discover their purpose or are is it more interested in bums on seats (and the income that is generated by this)? Has the church just become a reflection of the society we have created whereby our purpose is driven by our academic prowess? Yes we are all equal, but those with A*s and first class degrees are more equal than others. Where does that leave the rest of us? Probably feeling unworthy and unvalued, the two killers of potential. Has the church become so obsessed with second order matters, often consisting of trivia, that it has forgotten the ultimate purpose of its existence?

The point about the body of Christ is that we all have equal value. We don't create greater value by function. Yet in our judgement of each other, this is what we do. Within an environment of love we are all equal and all valued. We all have access to transformational love and we all have the power to be reflections of that love. I will return to a verse from the Beatitudes frequently, *the meek shall inherit the earth*. It seems counter-intuitive of the meritocratic culture we live in, but, in my experience, I have seen more genuine love expressed, more hope generated and crucially more potential for the body of Christ to move amongst those who have little or nothing, those who have suffered and those who have overcome great hardship to achieve small victories. It seems clear that it is from this least likely source that the kingdom will come. If you have nothing it is easier to see this transformational love than if you have everything in material terms. It is easier to become a Disciple and pursue your earthly purpose when you have nothing to lose than it is to put all you possess on the line and potentially sacrifice it all.

This theme of constantly stepping beyond our comfort zone is at the heart of this book. The key to being set free is to be free to live the life that God has planned for you. But you won't discover God's purpose for your life by standing still. It is constantly taking the next step beyond your comfort zone that will draw you nearer to God and his purpose. It is not until you are prepared to set out on a journey of faith – the *Disciple's Journey* – that you discover the God-given calling on your life. While the passage from Ephesians maps out the purpose of the journey, what better summary of what this means in our lives than the words of St Paul to the Romans,

Just as each of has one body with many members, and these members do not all have the same function, so in Christ we who are many form one body, and each member belongs to all the others. We have different gifts, according to the grace given us. If a man's gift is prophesying, let him use it in proportion to his faith. If it is serving, let him serve; if it is teaching, let him teach; if it is encouraging, let him encourage, let him encourage; if it is contributing to the needs of others, let him give generously; if it is leadership, let him govern diligently; if it is showing mercy, let him do it cheerfully.

Love must be sincere. Hate what is evil; cling to what is good. Be devoted to one another in brotherly love. Honour one another above yourselves. Never be lacking in zeal, but keep your spiritual fervour, serving the Lord. Be joyful in hope, patient in affliction, faithful in prayer. Share with

God's people who are in need. Practise hospitality.

Bless those who persecute you; bless and do not curse. Rejoice with those who rejoice; mourn with those who mourn. Live in harmony with one another. Do not be proud, but be willing to associate with people of low position. Do not be conceited.

Romans 12:4–16, NIV

To emphasise the criticality of this in our lives, Paul offers another, but similar perspective in this well known passage:

There are different kinds of gifts, but the same Spirit. There are different kinds of service, but the same Lord. There are different types of working, but the same God works all of them in all men. Now to each one of them the manifestation of the Spirit is given for the common good.

Now to each one the manifestation of the Spirit is given for the common good. To one there is given through the Spirit the message of wisdom, to another the message of knowledge by means of the same Spirit, to another faith by the same Spirit, to another gifts of healing by that one Spirit, to another miraculous powers, to another prophecy, to another distinguishing between spirits, to another speaking in different kinds of tongues, and to still another the interpretation of tongues.

1 Corinthians 12:4–10, NIV

It is interesting to note the number of times that the word 'Spirit' is used in this passage. It emphasises the point that what is needed to release our purpose is 'inspiration' [literally: *in Spirit*]. The Holy Spirit inspires the hearts of Christians, and he guides us. So we can find the truth about the purpose that God has placed on our lives. I use the analogy of a jigsaw. Within our hearts is a perfectly formed jigsaw piece – our truth. Once we have discovered our shape and removed the rough edges accumulated through life, we can sacrifice it to join up with the pieces with which we interlock and thereby, over time is built the perfect whole – the body of Christ. The word 'sacrifice' is derived from the Latin: to make holy or wholly. Believers are joined together in one body – united in Christ.

> The body is a unit, though it is made up of many parts; and though all its parts are many, they form one body. So it is with Christ. For we were all baptised by one Spirit into one body – whether Jews or Greeks, slave or free – and we were all given the one Spirit to drink.
>
> *1 Corinthians 12:12–13, NIV*

Paul continues, using the analogy of a human body to illustrate the 'body of Christ', which means believers in Jesus who have been baptised by the Holy Spirit.

All human endeavour calls for individuals who are prepared to step into the unknown. There is an enemy to defeat, more of which later, but partly it is a matter of finding the inner resilience to overcome the many challenges that will be thrown at the Disciple as he pursues his quest, but, *... I can do everything with the help of Christ who gives me the strength I need* (Philippians 4:13).

The *Disciple's Journey* is not just our personal journey, it is the journey of humanity. It is that Great Quest where we discover that the story that underpins our lives is universal. A Disciple is someone who has given his or her life to God in an act of 'passionate humility' as Stephen Cherry describes it in his book *The Barefoot Disciple*. The *Disciple's Journey* is underpinned by that concept of true humility, which is one of the great Christian virtues, not easily found, but which is the key to discovering the other great virtues expressed in

Colossians 3:12: compassion, kindness, gentleness, patience and, above all, love. This is where the journey becomes about more than just me. It is also about leadership, and by exercising self-control under the lordship of Christ I can become a leader to others. By embarking on my own *Disciple's Journey*, I am extending an invitation for others to do the same. In describing the various stages of the *Disciple's Journey* I will bring them alive through some of my experiences and lessons along the way.

At the start of *Disciple's Journey*, we are dead and lost, but by the end we find true life and have found our purpose in the kingdom. Throughout his earthly ministry, Jesus challenged people to become disciples by embarking on a journey of faith. He brings this alive most vividly with the invitation to Peter (and by extension all his disciples) to walk on water. *Take courage. It is I. Don't be afraid* (Matthew 14:27). Peter follows him and begins to walk on water until his courage fails him and he starts to sink. *Immediately Jesus reached out his hand and caught him. 'You of little faith' he said. 'Why did you doubt?* (Matthew 14:31).

This is a recurring theme of the *Disciple's Journey* as at each stage we face new challenges and fears. Climbing out of the boat is the most difficult first step, since it means walking away from everything that helps us feel secure. Often, like Peter, we take the step while leaving everyone else in the boat. It is painful and fearful and even though there may be high levels of confidence when you start, as Peter discovers, this can wane very quickly when reality kicks in. We lose courage and encounter self-doubt.

A key figure in the journey is the mentor, who helps by restoring faith and banishing self-doubt while holding the Disciple accountable for taking the next watery step. We may see in this something of a reflection of what Jesus did for Peter in that incident of walking on water.

We learn something important about faith from Jesus' ministry to Thomas who before he had seen the risen Lord had declared:

"Unless I see the nail marks in his hands and put my fingers where the nails were, and put my hand into his side, I will not believe it..." *John 20:25b, NIV.*

A week later, when Jesus was with the disciples, he said to Thomas:

"Put your finger here; see my hands. Reach out your hand and put it into my side. Stop doubting and believe."

John v. 27b, NIV

Notice that Jesus is compassionate to Thomas, but nowhere does he *commend* doubt. On the contrary the Disciple is told firmly to stop doubting! So there can be a battle to fight, and we see that the will is involved in faith, not just feelings. The disciple needs to be aware of that.

The *Disciple's Journey* is broken down into ten stages, which will be described in detail. They are symbolic of the steps we take as we step into the unknown. While it is tough, the reward for perseverance is the revelation of a virtue, which will provide the values that will underpin every aspect of your being. The journey has three key components: Believe, Become, Belong. The Believe phase is when we use our faith to step out of the comfort zone of our everyday lives, searching for our purpose. We will not discover ourselves by standing still and doing what we always do. It is tough because we are stepping away from what is known into what is unknown. Here we will begin believe in ourself and discern our future direction, overcome resistance and link up with a guide to accompany us at key moments in our journey. Within this phase there are four stages: Ordinary

World, Hearing the Call, Refusing the Call and Meeting the Mentor. The next phase is called Become since it is when we begin to discover our identity and purpose. It begins the journey of faith when we step into uncertainty often not knowing where we are going, only being able to discern the next step. It is the stage of commitment combined with the reality of what we have taken on. Those aspects of our character that no longer serve us will begin to emerge. Within this phase are three stages: Crossing the Line, Trials, Allies and Enemies and Facing the Darkness. The final stage is called Belong when we discover that we are just a small part of something much bigger and begin to take up our part. Within this phase are three stages:Contemplation, A New Perspective and the Return.

The Disciples heard the call, stepped out of the comfort zones of their ordinary worlds, had Jesus as a mentor, stepped across the line of faith and commitment, faced the darkness at the Cross, gained a new perspective of life at the resurrection and Pentecost, and then returned to preach the good news. It is rarely one complete journey. Indeed, as I will illustrate, journey builds on journey like a spiral, increasing our levels of consciousness and drawing us closer to our shared God-given destiny, in service to the world. You can be at different stages at different levels of your life at the same time and you can be certain that once you have made the return to your Ordinary World, the call to adventure does not subside. Indeed it is the Disciple's imperative that he returns to his Ordinary World to share his story to inspire and give tacit permission to others to set out on their journey too.

We understand the story of the Prodigal Son as a story of grace and forgiveness and these are important components of the *Disciple's Journey*, but surely it is also the story of the journey of the younger son. Seeing that his elder brother would inherit the farm, being a proud man, he set out on his own journey to discover what his purpose was all about. He cashes in his share of the inheritance and off he travels to the city where the temptation of the fleshpots is too great. He buries his sense of purpose, his dreams in an increasing spiral of depravity, moving well past the point where shame might have pulled him up. Like a drunk who drinks to forget, he continues until there is no more and he is left to eat nothing more than pig swill, the pain of what he has lost too hard to bear, his dreams shattered. It ended in utter shame and humiliation. There was nowhere to hide and his pride and self-sufficiency had blown away like a feather in a storm. But it is through this humiliation that he discovered the priceless gift of humility, which led him reluctantly and sheepishly to return to his father who he might have expected to judge and condemn him. Yet his father welcomed him home with open arms and forgiveness.

But we had to celebrate and be glad, because this brother of yours was dead and is alive again; he was lost and is found.

Luke 15:31, NIV

The rather stiff elder son who had never left home, nor had to, still had the material advantages of the farm, but none of the spiritual gifts acquired by his younger brother. No wonder there was envy. If we are honest, many of us are like the elder brother opting for the certain, safe, secure, material world. It is a place where it is easy to become pious and judgmental of others. Once you have experienced humiliation, it is virtually impossible to judge those who expose their vulnerability by risking the prospect of failure. The Disciple will take the risk of embarking on a journey, where he will mess up and fail, but will do so in a way that brings him closer to the Father and closer to his true being.

This is the nature of the internal journey that the Disciple is embarking upon. It is the classic battle between good and evil. It is only when we mess up that we are able to experience the true nature of grace. There is nothing so bad that grace can't heal. That is truly liberating.

While grace is there and available it should not be treated as the ultimate get out clause. *Because I know I am forgiven I can do what ever I like and stuff the consequences.* Grace is an acknowledgment of our sinful nature and is constantly available during our journey because God knows we will mess up. While we might like to kid ourselves that we are perfect, a moment's reflection reveals that we are not. Within us is a constant battle between the best of us and the worst of us. Some who professed to be Christians have inflicted great cruelty, and some have led the fight against cruelty. In living among us within the human condition, Jesus not only experienced our sinful nature, but in his death offered us, in grace, the freedom from it. In his book *Unapologetic*, Francis Spufford deliciously describes our sinful nature as the 'High Propensity to **** things Up'. Individually and collectively we always have and we always will, but at least let's face up to it and not hide behind a shield of self-righteousness or that as Christian I am better than everyone else. You're not and if you think you can do what you like and then use your 'get out of jail' card through grace, which you can, but do nothing to reflect on the particular sin that got you into trouble don't be surprised if it comes round and hits you in the face again.

We can self-righteously look back at some of the inhumanity man has inflicted on man and from our distance judge those involved. *How could someone do that?* we ask as we see skeletal survivors of Belsen stumbling past the bodies of those who didn't make it. Or the millions killed in Soviet pogroms or those Rwandan massacres. Or how could that man in the newspaper have killed his wife? As human beings we were there present and correct for all these atrocities. We stood by as we went about our daily business in the small town of Bergen, conscious each day of the sweet sickly smell that hung above us. We opted for the quiet life when our next door neighbour mysteriously disappeared in the night. *Oh I didn't want to get involved.*

I lived in Germany for many years when serving in the Army and I can recall every village having a church, every town having many and every city dominated by a beautiful cathedral. They had been there for centuries filled each Sunday with human beings worshipping the same God as we do today, listening to the stories of the same Jesus. No different to you and me. Yet the parents of those we met in the supermarket, drank with in the pubs, walked with in the parks elected Adolf Hitler and participated in some of the worst inhumanities man has committed during the course of history. And I bet quite a few went to church each Sunday and called themselves Christians.

I am perhaps labouring a point, but there was nothing in Nazi Germany that the human condition is not capable of today, whatever label we apply to ourselves. Certainly the way we behave to each other in our greed for wanting more and more and our envy when someone has more than us has laid the foundation for a society ill at ease with itself. And that is just for starters. And the Disciple needs to know this, since in embarking on an internal journey, he will encounter exactly the same traits within himself as inspired the Holocaust. That is why I began the book with the quote from the collect of the Royal Military Academy Sandhurst *help us to be masters of ourselves that we may be servants of others and teach us to Serve to Lead.*

And as for murdering the wife? One man I will never forget on frequent visits to Shepton Mallet prison is Sam, a gentle, deeply spiritual West Indian who was completing a life sentence for the murder of his wife. It was one of those moments that those of us who are married can identify with: a row, a loss of control and in Sam's case a moment of madness when he hit his wife in such a way that she died of head injuries. He had the rest of his life to reflect on this split second, which left him alone separated from his two daughters who would never see him again. Yet his faith was so strong and quietly infectious to all those around him. Sadly he was diagnosed with cancer and died a lonely death in the Royal United Hospital in Bath. But the grace he felt and displayed while alive encouraged others.

As Disciples we are not going to defeat our sinful nature, but we must be sufficiently self-aware to understand the impact that it can have and slowly, patiently over time begin to identify and draw out the virtues that will at least provide some balance. And as we do, we will draw others to us since we will begin to reflect the light that inspired them.

So where to start? Well where are you today?

6

The Ordinary World

We must be willing to let go of the life we planned so as to have the life that is waiting for us. *Joseph Campbell*

All journeys start where we are. I learned early in my work with offenders that it is vital to start where a person is and not where you want them to be. Often we think we can see the destination and thereby position ourselves further along our journey than we actually are. One of the first hard lessons is to be real and to be realistic. When we have a vision we think can see it in its final manifestation, but it does not materialise without dedication, patience and perseverance, essential companions to our journey. It is an early lesson for the Disciple to learn, for when he thinks that he can see the final destination, there is an overwhelming need to get there tomorrow. This can lead to unnecessary mistakes and shortcuts,

Dare yourself to do the unusual. You get a living by what you get; you get a life by what you give. *Winston Churchill*

The start point is the ordinary world we live in day by day. It is the world we are familiar with, where we feel secure and comfortable, where we hang onto all our hopes and fears. A huge amount of human energy is expended in maintaining this world. Sadly, most people move through life establishing and maintaining the financial security that allows them to stay in this world, earning a living to pay the rent or the mortgage, the household bills and, increasingly, the material items that give them status and credibility. If they are lucky they may be contributing to a pension scheme or saving for a rainy day. It is safe. It is the world that almost every aspect of our developed society encourages and demands. Or we become attached to ambition and status and never find the humility to realise that these are of nothing in the kingdom.

We have become a world of spectators and journalists. We go to the theatre and concerts, we watch films and TV, we are passionate about sport – mainly watching it, we have become addicted to twenty-four hour news and we go to church. When we witness riots on our streets, civil war in the Middle East, a collapse in the world markets, the eternal cry is lifted – *Something must be done*. And they are right something must be done, but the inference is that someone else must be doing it, never ourselves. And yet we are facing a future where we all need to take responsibility for change.

In our unconscious acceptance of this world we lose ourselves and our connection to God. We have forgotten what it is to be truly human. And that is why so many people feel unfulfilled, unhappy and seek reconnection through drink, drugs or extreme activities. It is a place that many Christians will recognise within themselves if they are honest: an ordinary world of church attendance on Sunday and maybe home group during the week, a rhythm that comforts and represses. Few of us are prepared to risk ridicule, criticism and judgement to step away from what we know, from what makes us feel secure. We have few moments in our lives when we have the chance to reflect and understand what our world has become. This is the opportunity to do an audit of your life. We all need to discern our calling. Knowing what is really important to us, what is of real value in our lives is the key to us taking the choices that are right for us. Successful leaders know the importance of having virtues that underpin all they do. They become their moral compass. Within each stage of the *Disciple's Journey* a virtue is revealed, which not only provides the learning from that stage, but equips us for the next stage.

My Ordinary world at the time of the start of my *Disciple's Journey* had taken me from a happy childhood in Essex, to university in Newcastle, where, reading law, I discovered the Officer Training Corps. An Army career was the least likely course for my life to take, but when my interest in matters military trumped my interest in the law, the choice between the two was taken away and I found myself joining up as a soldier. After graduation from the Royal Military Academy Sandhurst, I joined my regiment, the 15/19th King's Royal Hussars in Germany. I became what would now be termed a Cold War warrior. I have used the expression 'echoes of the future' before and looking back my early Army experience was in armoured reconnaissance. Part of our role was to advance before the main force to attract the enemy's fire so that it could be identified. Having identified the enemy's main positions we shaped the battlefield for the main force behind us to advance and destroy the enemy. It proved to be an interesting metaphor for my *Disciple's Journey* as I found myself as a pioneer for those greater than myself, opening up a space to exploit the new approaches to entrenched problems that I was called to create. Along the way I had to draw the fire of my internal enemies in order to be effective; but more of this later. I had joined the Army a short service officer on a three year commission. I was easily persuaded to extend this to a regular commission, which would offer me a career until I was 55. For this I had to return to Sandhurst for six months to complete the academic part of the syllabus, something I loved. I was able to live out of the academy and shared a house with an officer from my regiment, who went on to be Commandant of Sandhurst, and two Irish Ranger officers, one of whom had four sisters. I have spoken to people who knew in a moment that they would marry someone and then later fell in love. This happened to me and so on a glorious late summer day Cerys and I were married in the centre of Athens where her father was Defence Attache.

Over the next ten years we moved eleven times including a year in Cyprus and many years in Germany before I emerged into civilian life with four daughters in tow. I will describe how we hear the call to change in the next chapter, but at this stage it is sufficient to say that I followed an internal prompt to leave. As I left I didn't have a clue as to what I was going to do, but I had a strong sense that I wasn't going to exchange one hierarchical organisation for another. Without having a clue about business, I decided to acquire a derelict site below Pulteney Bridge by the River Avon in Bath and within two and half months turned it into a successful restaurant. Looking back it was essential to have become an entrepreneur since so much of what followed required this experience. We moved to a village suburb of Bath, Combe Down, where we brought up our children and still live there today. Echoes of the past will be revealed as the story unfolds. As someone I worked for in the Army put it, *we are all victims of our experience.* This is true in that the past shapes us. Whether it defines us for the future is down to us. The *Disciple's Journey* offers us the opportunity to reflect in a way that allows us to learn from our failures and disappointments in order that we don't become attached to them. It also allows us to see the best in ourselves so that we can reinforce achievement and truly believe in ourselves. At the end of each section is a list of questions to reflect upon. You can, of course, do this on your own, but it is a much richer experience to do it with someone else, and maybe, as the journey unfolds, with your mentor.

Virtue

In my Ordinary World I needed to discover something that would boot me out of my complacency. The virtue I found was *Inspiration*; a word that literally means in spirit. It comes from the Holy Spirit, and may be heard like promptings in the soul which cannot be ignored. It is a personal sign to act based on a persistent inner voice. It will continue to prompt until action is taken since it is there to support the Disciple on his journey of self-discovery. When we are inspired we become inspirational. The option to stay where we are no longer exists. Our inspiration is the source of our personal leadership, our creative energy and our relationships with other people. Leadership without inspiration is dry and managerial.

Those historical figures who have been acknowledged as great leaders, for all their flaws, have had an ability to inspire others, and that has been perceived as 'greatness'. We could all make our own lists of those whom we feel were in some way 'great'.

Of course the perfect leader was and is Jesus himself, and we can see how people were drawn to him, as recorded in the Gospel accounts. Some of the people began to see who he was, though many misunderstood his mission and many rejected him, even calling for his crucifixion.

Field Marshal Sir William Slim, every soldier's leadership icon, came up with rather a good quote on leadership when addressing the Australian Institute of Management in 1957:

There is a difference between leadership and management. The leader and the men who follow him represent one of the oldest, most natural and most effective of all human relationships. The manager and those he manages are a later product, with neither so romantic nor so inspiring a history. Leadership is of the spirit, compounded of personality and vision: its practice is an art. Management is of the mind, more a matter of accurate calculation, of statistics, of methods, timetables and routine; its practice is a science. Managers are necessary; leaders are essential.

The world needs leaders who inspire. The most compelling leaders from history are those that have seen a need and done something about it rather than walking by on the others side. Without 'spirit' there would have been no Agincourt, no Waterloo, no Goose Green. These were all military victories where young men overcame the odds, defying logic and reason and won all the same. It is the qualities of inspiration, courage and resilience that are needed now as we embark upon the various battles to defeat the challenges facing the world today.

There is so much need in the world and Christians should be witness to the leadership epitomised in the story of the Good Samaritan, which is preceded by the following words:

He answered, "'Love the Lord your God with all your heart and with all your soul and with all your strength and with all your mind'; and, 'Love your neighbour as yourself.'"

"You have answered correctly," Jesus replied. "Do this and you will live."

Luke 10:27–28, NIV

The story of the Good Samaritan is an inspiration to be relevant to the need in the world. In the cold, hard world of the mind, driven by targets, statistics and that awful phrase 'evidence based', we need inspiration. Because it comes from the heart, it touches other hearts. It provides a balance and reflects the fact that as human beings we are not numbers, however convenient that might be to the bureaucrat. We have hearts and emotions. Indeed our emotions run our lives most of the time if we are honest. If we are only using our minds, we are only using half our armoury and cannot be effective performers in any arena.

We are invited to be different; we have been released from the cold, hard legalistic world of the mind. If we can be mirrors of the love we have been released into, the world will be inspired to look at Christianity as something relevant to all of us. In a world where Christianity is seen as increasingly irrelevant and judgmental, what greater gift can the Disciple bring than to be a servant to others in the world?

REFLECTION

- **Who am I? What is my Ordinary World? What are the key elements?**
- **Who are the key people in your life?**
- **What are you really grateful for?**
- **What have you learned about yourself and your potential from what you have already done in your life?**
- **List the things that make you happy/unhappy at work; things that make you happy/unhappy at home.**
- **What do you currently enjoy doing?**

- What are your greatest achievements? Your proudest moment?
- What are your greatest failures and disappointments?
- Who are the great leaders that you admire? Who is your hero and why? What are the qualities they possess?
- What is important to you? What are your values? List the three values in your life that are most important.

7

Hearing the Call

For he chose us in him before the creation of the world to be holy and blameless in his sight. In love he predestined us to be adopted as his sons through Jesus Christ, in accordance with his pleasure and will – to the praise of his glorious grace, which he has freely given us in the One he loves.

Ephesians 1:4–6, NIV

One of the more interesting questions discussed at some point in life is whether our lives are governed by destiny or by fate. We live in a very fatalistic society where we have convinced ourselves that we have little control over our lives – stuff happens. But in this opening passage from Ephesians, Paul specifically uses the word 'predestined'. The very word, for some, can reinforce the view that our lives have been mapped out from the moment of conception. This passage is central to the *Disciple's Journey* since it highlights the paradox between destiny and free will and choice. Some would argue that you can't have both – that they are extremes incompatible with one another. We often fall into the trap of trying to understand the world and our faith in black and white terms. But the most interesting truths usually come with a paradox. This is one that is fundamental to our faith.

It is interesting that the word 'predestination' is preceded with the words 'In love', since this provides the essence of the *Disciple's Journey*. Whatever happens, whatever we do is underpinned by God's love. Even when our world seems to be falling apart God's love is ever present and available. So when love is used in the context of predestination it is in the context that in creating the world he gave each of us the opportunity to choose whether to step into the destiny he has planned for us: *to be adopted as his sons through Jesus Christ, in accordance with his pleasure and will – to the praise of his glorious grace, which he has freely given us in the One he loves.* Equally we have the human choice not to step into the destiny that has been planned for us. At each step in the journey we are confronted with choice. It may be simply the choice as to whether to take the next step or not. It may be the choice of how we want to be from day to day and the values that we choose to underpin our actions. It is a constant tightrope, but as long as we continue, however unsteadily, to pursue the path that has been predestined for us, we will continue to grow as children of God. We will examine how we hear the call to our predestination, but for now it is crucial that the Disciple understands that the ultimate choice lies with him.

As Carlos Ruiz Zafon writes in *The Shadow of the Wind*, *Destiny is just around the corner like a thief, but what destiny doesn't do home visits.* We have to go out and grab it. In so doing we begin fulfilling the destiny God has planned for each of us.

> Now to him who is able to do immeasurably more than all we ask or imagine, according to his power that is at work within us, to him be glory in the church and in Christ Jesus throughout all generations, for ever and ever! Amen.
> *Ephesians 3:20–21, NIV*

Even to use the word 'calling' in our culture is unfashionable.

Yet it is noticeable how many young people are seeking something beyond career and wealth. They are seeking meaning in their lives, for something less material and more spiritual – a quest. This is no coincidence as the culture that led to the credit crunch is so apparently lacking. The world is looking for leaders who look beyond the narrow self-interest of their organisations into the wider interest of an increasingly vulnerable world.

You are probably asking where all these leaders are going to come from. There is a widespread quest for meaning; people are looking for real insight into their own significance and that of life itself, and many young people are part of this, even though they may be stumbling uncertainly or unconsciously towards it. It is my hope that (reading this book) you are a disciple who is keen to go on learning, but you will have to get out of the comfort zone of your Ordinary World. Our natural inclination is to cling on to what we know, but the truth is we cannot grow, nor can we reveal our vocation, by standing still. Some of the unhappiest people are those who have not been able to walk through their fears since at a profound level they know that there is a widening gulf between the life they are living and the life that is intended for them.

Some of us seek change, some of us have change thrust upon us. For the Disciple hearing the call comes from three sources. Firstly, it is either forced through crisis such as losing a job or suffering bereavement. It is one of those moments in life, when as much as we want things to return to the way they were back in our Ordinary World, this is no longer possible. Lee is a veteran of the Afghan conflict. Every day he went out on patrol and sometimes as the lead. Stepping into the unknown became a minute by minute challenge, as he didn't know what he would step on next. Imagine the pressure we put on young men who are often no older than 18. Lee hadn't really wanted to join the Army, but unemployment on Tyneside was high, the recession was getting deeper and the prospect of a job receding. His father had left home when he was two, so he never had a male role model in his life. His single mum did the best she could but she had to work all the hours God sent to make ends meet. He never really engaged at school but managed to get 3 GCSEs before he left at the age of 16. He found himself in that growing group of NEETs (not engaged in employment, education or training) signing on and hanging out all day until a mate persuaded him to come along to the recruiting office. He didn't want to join and his mother was dead against it, but his mate, on leave from basic training, told him it was not so bad and after a few beers he decided to sign on. Taking a single step into the unknown, he didn't see the IED that would prevent his legs taking another step. He did not lose consciousness as the Americans flew him back to field hospital and nor did he lose his unselfishness. His only concern was for his mates and for his mother back home, who he knew would react badly. I met him when he was well on the road to recovery with two new prosthetics fitted in America, giving him a level of mobility he never anticipated he would have again.

Lee's life has changed irreversibly. By taking the step into the unknown that blew off his legs, he, without knowing it, took a bigger step into an unknown future, where he discovered the humility to realise that, despite what had happened to him, he could still be of service to the world. He told me that he wouldn't have changed what happened to him, because he discovered things within himself that he would never have found otherwise. He turned tragedy into revelation.

I am not saying that stepping into the unknown will have such a dramatic impact on the Disciple. It is to show that we can be encouraged by the fact that these moments in our lives can bring us into a more profound purpose for our lives. Loss is particularly hard to bear, but we always have the choice as to how we respond to it, as I will illustrate later in the book. Usually there is a choice between freezing in self-pity and regret or being grateful for what is still available and using this point of change to step into a new destiny. It is at these points of vulnerability when God can often be most available if only we let him.

Secondly, it comes through the inspiration of another: 'Have you ever thought of doing…?' Someone just showing up in your life and making that suggestion that creates an internal connection that suddenly makes sense of your life as happened to the early disciples,

As Jesus walked beside the Sea of Galilee, he saw Simon and his brother Andrew casting a net into the lake, for they were fishermen. "Come, follow me," Jesus said, "and I will make you fishers of men." At once they left their nets and followed him.

Mark 1:16–18, NIV

When Jesus called his early disciples they were quite happily existing in their Ordinary World, fishing. But they couldn't stay there and follow him, and neither can you. There was no hesitation – maybe fear, but they realised in a moment that in order to fulfil their destiny they would have to leave everything that was familiar to them and step into the unknown, unaware of the destination. They made a choice and in so doing allowed themselves to fulfil the predestination that God has planned for us all. It is an inspiring thought that we are no different to those early disciples in God's eyes. Everything they chose to do and achieved by so doing is similarly available to us right now.

Thirdly, the call comes through that nagging internal voice of the Holy Spirit that is seeking something better than the current reality. The word 'vocation' is rooted in the Latin word for voice. On one hand we need to discern that inner voice of God, which can be difficult. On the other, and in my case this is what happened, I found myself articulating my calling. Articulation not only releases a calling but it allows others to respond. In other words your being speaks. In your being, as opposed to your doing, your calling will emerge. If we believe that we were born on purpose for a purpose defined by God, something inside us will be expressing its discontent with the status quo as long as we don't answer the call. It is that big question: To be or not to be? And if you only hear silence, ask God to reveal his purpose to you.

"Ask and it will be given to you; seek and you will find; knock and the door will be opened to you. For everyone who asks receives; he who seeks finds; and to him who knocks, the door will be opened."

Matthew 7:7–8, NIV

It is important to really discern the vision for your future direction. We may be inspired by the vision of others and try and make it our own. It won't work and just leads to unhappiness and frustration. Humanly, it is too easy for us to do what we want and then justify it as God's will. This can be exacerbated by a strong spiritual experience. It is tempting to remain attached to these moments and to try to repeat them; but they are only prompts and signals to get us on track.

As Jesus was getting into the boat, the man who had been demon-possessed begged to go with him. Jesus did not let him, but said, "Go home to your family and tell them how much the Lord has done for you, and how he has had mercy on you." So the man went away and began to tell in the Decapolis how much Jesus had done for him. And all the people were amazed.

Mark 5:18–20, NIV

As we are healed it is tempting to 'stay in the boat' where we know we have sensed feeling close to Jesus, but the task of the Disciple is then also to step out in faith and be a living example to others. Of course in reality Jesus will still be with us. The apparent security of the past can be a comfort zone that we need to escape, important and precious as moments of great encouragement may be.

In a world now obsessed with happiness, the secret is to be aware of our path through life – our purpose – and to accept it. Joseph Campbell says that we must strive to achieve, and when we have achieved our goals it is time to realise: *This is it – I am in that place and this moment is of value in and of itself.... It's beautiful.*

It all starts with a dream and usually it will be big. Big dreams inspire others, one of the first steps in the journey, as we have seen. Leaders can't exist without a dream; it is fuel for the journey. The dream is simply an echo of the future and every great human accomplishment has evolved from the heart of man. Dreamers are able to think beyond the paradigm of the Ordinary World allowing themselves to be unbounded by the narrow margins of our day to day existence. My dream today is to set people free to be everything they were born to be and, by linking up with others, create an impact on the world that draws society back to the essence of Christ. But it didn't start that way.

It all started for me when the crisis and the inner voice collided on 1st June 2000. I had become increasingly disillusioned by the monster, Pierre Victoire, a national restaurant group I had taken on two years before. The politics of business had become overwhelming. Having secured a bad deal in a buy out, I had persevered with others to keep the debt-ridden company afloat, while re-branding it and introducing a new concept. It was too ambitious. We had brought in a new Chief Executive and Financial Director. The Chief Executive was out of his depth and the Financial Director was desperately trying to trim costs. I had been trying to encourage shareholders to relinquish some of their equity in order to raise money to allow us to expand and thereby save the company. It was not a happy time. And on that fateful day I went into work to discover that I had been sacked. I remember walking out of the office at the back of our Leith restaurant outside Edinburgh in a daze.

I walked around Leith docks trying to work out what I was going to say to Cerys my wife. The old tongue twister 'The Leith police dismisseth us' kept going round in my head. I had been dismissed for the first time in my professional life and couldn't make sense of it. But we were losing money and the only way of rescuing the company was to raise more. The shareholders would have to give up equity and voting rights to the bank and neither was likely to be accepted by them. So savings had to be made. It was a cruel irony to be made redundant by the very people I had recruited to work with me, but, although I didn't know it then, it was part of my destiny. In fact I would not be writing this now if it had not happened. One of my great friends subsequently said to me *You should live your life looking forward, but understand it looking back*. At some point in our lives, usually at Christmas, we have watched that classic film, A Wonderful Life. It is the story of a man who believes he has let everyone down and that his continued existence on earth is pointless. He is about to commit suicide when he is taken on a journey of his life that makes him realize that he is important and his existence has had a profound impact on the lives of others. If we can believe this to be true, we can accept even the toughest experiences of our lives. For it is in these moments that we have the greatest opportunity to learn both about our life and ourselves. This is where God can engage with us and if we don't listen to those internal prompts, a crisis can occur which gives us no choice but to listen.

I have no idea why I decided to go Bath Abbey that June day. Sometimes we are given a prompting from the Holy Spirit. It is as though we are simply being guided by some unknown hand – which is in fact that of God. Again it reinforces the concept of predestination where God offers us prompts, which we can respond to or ignore. Listening, and discerning that voice, becomes the Disciple's greatest challenge. Sometimes the prompts can be so incredible we rationalise them out completely. God can create what is truly amazing through each of us, and the Disciple has to learn and embrace that. I wish I could say that it was easy.

It was a beautiful summer's day, the sunlight streaming through the high windows of the Abbey, the Lantern of the West where earth meets heaven, lighting up the congregation within. The Abbey was half full. We sang hymns, we prayed and we listened to the sermon. To this day I don't know who preached it, so he will never know the profound effect it had on me. I suppose it is true of life that we rarely see the consequences of our actions, good or bad. The sermon was on the well-worn text from Isaiah 6:8, *Then I heard the Lord asking 'Whom shall I send as a messenger to my people? Who will go for us? And I said 'Lord, I'll go! Send me.'* I was unusually attentive. It seemed as though the preacher was talking directly to me. I sat next to one of the pillars with a shaft of sun setting me in a spotlight and I found I couldn't move. I found myself weeping uncontrollably rooted to the spot. I knew that something profound was happening; I had read of others having a similar experience. I don't recall the rest of the service. All I know is that at its end I was still sitting next to the pillar unable to move with the words *'Send me'* reverberating around my mind. I don't recall getting home, but I do recall picking up the Sunday Times and turning it, again as though I was a puppet at the end of destiny's strings, to an article by Jonathan Aitken, who had just been released from prison following a conviction for perjury. He wrote of his time in prison and the lessons he took away from the experience. In a moment my experience in the Glen Parva Young Offenders Institution came flooding back.

I was on a tour of thirty prisons completing contingency plans for a Prison Officers' strike while serving in the army after a year at the Army Staff College. It was 1988 and Margaret Thatcher had secured significant victories against some of the biggest unions in the country including the National Union of Miners and the print unions. It was a period in history when the power of the unions was being broken. The Prison Officers' Association (POA) was, and remains today, one of the most conservative of unions, highly resistant to change. No Prime Minister has really bitten the bullet in radically reforming a prisons system that continues to fail in its attempts to reduce reoffending. It is a particular part of the public sector that reflects the unforgiving nature of the electorate. I believe it should be compulsory for every adult to visit a prison, not only to meet the people who are locked up there, but to understand that in most cases it makes bad criminals worse. Prison should serve a three-fold purpose: prevention through deterrence, punishment and rehabilitation. The latter is the Cinderella to the two Ugly Sisters of the former, and on present form is unlikely to get to the ball. There is no Fairy Godmother for rehabilitation and every prince who has even thought of courting her has soon been persuaded to shy away by the sages of the Daily Mail.

Every attempt at reform has failed. When Margaret Thatcher threatened to make changes, the POA didn't like it. So there was the threat of a strike. In such event the police would secure the inside of prisons, the Army the outside. I was tasked with putting together security plans for all the prisons in the East of England from young offenders institutions like Glen Parva to HMP Gartree, one of a few maximum security prisons in the country, which was at that time the home to a number of IRA terrorists. The prison became infamous just before I visited it, when it experienced the first (and last) helicopter escape on the UK mainland. When I rang the governor, confidentially, of course, since my presence was highly secret, I told him that due to the pressure of time and the numbers of prisons I had to visit, I would be arriving by helicopter. The silence was deafening until he heard my gentle chuckle and realised it was a wind up. He turned out to be the most helpful of all the governors I met, allowing me access within the prison where I was able to meet and talk to staff and prisoners and begin to get an insight. In the kitchens I was introduced to a quietly spoken elderly Welshman. He looked so out of place, I asked the prison officer what he was in for. *Oh he chopped up his wife, but we have put his skills to good use; he is our master butcher.*

But it was Glen Parva that moved me most. What I witnessed horrified me: hundreds of young men without hope, written off by a society that was the fifth richest in the world. Discarded as a child would discard a toy it had no further use for. And of course we can afford to lock up more and more young men, because we are so wealthy. Interestingly. poorer societies, such as the Aboriginal, use a restorative form of justice because they can't afford to build prisons.

During life we witness many things and things happen to us. Often we put it down to fate and move on. But destiny kicks in when we decide to do something about it. It is difficult to separate destiny from coincidence, but whichever way you look at it my father's childhood home was Bulwood Hall near Hockley in Essex. Today it is a Category C prison, having been a women's prison for many years before that. There is something about going into a prison which profoundly changes your perspective on life. It is something we just take for granted – a place to which we send bad people. It is easy in our tabloid world to demonise criminals, but the first thing that hits you is that they are just human beings like you and me. Young men who had never had a chance from the moment they were born. I knew young men like this. Young men who had come from similar backgrounds, faced similar challenges, probably done the same things. The difference: they hadn't been caught. They ended up enlisting in the Army, which offered them a purpose, discipline, training, comradeship and a cause greater than they were. I was to learn a lot about young men and the way that we betray them in our society. We have become increasingly fearful of the wild energy that is contained in all young men which needs a natural outlet. In more tribal cultures they still understand the importance of a rite of passage. The young man is separated from the feminine influence of their early years and taken away by the elder men in the tribe to be initiated in the ways of manhood. Their hard wiring is understood and celebrated. Their wildness, which used to serve the purpose of becoming a hunter/warrior, is found productive outlets.

Until a generation ago National Service provided such an outlet. The young man was initiated by older men; the infamous NCOs often parodied, but who provided ever-lasting memories to those who experienced their tough love. For it was tough love. Despite the perceived brutality and withering sarcasm of the average NCO, there was a passion to bring out the best in the young men they trained. There was a clear understanding that team mattered. Whatever the rank, all relied on each other. Each brought a set of skills to the whole and through this mutual support, the British Army became the efficient fighting machine for which it is world-renowned. In our current troubled times with the return of riots to the streets of our cities, I am proposing the establishment of a non-military national service that reaches into the most difficult communities and the gangs to offer alternative positive role models and opportunities to serve. Yet again, it is in service that I believe we can tackle some of our most insoluble social problems. This is the conclusion that my journey has brought me to and is a reflection of the work with many of the young men I have worked with over the last 10 years. But this is for later.

Virtue

The reason we don't discern our calling is that we have not discovered my second virtue: confidence. The word 'confidence' is derived from the Latin word 'confide', which means *to reveal the truth within*. We step into our truth once we answer the call to change. A good education will focus on uncovering that unique set of strengths and talents that will set us free to live authentic and fulfilled lives, but sadly our educational system has become a reflection of the culture we have created. It is the culture of targets and league tables where performance in academic exams is the only real measure. What chance does the non-academic, vocationally driven young person have? Education provides the best opportunity in life to discover our inner confidence. Indeed it should be its primary purpose. By so doing the savings in human misery and to the Exchequer would be enormous. The focus yet again is fear, fear of not being as good as the school next door, fear of failure, the fear of trusting young people to take responsibility for their own learning and fear of trying something new. Interestingly, another meaning of the word 'confide' is 'together I trust', which gives us a clue, revealed later, as to how we use our talents.

Fear is inevitable whenever you try something new. In setting up *Believe* and since then, *Mowgli* and a mentoring programme for ex-servicemen, I was taking a new paradigm into some highly conservative cultures: the criminal justice system, the Middle East and the Services. The fear that comes in challenging the status quo can be crippling, but success is impossible if you give into it. It is also the fear of failure. It is indicative of our self-absorption that we kid ourselves into thinking that we are the only people who fail. The fact is that we all fail; we just don't boast about it. The failure rate of the human race is one hundred per cent and everyone qualifies as members of the club. And the failure rate of those who are prepared to put everything on the line to create something new is even higher! When we choose to play safe with life our lives can become like a barren wasteland.

A huge amount of human energy is expended in maintaining this world. Sadly most people move through life establishing and maintaining the financial security that allows them to stay in this world – earning a living to pay the material items that give them emotional rewards, status and credibility. It is safe. It is the world that almost every aspect of our developed society encourages and demands. It is a world based on competition, where we stress ourselves out trying to attain more and look better than each other, whether corporately or individually. It is a world that has made a virtue out of greed and envy. Carlos Ruiz Zafon in his book *The Angels Game* puts it like this:

Envy is the religion of the mediocre. It comforts them – it responds to the worries that gnaw at them and finally it rots their souls allowing them to justify their meanness and their greed until they believe these to be virtues.

And it is all so soulless. The key is being you and finding that one thing where, as we have seen, that natural talent meets your passion – as I have said earlier, your own perfectly shaped jigsaw piece where what you are naturally good at and what you love combine. Life is simply about discovering the shape of your piece and then seeking out those pieces with which it fits. It is essential for human fulfilment and the pursuit of that elusive word happiness. It is also essential in terms of finding personal authenticity, integrity and the moral compass, which allows us to respond to the challenges of life in the right way. But it is also essential for the health of wider society. If people are disconnected from themselves they are more likely to cause problems to themselves and others. So confidence is not the shallow kind often displayed by those who lack it. It is a deep inner confidence that comes from being comfortable in our own shoes. We know it when we see it. Not only that, others can see it in us. When you are confident, people are more likely to trust you, often because your authenticity shines like a light. Opportunities open up and our confidence becomes like fuel igniting and propelling us forward. When we are confident we can stop wondering whether it is the right thing to do and just do it anyway. As we do we draw others in and suddenly discover that we are living out our purpose.

Jesus tells the parable of the talents, when a master gives one of his workers five talents, another two and the other one. These are a gift from God to us to use to fulfil the purpose he has for our lives. They are generous gifts given to us to be used. When the master returns and discovers that the first two have used their gifts wisely, he rewards them. The third worker, who had just buried his talent, afraid to lose it by using it, is condemned. The *Disciple's Journey* gives us the opportunity of revealing our talents and then using them as our contribution to the kingdom. So many of us are like the third worker, burying them away, afraid to use them or, through false pride, feel unworthy of them and fail to appreciate their value. This is narcissistic since we take on the individualistic approach of the world and assume that it was all about us.

This is the true joy in life, the being used for a purpose recognised by yourself as a mighty one...the being a force of nature instead of a feverish, selfish little clot of ailments and grievances complaining that the world will not devote itself to making you happy. I am of the opinion that my life belongs to the whole community, and as long as I live it is my privilege to do for it whatever I can....

I want to be thoroughly used up when I die, for the harder I work, the more I live. I rejoice in life for its own sake. Life is no brief candle to me; it is a sort of splendid torch, which I have got hold of for the moment, and I want to make it burn as brightly as possible before handing it on to future generations.

George Bernard Shaw

Reflection

- How much do you embrace change, pick up challenges or try and make a difference? (Score yourself out of 10.)
- Complete a timeline of your life tracking those moments of change. Look back at your timeline and understand the events that have shaped you – look at all aspects of your life.
- From this, list the major changes you have made in your life.
- What has led to change in your past?
- Make a list of those things that you spend significant time on in your life.
- What are you naturally curious about?
- Do you know what you are searching for? How open to change are you?
- What is your dream? Do you have one?
- What have been your successes? What have been your disappointments? What did you learn from them?
- What would you wish to change in your life and the wider world?
- Where do my natural talents and my passions come together?
- What is effortless for you? When in your life have you felt most in the flow?
- What are you doing when time flies and what are you doing when time stands still?
- When are you completely present? (This is a time when we are at our most effective since we are doing what comes naturally to us. We don't have to think about it. This will give you a clue to where your natural strengths lie.)

- You have one life. Pray and work out what it is you really want from it.
- Test all your desires with five 'Whys?' (This is to really dig deep to establish your true motivation. Since motivation will fuel your success, it is important to get it right.)
- Write a ten word epitaph.   How do you want people to remember you?
- Who is in charge of your life?
- Write down dream, vision, goals and actions.

8

Refusing the Call

"Enter through the narrow gate. For wide is the gate and broad is the road that leads to destruction, and many enter through it. But small is the gate and narrow the road that leads to life, and only a few find it."

Matthew 7:13–14, NIV

It was 6.03 in the morning. I woke with a start. The name '*Believe*' came to me from nowhere and immediately I knew it was the right name for the charity I was setting up. Like most people I would say that I am invulnerable to the advertiser's art. I cannot claim to have originated the name. The suggestion came from a series of, as always, excellent TV advertisements for Guinness. The silent slow motion sequence of a rugby player shaping up to take a conversion in wet and muddy conditions was simply underlined by the word *Believe* with the Guinness logo replacing one of the letters. Believe – the essential ingredient to any human achievement. Yet there are so many people who have no self-belief, particularly those that have had no opportunities in life. What would make a difference to them? What would help them fulfil their potential? It seemed so simple: believe in people so that they could believe in themselves; believe in the best in people rather than the worst.

Along with the name *Believe* came a philosophy that was to underpin it. I am not sure where I found it, but it is indicative of the *Disciple's Journey* that the right thing turns up just when you need it. It came from Goethe, *Treat a man as he is and he remains as he is; treat a man as he can and should be and he will become all he can and should be.* The next five years were to be a rollercoaster as I battled to introduce this philosophy into both educational and criminal justice systems as a means of preventing young people getting into crime and reducing reoffending for those that do.

The greatest asset to the Disciple when starting a new venture is naivety, since, if you knew what you were going to be taking on, you would never start. But as I was to learn, it is not the end but the journey which is important, since this is when you meet that stranger inside all of us – our true selves. That is the gift of risk: if you can step through the pain that risk entails, you will discover pure gold on the other side. That pure gold is the person you were meant to be. Charles Handy tells the story of the young man who was down on his luck. He had no job, no home, no money. He was living on the street. He was feeling suicidal. Six months later he was transformed. He had a job, a smart suit, a flat and a girlfriend. He was asked what had happened to bring about the transformation. He related how he had decided to end it all, but before he did he wanted to hear his father's voice just one more time. When he rang him, it was as though his father knew. *Son*, he said, *when you get to heaven you will discover the man you were meant to be.* What a frightening thought. We could drift unconsciously through life and then discover at the end the person we might have been if only we had pursued our destiny.

Yet at this stage refusing the call seems much easier. Questions start circulating round and round. Would I have carried on if I knew how it would end? Would I have allowed myself to be inspired if I knew the pain and despair I would feel, the utter helplessness, the dark nights of the soul? Would my family have supported me if they knew the sacrifices they would have to endure, while I pursued my dream? If we knew what was to come, who would have the courage to start? And yet we do. The course of history is defined by those who have taken risks in order to make a difference, leave their mark, pursue their dream. And thank goodness they have, for the world is a much better place for them. *Better to have tried and failed than never to have tried at all.* Creativity is the essence of life. None of the great biblical figures had an easy ride, nor did they start from a foundation of perfection. Many were very flawed. But they all responded to their calling.

Discipleship is at its essence an attitude of mind. It is an intensely human experience full of emotion. It requires wholehearted focus and reserves of dogged perseverance that most of us mere mortals are unaware we possess. The world is crying out for spiritual entrepreneurs. All human endeavour, all human achievement is dependent upon individuals who are prepared to step into the unknown and discover their own unique truth. *Consciousness is moulded by the sacred story to which it awakens.*

And so it was for me that this call to change came about and another famous verse from Isaiah, used by Jesus, became my guide:

> The Spirit of the Lord is on me,
> because he has anointed me
> to preach good news to the poor.
> He has sent me to proclaim
> freedom for the prisoners
> and recovery of sight for the blind,
> to release the oppressed,

to proclaim the year of the Lord's favour."
Luke 4:18–19, NIV

It was only later in the journey that I was to realise that the prison I was being sent into was allegorical to something deeper within the human condition. But I would have to embark on my own journey before this became apparent. It is important to remember that we won't get the full picture at this stage, but we have enough information to take that first vital step. At this stage it was simply to set up a charity to work with those in prison, using a combination of coaching and mentoring to help prisoners find something good within themselves in order to rebuild their lives.

The word 'vocation' implies a relationship. If someone is called, it follows that someone must be doing the calling. This 'someone' can only be God. But God has given us free will and it follows that we have the choice to refuse God's calling. This is where the resistance to accept the call stops many potential Disciples in their tracks, since it involves change. Our natural response to change is to refuse it. It all looks too hard; the wide gate along with the herd looks much more attractive. Our ordinary world suddenly doesn't seem so bad after all. At least we know where we stand and so do our friends and family. Those who change threaten those who won't. They have all placed expectations on us that suit them. How many unhappy people are living the lives they feel they ought to rather than pursue their God given calling, their destiny? So many people arrive at the end of their lives regretting the fact they have lived the life expected of them rather than the one God gave them. And regret is simply an insight come too late to do anything about it. In our unconscious refusal of change we lose ourselves further. We forget what it is to be truly human. So many people are locked into a self-constructed prison of fear and doubt. We run away from change rather than face ourselves. And the experience of our past often stops us dead in our tracks.

He said to another man, "Follow me."

But the man replied, "Lord, first let me go and bury my father."

Jesus said to him, "Let the dead bury their own dead, but you go and proclaim the kingdom of God."

Still another said, "I will follow you, Lord; but first let me go back and say good-bye to my family."

Jesus replied, "No one who puts his hand to the plough and looks back is fit for service in the kingdom of God."

Luke 9:59–62, NIV

These verses seem so harsh, but the lesson Christ is imparting to us is that in life we will always find the justification to refuse the call on our lives. This is even more so today in our multi-media, high achieving world with the potential for distraction in every moment. Distraction and procrastination, as we shall see, become perpetual enemies. For the modern disciple true service requires focus and dedication. We just have to continue to have faith that it is possible, since the future isn't inevitable. God gives us the opportunity to shape it in his will. Some people only discover themselves later in life often through some sort of crisis when they are forced to take a risk. Others are self-aware and respond to that voice of the Holy Spirit inside which is often buried deep. The voice of our true self cries out to be heard. The clue is in our dreams. What do we dream of being? Often we convince ourselves that we are not good enough, worthy enough to follow our dreams and we end up following the herd. I have discovered that the first secret is to take the risk of articulating your dream. Once you do so the Holy Spirit can work in a way that allows you to start the journey towards achieving it. As some wise person said *You can live your life dreaming or you can give your dream some life*. The alternative is the regret of a life unlived and that must be unbearable.

But as soon as the dream is out there, the mind begins to convince us that it will never work. There will be many people who will convince us that our mind is spot on. The Disciple will constantly walk the tightrope between the potential for the life unlived and the fear of living out the life determined by their calling. Sometimes the tension between the two can become unbearable and freeze future action. With every step into the unknown there is fear and doubt, but with every step successfully taken there is faith. Doubt makes every decision difficult. It keeps the Disciple from seeing the easy solution. It prevents us from being all that we could be and realising our full potential. Worse still, doubt breeds doubt – those who see the doubt in us begin to doubt us and lose confidence in us. We procrastinate and miss opportunities, and the dream that seemed so vivid begins to fade.

Where does this doubt come from? It is in our past, our previous traumas, failures and pain. *The past is another country.* One of the great openings to a novel, *The Go Between* by LP Hartley. And this is how we should treat it. The future is a blank canvas, both exciting and frightening. But we allow our past to cast a shadow over that blank canvas, preventing us from fulfilling God's purpose for our lives. The problem with the past is that it is just that – it has happened. It is just a collection of moments that we allow our psyche to shape depending on the mood we are in. This is true both collectively and individually. We allow ourselves to be trapped by what we cannot change.

Each moment of our lives may be shaped by a past moment and our response to it. I can still allow myself to feel a sense of utter worthlessness by something that was said or done fifty years ago, whether by a teacher or a school bully. Allowing that sense of worthlessness to hang around and build up leads inevitably to depression, closing down the joy of the present and completely denying the future. What a waste of the blessing of life. The past is another country and we should treat it as such: with respect and with the knowledge that it has given us the opportunity to learn. Once we recognise that none of us is perfect, no situation is perfect and the present is just that, a gift, we can learn to grow and treat everything as a growing opportunity. We will look at doubt in more detail later, since, as the Disciple's constant companion and shadow of faith, it is worthy of greater study.

The Disciple soon learns that standing still is not an option. Notwithstanding my fear of being ridiculed, I suddenly found myself articulating my dream. As soon as I did the fear and doubt kicked in again and I found myself saying, What do you know about prisons and what could you do? Equally I began to reflect on past failure and convinced myself that I wasn't worthy to pursue the idea. I wanted to push away the very essence of my life.

When Simon Peter saw this, he fell at Jesus' knees and said, "Go away from me, Lord; I am a sinful man!"

Luke 5:8, NIV

The refusal of the call had begun.

Virtue

Remember how the fishermen pulled up their boats on shore, left their nets and followed Jesus.

How do we overcome refusal? Symptomatic of *Don't be afraid* is my next virtue: **courage**. The word courage is derived from the French word 'coeur', meaning heart. This is the root of our courage; it doesn't come from the head but rather from the heart. It is to do with our moral compass, our core values, which shape the people we are, and of course we need the help of the Holy Spirit with this.

To act we need courage; to take tough decisions we need courage, to do what is right takes courage. We need courage to take responsibility, something we are so short of in the world currently. By taking responsibility we set us ourselves free from the chains of the past. When we take responsibility for something that isn't working, we can claim the power to change it and this increasingly engenders respect. But to start something new or to embark on change needs exceptional courage. If we are to become the leader we aspire to be we have to start from where we are and dig deep to find the courage to change; to create the *me I was born to be*. And that is a risk because we have to part company with the comfortable world in which we have lived to embark on a journey of self-discovery. It is not for the faint hearted.

At some point the Disciple is going to have to summon up the courage to take the risk to step outside his comfort zone if he is truly going to find himself. I was to reflect on this stage in the journey later in my diary recording a short talk I gave,

Faith without risk is impossible. When I pursued my calling to set up Believe I went without an income for two years. With four teenage children, this would seem crazy

to the rational world. It was not without pain and a great deal of stress but through the grace of God we survived. I urge anyone who feels similarly called to take the risk and follow their heart. Our greatest enemy in the material world in which we live is the perceived need for financial security. I meet so many people who say that they will commit their lives to God or follow their dream, once they are financially secure. This of course never happens as the more we accumulate the more insecure we become. God wants it to be the other way around. It was at this stage that the vision for the *Disciple's Journey* unwittingly began to emerge. I recorded a vision called *Risk it for Christ*, in which I said *People need shaking up if Christians are going to make a real impact in the world around us.*

As a soldier I remember being told that there is a very fine line between courage and stupidity. I was never sure which side of the line I was, but I believe that courage stems from something deep within us. Talking to soldiers who daily risk their lives on patrol in Afghanistan, I am deeply impressed at their ability to confront the deepest fear on a daily basis. What courage, we think. But the courage came from a love of their fellow man, whom they did not want to let down. There is an honour and a camaraderie between soldiers that is unique.

The true soldier fights not because he hates what is in front of him, but because he loves what is behind him.

GK Chesterton

For those who have not experienced this it is hard to relate to. It can be as powerful as the love by a mother of her child. While rarely confronting the fear of death in the way that a soldier does, the Disciple will experience the fear of risk and the constant doubt that pursuing our faith is stupid.

The greatest commandment is that we should love the Lord our God – and we should also love our neighbours as ourselves. Through obeying these commands the Disciple will unlock the courage within. It allows us to go for the impossible and to discover that we have capabilities that we never dreamt possible.

We need courage to overcome the anticipation of failure. Since failure is inevitable somewhere along the way, it is best to anticipate it, even embrace it. Although in our rational world where failure is 'not an option', for the Disciple failure indicates progress. At least he is trying. Failure is just a rehearsal for the real thing. I have found failure to be my greatest teacher and, when, at a later stage in the journey, I am able to view the world through a new perspective, it has been a time of great learning. Failure is only failure when you give up and return to the more predictable, safe ordinary world you left. That is not to say that we won't fear failure. The Disciple lives with it every day, and often every night. But the thought of failure can freeze us and prevent us living out our destiny.

A nurse who worked in a hospice for 25 years wrote about the five greatest regrets of those who were facing the fear of imminent death.

She writes,

For many years I worked in palliative care. My patients were those who had gone home to die. Some incredibly special times were shared. I was with them for the last three to twelve weeks of their lives. People grow a lot when they are faced with their own mortality. I learned never to underestimate someone's capacity for growth. Some changes were phenomenal. Each experienced a variety of emotions, as expected, denial, fear, anger, remorse, more denial and eventually acceptance. Every single patient found their peace before they departed though, every one of them. When questioned about any regrets they had or anything they would do differently, common themes surfaced again and again. The most common regret of all:

I wish I'd had the courage to live a life true to myself, not the life others expected of me.

When people realise that their life is almost over and look back clearly on it, it is easy to see how many dreams have gone unfulfilled. Most people have had not honoured even a half of their dreams and had to die knowing that it was due to choices they had made, or not made. It is very important to try and honour at least some of your dreams along the way. From the moment that you lose your health, it is too late. Health brings a freedom very few realise, until they no longer have it.

Courage is about being authentic, standing forth as we truly are, facing the potential ridicule and rejection that can come with it. It is about standing up for what we believe in, risking the judgement of others. It is being prepared to stand out from the crowd whatever the cost. It is allowing ourselves to be uniquely different standing alone in our perspective while following the promptings of our soul. How often do we see this type of courage in our world today? Too rarely, but it is this courage that the Disciple is invited to dig deep to find. A disciple will always be accountable not only for his soul, but for his actions and behaviour. This takes great courage too. One of the many failings of contemporary leadership in politics and the corporate world is a lack of accountability. How often do we hear government ministers and CEOs exonerating themselves, denying any responsibility when something goes wrong, delegating accountability to a subordinate. This is moral cowardice. Power and pay packages come with a heavy price – the buck simply stops there. How few leaders we have who understand that and have the courage to stand up when things go wrong. By taking the first step the Disciple begins the journey away from this culture into something far richer.

Reflection

- **What is your greatest fear?**
- **What situation right now is weighing on your mind? What is draining you and just feels like hard work?**
- **Refer to your timeline – how many false starts have you had?**
- **What are your greatest failures?**
- **How do you respond to failure? What is failure?**
- **What would you do if you couldn't fail?**
- **What would it feel like to get rid of all those things you feel you 'ought' to do or those things that others expect of you?**
- **What are your possible people problems? How will they affect you?**
- **What is holding you back inside?**
- **Who can help you?**

9

Meeting the Mentor

"If you love me, you will obey what I command. And I will ask the Father, and he will give you another Counsellor to be with you for ever— the Spirit of truth. The world cannot accept him, because it neither sees him nor knows him. But you know him, for he lives with you and will be in you."

John 14:15–17, NIV

The *Disciple's Journey* can be a lonely one. Loneliness can be your greatest companion. For however strong your faith and your support network, the truth is that when you take up the challenge, in human terms, you take it up alone. The truth is that all key moments in our life from birth to death are faced alone; at least we feel we are alone. This can be true even amongst those closest to us; sometimes particularly so.

I have always been struck by the following passage,

Jesus left there and went to his home town, accompanied by his disciples. When the Sabbath came, he began to teach in the synagogue, and many who heard him were amazed.

"Where did this man get these things?" they asked. "What's this wisdom that has been given him, that he even does miracles! Isn't this the carpenter? Isn't this Mary's son and the brother of James, Joseph, Judas and Simon? Aren't his sisters here with us?" And they took offence at him.

Jesus said to them, "Only in his own town, among his relatives and in his own house is a prophet without honour." He could not do any miracles there, except lay his hands on a few sick people and heal them. And he was amazed at their lack of faith.

Mark 6:1–6, NIV

It didn't seem to make much sense until I embarked on my own *Disciple's Journey*. The Disciple will discover the truth of the phrase *familiarity breeds contempt*. Those closest to us know us well, flaws and all. Different people see different sides of our character and can find it hard to accept that someone so fallen can receive a calling to serve. In his hometown and with his family, Jesus was probably seen locally as as a carpenter. Neighbours who had watched him grow from boyhood to manhood might have found it hard to accept that the man they knew so well would be a great healer, prophet and teacher.

We can have a feeling of loneliness and rejection. Of course we never are truly alone because God is with us; we are in Christ. We always have access to him through prayer.

"Therefore I tell you, whatever you ask for in prayer, believe that you have received it, and it will be yours."

Mark 11:24

In this sense we always have a mentor. Prayer is the great reinforcer of faith. We must believe that we will receive (see the teaching of Jesus in Mark). If our prayer is in God's will, it will be answered, although not necessarily in our timing, nor perhaps in the way we expect.

Prayer allows us to have expectation of a response from God. It is a radical response to the challenges of life. It is thought by many not to be rational, so in the age of reason, its supernatural quality is easily rejected. However prayer is useless unless translated into meaningful radical action. God wants us to cooperate with him. If we have turned our back on him, we have to roll over towards him. And if our prayer is in line with his will, and if we act upon the thing we are praying for, he will act too. Prayer is not a passive activity, although its practice may seem to be. As I have already pointed out, it is radical. Interestingly, the root of the word 'radical' is 'radix' which means to get to the root of things. As we arm ourselves for the battle for social justice in our world, it is essential that we do so by addressing root causes, not by devoting our personal and corporate efforts toward merely superficial symptoms (and, of course, there are important implications about how resources should be deployed in our society).

Discipleship involves learning in a way that is so everyday and ordinary that it is easily overlooked. It is the kind of learning that happens when people are challenged at a deep level and know that they need to think differently to understand, accept and live with the experience. This is the gracious, often relational learning that changes lives. This kind of learning is not an achievement of the self so much as a forming of the self; a formation of the self into something both more realistic and holy.

Stephen Cherry *The Barefoot Disciple*

It is extraordinary but true that in all the great epics a human mentor has appeared to support the hero/disciple on his journey. The mentor is often unknown to the Disciple so will be able to see the best side without that contempt that comes from familiarity. A mentor is driven by one thing: a desire to bring out the very best in the Disciple. It is a human expression of God's love since God has created us uniquely to be all that we can be. In loving his neighbour as himself, a mentor is helping us to see the best in ourselves and then use this inner knowledge in service to the world. It is a deeply human relationship built upon high levels of trust.

In biblical accounts of incidents which might share some features with what we understand by 'mentoring', God may give either some foreknowledge or immediate guidance about the *Disciple's Journey*. A good mentor is a gift from God, and needs God's guidance in the task. Elijah got alongside Elisha. *Tell me what I can do for you?* (2 Kings 9). That is the most profoundly liberating question for the aspirant disciple, since it is a clear sign that he is no longer on his own. Usually the mentor will have the wisdom of the journey wrought out of many years of journeying himself. More than anything the mentor will believe in you. This creates the foundation for self-belief and will be a constant theme in the journey. As the challenges grow (and self-doubt may grow with them), to have someone walking alongside you reminding you of your dream, bearing witness to your progress and encouraging you when it seems impossible, is the most powerful contribution to success. But the mentor's first duty is to help you commit: to cross that line into faith. At a spiritual level, if you allow it, your most constant companion and mentor is the Holy Spirit, but we all need that human support too.

There are times in life when we are called upon to be bridges
not a great monument spanning a distance and carrying

loads of heavy traffic,
but a simple bridge to help one person from here to there
over some difficulty
such as pain or grief, fear, loneliness,
a bridge which opens the way for ongoing journey.
When I become a bridge for another,
I bring upon myself a blessing for I escape from the
prison of self
and exist in a wider world, breaking out to be a larger
being
who can enter another's pain and rejoice in another's
triumph.
I know of only one greater blessing in this life and that is
to allow someone else to be a bridge for me.

Joy Cowley

Mentoring is one of the strongest weapons in the Disciple's armoury. Since loneliness can be the greatest enemy, the knowledge that you have another person walking alongside you, or providing that bridge is highly motivating. I have learned that most problems can be alleviated through the power of human relationship. Well structured mentoring has a hugely beneficial effect on both the mentor and the one being mentored since, to be effective, it has to be built on trust. Mentoring is a genuinely voluntary activity whereby the mentor gives of himself with no expectation of return. This is vital since in most of our relationships there is an 'agenda'.

There is a road from the eye to the heart that does not go through the intellect. *G K Chesterton*

Why am I such a passionate advocate of mentoring? I believe that in the highly technical world we now live in, despite the huge growth in social media, we have become more disconnected from each other. In creating a global community we have forgotten about the person next door. Someone can have 500 friends on Facebook and yet not know the name of their next-door neighbour. Until the industrial age, we lived in self-supporting communities. We all knew each other and understood the importance of relationship. Because there was little state intervention in our lives, for good or bad, we had to look after each other. I am not advocating a return to some idealized bucolic world that looks blissful on film and television. For most people it was a grim existence of survival. The industrial age has brought many advantages and a welfare state that has provided a safety net for the most vulnerable. But humanity is out of balance. In pursuing our self-interest we have forgotten that we are part of a wider community, leading to huge disparities in wealth across the world. The crisis that we face is the crisis of the common good.

So we need to find a way of remembering the values that allowed us to live together as human beings. Mentoring is one way of achieving this: connecting strangers in service to each other. Ultimately mentoring sets us free from the bondage of self-absorption to serve the interests of others. Through the intimate relationship of mentoring we begin to realise that all the anxieties that hold us back from our natural generosity are common to all. In other words, by understanding that my anxieties are the same as your anxieties, that the bad things in my life are common to everyone, I am able to step into the search for the common good. And once this energy of human kindness is unleashed it will take on a life of its own since there is an unwritten rule within mentoring that if you have been mentored you pass that gift on by mentoring another.

Many of the symptoms of the ills that we invest a fortune

in to treat can be prevented or addressed at their roots through a restoration of relationship. I have not worked in any context where mentoring hasn't contributed to a profound and transformational effect on those who have participated. And the contexts have been diverse: from a prolific offender in prison to a young Syrian entrepreneur. It works because it relates to something deep within us, because we are principally relational beings. Because we live in a rational age we have become conditioned to the fact that we must rely on the intellect to find solutions to the challenges we face. Mentoring talks to the soul.

Instead, speaking the truth in love, we will in all things grow up into him who is the Head, that is, Christ. From him the whole body, joined and held together by every supporting ligament, grows and builds itself up in love, as each part does its work.

Ephesians 4:15–16, NIV

The key is speaking the truth in love in a way that is difficult in all our other relationships, which, whether we like it or not, are not entirely neutral and objective. Even, and maybe especially, in our most intimate relationships it is difficult to have those profound conversations within which we can explore questions such as *Who am I* and *why am I here?* Within a mentoring relationship, it is possible to have those conversations that maybe we have with no other person. Mentoring is a process that always involves communication and is relationship based, but its precise definition is elusive. My own definition of mentoring is: ***a relationship which inspires, empowers and guides another in achieving their personal and career potential especially during times of change***

We have already noted that our culture is underpinned by

fear. The alternative to fear is love, releasing individuals into responsibility and the principal means of achieving this is through relationship. At heart we all want take responsibility for our lives but we are either afraid to do so or the system works actively against us so doing. The *Disciple's Journey* offers a meta-narrative for a life that does set out to take responsibility and discover its purpose. The reason for life is to discover our purpose; why are we here? The meaning of life, once purpose is discovered, is to use that purpose for a cause greater than ourselves. And the key character in the *Disciple's Journey* is the mentor. And if ever there was a time for good mentors it is now.

It is my experience, and research shows, that progress is achieved more quickly when working together. In a practical sense a mentor can be of most value during times of transition and change when we are vulnerable and uncertain. Be careful in selecting a mentor. The best will be able to step into your shoes, since they have been there before. Traditionally parents or elders fulfilled the role of mentor, but increasingly it has become somebody outside the family who is able to get alongside you and help you see for yourself those gifts that you take for granted. It is a strange truth but the very essence of ourselves is often hidden to us because we take it for granted, assuming everyone else is the same. We spend life acquiring education, qualifications, wealth, relationships, material possessions, all of which can become masks that shield us from our true identity. Some have likened the role of the mentor to that of a midwife facilitating the birth of the person we were born to be.

Michaelangelo was once asked where he found the inspiration to create the wonderful sculpture of David. He said: I did not make David. I revealed him in the stone. All I had to do was to remove the parts of the stone that were not David and reveal the perfect David. That is what a good mentor will do for you: cut through all the 'stone' that hides us and reveal the you that exists inside. Because the relationship is largely conducted on the emotional spectrum it provides an antidote to the analytical, rational world we inhabit. As someone being mentored once said: You may not remember what was said; you may not remember what you did, but you will always remember how your mentor made you feel.

Like all relationships, mentoring is richer for being a two way process. This richness emerges when both parties are communicating from a position of authenticity and humility. By doing so it allows us to connect at a deeply human level. It is about wanting unconditionally the best for another person, getting alongside them while they discover the best in themselves. The mentor draws on the wisdom of experience to challenge and guide the person being mentored on different stages of life's journey.

A mentor will listen. In our busy lives it is extraordinary how little we really listen to each other. There are always distractions externally and internally as we try and shut out noise while switching off our inner journalist who is reinterpreting what we hear to fit our own experience or working out how to respond. The power of really listening is liberating. The disciple will constantly be facing choice and challenge. To have a sounding board to test ideas and get a second opinion or to look at alternatives can prevent a lot of heartache. Equally, a mentor will help the Disciple maintain perspective and keep a work/life balance. He will challenge when the Disciple is flying and encourage when all seems lost. There will be failure and disappointment so the mentor will help the Disciple to pick himself up and persevere especially when confidence levels are low. Most importantly, the mentor will provide accountability in regard to the vision and what has been promised – and can remind the Disciple of progress made. This is highly motivational.

A good mentor will hold a mirror up to the other person, allowing them to see themselves as they are. The mirror will help them discover unique gifts and talents, but also barriers to progress. The mirror is, of course, a profound knowledge of ourselves and the human condition. It is through a strong mentoring relationship that we discover our own identity. The mentor is able to draw on the wisdom of experience to challenge and guide their mentees towards achieving their goals. A key theme of mentoring is to give new purpose to life and to open up opportunities to widen horizons so that we can fulfil our potential. As highlighted earlier, the mentor talks to the soul wherein lies our truth. I am struck by the number of times within my mentoring relationships, where a question is asked that cuts through everything to the core of our being and a gentle tear runs down a cheek in salute. A mentor helps us to overcome doubt, when the past is telling you lies about the future. When the mind starts making up stories that prevent progress, the mentor's role is to earth the Disciple in the present. This will often involve simply taking the one task that can be done today and doing it. For me at this stage, a mentor drew alongside me, a complete stranger at first. He immediately believed in me and gave me the encouragement to set up *Believe*. We would work together through the many trials that followed. When I lost heart, which I frequently did, he reminded me of the vision. Ultimately the mentor holds onto your dream even when it seems that it will never become a reality.

It's a hard road that's walked alone. *Celtic proverb*

So what does a mentor bring? What are the qualities that allow the mentor to be fully in service to the Disciple? This is not an exhaustive list, but a reflection of what I have observed in myself and in others as I have facilitated mentoring in a wide range of contexts.

Humility
The essence of mentoring is service with no expectation of return. Mentors need to understand that they are servants to those they mentor and this requires humility. Within a mentoring relationship the recipient is in charge. This requires the mentor to be non-judgmental and empowering, allowing the other person to make the best choices for him/her. It is their journey not the mentor's.

Belief
Belief in another is the most powerful of transactions. When you believe in someone it allows them to believe in themselves, which is the first step towards them finding new purpose to their lives. A mentor will relentlessly pursue the positive traits in the one being mentored and maintain their confidence.It is the greatest antidote to doubt.

Inspiration
Inspiration literally means 'in spirit'. It comes from something that is beyond ourselves and is transmitted to others in a way that creates a positive response. We have discussed inspiration, but what a mentor does is inspire disciples to find the best within themselves and, of course, to be open to the help that God can give in their situations – and encouraging them to hold to the highest vision when the temptation is to dwell in the weeds of detail.

Experience
The best mentors will be able to step into the Disciple's shoes. As we have discussed before, a mentor will empathise with the challenges the Disciple is facing at any moment,

since they have been there facing the same hopes and dreams while confronted with their inner demons.

Holistic

There will be many different strands to a disciple's life. We are whole human beings and can't be compartmentalised. What happens at home will affect us at work. What happens at work will affect our relationships at home. Too much focus on one at the expense of the other will leave the Disciple out of balance. A mentor will be aware of this and will work to hold the Disciple's life in balance and integrate everything to ensure that potential is achieved.

Patience

Allowing people to work at their own pace. Mentors should not allow their own 'need' for success to force the pace. The disciple is in charge. Because the mentor has been there before he will be patient with mistakes and failure, constantly reminding the Disciple of the destination, not worrying about what seems to be a current crisis.

Listening Skills

The art of mentoring is listening. This requires complete presence and the capacity to 'listen with your eyes' too: an ability to pick up non-verbal cues is crucial to understanding the inner state of the Disciple in the moment. Communication is key to mentoring; but a lot can get in the way. Often when we are 'listening', we are working out our own response or we are allowing our inner 'journalist' to make judgements based on our own view of the world. For example, at one stage in my life I had a restaurant and discovered that the reality of running such a business was far more complicated than my original vision took into account. I have had to pull myself up when someone has expressed a wish to open a restaurant. My 'journalistic' response was to say, Don't, and in that one word potentially kill someone's legitimate dream. What a good mentor will do is take their own bad experience and use it to help the Disciple avoid the mistakes that motivated that negative response.

Perspective

Because the mentor has experience of life, he is able to offer perspective. So many times we are faced with challenges that we believe to be insurmountable or we beat ourselves up with self-doubt. Having faced the same things at some point, a mentor is able to set the problem in a long-term perspective. Equally, a mentor is able to see the Disciple from a different perspective. Mentors can often see things that disciples can't see in themselves.

Creativity

Transition delivers an array of fears, choices and opportunities. The main objective is the creation of a new future. Creative thinking is needed to ensure that the Disciple has explored all possibilities. Furthermore, some of the challenges will need creative solutions. When two people are in a deep relationship, conversations can open up possibilities which can turn into opportunities that generate actions which create something new.

Feedback

We learn through experience and reflection. Mentors should avoid judgment and criticism. Positive feedback will allow a disciple to discern what they are doing well while helping them to discover what they could be doing better. A mentor will particularly affirm those things that the Disciple should keep on doing.

Accountability

How often do we commit to doing something and not follow it through? It is very easy when we are on our own to let things quietly slip and justify our reasons for that happening. A good mentor will understand the Disciple's objectives and how he/she is going to achieve them. But most importantly he will hold the Disciple accountable. 'You said you were going to do that. How are you getting on?' Sometimes this will be to spur him/her into action, but equally sometimes it will be to remind him/her of the progress made. The mentor will keep the Disciple focused on what is important.

Challenge

A good mentor will know when to challenge. If the relationship is based on a strong foundation of trust, the ability to challenge and push will be expanded. The mentor will use feedback and have an armoury of insightful questions and techniques to get to the 'core issue'.

Encouragement

The mentor needs to know when to encourage. There will be times when the Disciple is facing tough times and wants to give up. Having someone to keep us on track when every fibre of our being wants to stop is vital.

Advocacy

The mentor will sometimes act as an advocate, both signposting and facilitating opportunities through networks, often overcoming the barriers that prevent the Disciple making progress.

Virtue

Trust is like a vase....once it is broken, though you can fix it, the vase will never be the same again. *Anon*

Mentoring is based on trust. Trust is achieved through relationship. But trust is like a vulnerable flower. It encourages openness. In a rich mentoring relationship the Disciple will talk about what is really going on in life behind the façade. This can create a truly authentic relationship. This works because the mentor is genuinely serving the mentee with no expectation of return. If at any stage the mentor allows his agenda to intrude into the relationship, trust can quickly become eroded. Trust is like a bank account. We can put in a lot of credit over time, but one action can break that trust and the credit disappears. Trust, once broken, is rarely restored.

Trust is a big issue in the world today. On a global scale, it is when there is a breakdown in trust that nations may embark on warfare, with all the resultant suffering. On a more parochial level, trust has broken down in such a way that we have introduced expensive processes, such as the Criminal Records Bureau (CRB) checks, to protect, but inhibit, many of our relationships. What used to be natural to us is now condemned. Because of a few isolated cases of abuse, the normal healthy relationship between adult and child is now regulated by the state in such a way as to threaten the cohesion of our society. Yet trust can only be achieved through relationship. One of the root causes of social breakdown is fear stemming from a lack of collective trust. Failures in leadership usually stem from a breakdown in trust. Human beings are naturally relational. At all stages of our lives we are dependent upon our relationships since it is through them that we discover our own identity – through family, friends and teachers.

Trust is so important in a mentoring relationship since within it exists those conversations that allow complete vulnerability where wildest dreams can be articulated and turned into reality. The mentor is there to be objective and to help keep the vision realistic and achievable. Sometimes this means having to confront our limitations. I have had to face up to the pain of some of my failures and try and learn from them, but it is not easy. The temptation is to blame others for the failure and then carry on as before. One of the hardest lessons I have had to learn is that I am a creator not a manager, which has meant setting up a venture and then turning away from the pleasure of leading it. When we face up to our limitations it can be liberating. It helps you realise that you don't have to be self-sufficient any more. It allows you to trust others to delegate effectively. The mentor is there to help draw out the gift and then to help refine it by holding a mirror up to those areas to which we are blind. Only this way do we grow into the self-awareness that underpins good leadership.

Ultimately, whilst each person is a distinct individual, he/she has a variety of relationships with other persons. The most important relationship is with God. If I don't trust him, then how will I trust anyone?

One of the growing needs in our society is to fill the gap in many young lives of a lack of parental leadership and role models. And I mean proper human relationship, not the Facebook relationship since it is through human contact that we learn and grow and feel fulfilled as human beings. More of which later.

Reflection

- Are you ready to take responsibility for your future?
- With whom would you like to surround yourself?
- When have you had good mentors and what did you do?
- What are the qualities you see in mentor?
- How are you going to work together?
- What boundaries are you going to set?
- How often are we going to meet/speak?
- What structure are we going to put around our meetings?
- As a mentor, how am I going to help you find your blind spots?
- How do you like to receive feedback?
- What has someone else seen in you that you had not seen for yourself?

10

Crossing the Line
— the Separation

C S Lewis observed that nowhere in the universe is there neutral ground, commenting that all space and time is 'claimed by God and counter claimed by Satan'. The fact is that you cannot be uncommitted. Not to choose is to choose. Crossing the line is a demonstration of that commitment. Often it is something that we will resist. Procrastination can become your greatest friend as you find all those things to do to avoid the one thing you need to do. As a Christian the greatest sign of commitment is baptism. Baptism is the rite of passage into the *Disciple's Journey*. It was after all what marked the start of Christ's ministry.

Then Jesus came from Galilee to the Jordan to be baptised by John. But John tried to deter him, saying, "I need to be baptized by you, and do you come to me?"

Jesus replied, "Let it be so now; it is proper for us to do this to fulfil all righteousness." Then John consented.

As soon as Jesus was baptised, he went up out of the water. At that moment heaven was opened, and he saw the Spirit of God descending like a dove and lighting on him.

And a voice from heaven said, "This is my Son, whom I love; with him I am well pleased."

Matthew 3:13–17, NIV

As each of us makes that commitment, we receive the same blessing. Within that blessing are contained the three 'A's I have referred to before, so essential to a fulfilled life: attention (*this is my Son*), affection (*whom I love*) affirmation (*in whom I am well pleased*). It was not Jesus who needed to hear these words, but each one of us. They are the words that every child needs to hear as they pass into adulthood. They become the foundation to life and the fuel to keep going when, as it will, everything seems to be falling apart. There is so much pain around as a result of not hearing those three 'A's. Every parent and every teacher should have them deeply ingrained before they are allowed anywhere near children. In a world that is obsessed with the cost of everything and the value of nothing, the accountants in the Treasury might like to interview those who daily deal with those whose parents and teachers failed to provide the right levels of attention, affirmation and affection. There are the obvious candidates on the streets draining the empty can as a nightcap before curling up under the cardboard boxes, There are the prostitutes plying their trade, their lack of self esteem corroding their souls. And there are the less likely, driven by an ambition born out of a lack of love – we have all worked for one of them and witnessed the fear they wreak. So when your boss loses it again, maybe just offer that poor little person inside the three 'A's!

Jesus had crossed the line and in doing so became vulnerable, the impact of which we will see in the next stage. Having received the blessing of his Father he was commissioned to release others from themselves and into their individual and collective ministries. We remember that call to the fishermen who left their nets (Mark 1:17–18). That is crossing the line; that is commitment. The disciples gave up everything they had without having a clue as to what they were stepping into. When you cross the line you are stepping into the groundless ground of uncertainty. You may only be equipped to take the next step. There is no hiding place when you step across the clear line of commitment. You either hover indecisively on one side, feeling all the stress of a decision untaken or you go for it. If you are like me and there is a big decision to be taken, a great diversionary tactic is to repeat the word 'procrastinate'. You can enunciate it very slowly and use up many hours and minutes. Again it is something common to the human condition. We hate taking a decision, we are frightened of the consequences, and as soon as we have taken it we regret it and begin to think another choice would have been better. But this is where we need to be bold and remember the power of grace. How many times do we hear cry, Have faith! You will never really understand faith until you step into it. Faith cannot be lukewarm. You have to lay everything on the line, being prepared to make the ultimate sacrifice. Faith needs constant exercise. We need to be proactive, constantly seeking to move forward. When we remain static, faith begins to wither.

When you cross the line you are committing to your path, not knowing where it will lead. There is no going back at this stage since you have now left your Ordinary World and made your commitment. But it is an extraordinary place to be. I illustrate it using that wonderful scene in *Lord of the Rings* when the Fellowship has been arguing amongst itself as to who should return the ring to Mordor, the place of evil. Each of the characters is finding a good reason as to why it should not be them who commits, while Frodo, the smallest, the apparently least equipped of all, sits and watches from the sidelines. During the heat of the argument Frodo silently slips through the crowd and picks up the ring lying in the centre of the circle saying quietly, *I will return the ring, although I don't know the way.* This is the classic Disciple's response. So often we know something has to be done or that something isn't right. The usual response is to discuss the problem, set up an enquiry into it or write papers with recommendations which never get enacted. The Disciple acts. And when he does he unleashes a whole range of possibilities that didn't exist before he acted.

We can't become too attached to what we have lost or the life that we can never return to. We have crossed a new frontier. There is a wonderful line from the film Motorbike Diaries about the journey the young Che Guevara took around South America with a friend, as a young trainee doctor. It was journey that took him from a comfortable middle class existence in Buenos Aires to the revolutionary he subsequently became, as the injustice that existed across his continent became increasingly apparent. *What do we feel when we cross a frontier? Melancholy for what we leave behind, but excitement for what is to come.*

Start by doing what is necessary, then what is possible, and suddenly you are doing the impossible. *St Francis of Assisi*

This is the way it works. Just start with what is necessary in that moment. It maybe something small, but from that act something will follow. As I have said, faith cannot be lukewarm. You have to lay everything on the line, being prepared to make the ultimate sacrifice, a word I will return to. God gave me the gifts of a lovely wife, four daughters, some wonderful friends and family and a beautiful house in Bath. The last thing I needed with a huge mortgage, no income and my daughters all entering their teens, developing the same proclivities to shoes and clothes as Imelda Marcos with the spending habits to match, was a clear call to lay it all on the line. Since then I have remortgaged the house twice, used up all my life savings, sold all my life assurance policies, but the journey was on. Since then we have lived life on a perpetual financial knife-edge, a life of constant uncertainty. I could not have done it without the support of my wife, Cerys whose faith I suspect is stronger than mine. She, with my children, has borne the brunt of my sacrifice. And I mind that but I don't mind giving everything up if I have to, because I have found a far greater wealth. And that wealth is love. It is the gift of occasionally being able to see the world through the eyes of Christ. My security lies in that love – not in money, personal ambition or the acquisition of qualifications. And God doesn't want me to stand still. He constantly challenges me to grow, opens up new horizons and new callings. It seems that once you step into his will there is no stopping him. As soon as I feel comfortable, God challenges me to go further.

True disciples are those who absorb Jesus' wisdom by becoming travelling companions on the way. What happens to us on the road is a vital source of deep learning and real insight. The journey of discipleship involves crossing the boundaries of our personal comfort zone again and again. This is always going to be disconcerting, and sometimes painful, but it seems to me be the way in which God organizes our apprenticeship in Christ. We are true disciples when we are doing our best to latch on to Jesus' way of life by being open to the adventures that God has given us. It is then that we take three things together: learning from Scripture, learning from Christ's travelling companions and learning from our experience of the journey that we open ourselves up to being constantly renewed.

Stephen Cherry *The Barefoot Disciple*

The great thing that comes with commitment is confirmation. As with all callings, the Disciple doesn't just hear it once. God does not reveal something and then leave the Disciple hung out to dry. There will be confirmation in many different ways, some small, some quite dramatic. For me the confirmation came firstly in a gentle and surprising way. I had gone on retreat to Harnhill to reflect on where I was being led. It was a cold but sunny autumn day when I decided to go out for a long walk around the surrounding Gloucestershire countryside. On arrival in my room at the beginning of the week, a Bible lay open at Psalm 41, the opening verse of which says:

> Blessed is he who has regard for the weak;
> the Lord delivers him in times of trouble.

Another verse lay on the desk from Ephesians 4, a chapter that had a profound effect on me, as is reflected in the chapter on discipleship:

> Get rid of all bitterness, rage and anger, brawling and slander, along with every form of malice. Be kind and compassionate to one another, forgiving each other, just as in Christ God forgave you.
>
> *Ephesians 4:31, NIV*

In those two passages lay the prize and the cost. As I walked I reflected on my own bitterness, rage and anger. As we will, see the *Disciple's Journey* is an opportunity to reflect on all those aspects of our character that don't serve us. This was just the start. I reflected on the bitterness, rage and anger that I was in bondage to: being sent away to school at 7, the beatings that followed, the bullying, the sense of never being good enough, the failures, the high expectations that I never delivered, the inability to focus, the wasted potential. All had contributed to an inability to deal with authority, an inability to ask for help, a fear of rejection and a self-sufficiency that couldn't ask for help. I felt unworthy of any blessing. I realised that I had created a prison of my own making. It was at least the first step since, until we realise that we are in prison, no escape is possible. Looking back, I realise that concepts such as compassion and forgiveness were simply words. It would be some time before I truly understood them. But at least I was in a position where I was searching for answers.

And an answer came quickly and in a surprisingly unexpected way. I had been reading in my room, ironically a book called "How can I hear God?' I was about to get a direct answer. It was 10.30 at night. I had finished the book and was returning it to the library. As I walked along the darkened corridors of the retreat house, I ran into an Afro-Caribbean lady from Birmingham. I smiled, and as I was about to walk past, she grabbed my arm and said, *I have been wanting to talk to you*. Having just been beating myself up, she said that God loved me just the way I was. She told me that God would fulfil everything that was on my heart. *He won't let you down. Don't push yourself or try and pursue deadlines. Let him take control. He will provide for all your needs if not all your desires*. She compared my situation with George Muller, whose biography, 'coincidentally', I had been given the year before as an inspiration. *Protect yourself when you leave here. I can see God so clearly in you, but be prepared to be attacked*.

Further confirmation came in more dramatic style while I was training for a half marathon in the Devon countryside. I call it the Penquit revelation, since this is where it happened: a small hamlet called Penquit. In itself the name is symbolic since in its two syllables 'Pen' and 'Quit' lies the clue. 'Pen' I saw as 'penal', which linked with 'quit', revealing the whole purpose for the vision. It was a beautiful midsummer day. The countryside was stunning, with rich fields, narrow lanes and rolling hills. I had been running for three miles when I was confronted by a very steep hill. Steep hills have become very symbolic of the *Disciple's Journey* since they are consistent features of the landscape. The narrow road wound its way up the hill to the point that I was only able to maintain a fast walking pace. When the road flattened out at the top there was a sense not only of physical relief, but also huge spiritual energy. In that moment I heard the following words: *I have a dream of the day when our prisons will be run by Christians based on Christian principles where a man will be genuinely given a second chance; where bad is turned into good; where the bad things that a man has done can be turned into the good for others. Use* Believe *as a spearhead into our prisons. Make my church relevant to your world in a way that proclaims the glory of God.*

Virtue

At some stage we have to commit to the call to change. We can no longer prevaricate. So what does this commitment unleash? Another virtue – *creativity.* I believe that as we step into our truth we begin to create the life we are destined to live. We unlock the creativity that not only changes our world but has an impact on the world around us. Many people when asked whether they consider themselves to be creative say that they are not. But we all have the potential to be creative, if only in creating the life we are meant to live. This starts when we make the commitment to do so. And creativity doesn't need to be big picture stuff. Walking into an office with a smile on your face creates warmth. Providing support to a friend having a challenging time creates gratitude. There are many small ways in which we are creating, all the time, but for the bigger picture stuff, creativity in retrospect seems so neat. We think of the finished work of art, the sublime piece of music, the classic book. It seems so effortless, so simple, and sometimes it is. Picasso could knock up a painting in his lunch hour. Mozart could rattle off a tune at the age of four. But for most of us mere mortals creativity is relentlessly hard work and messy. It takes us into places we didn't know existed. It gives us extreme highs and desperate lows. But somewhere in between is life. And life is where we work out our truth.

The world is desperate for creators. We have an opportunity, according to Tom Wright, to create the kingdom. And this needs boldness, particularly by the young. It is the duty of the generations above to empower and support them in delivering the changes that are needed to our economies, our environment, politics, education and the way we live and what we value. The industrial age has created the world we live in and many of its advantages, but it is no longer sustainable to a world population that has just crossed the seven billion threshold. The capitalist model in itself isn't bankrupt. We will still need a means of creating jobs and the means to exchange goods and services. But we need to change our intent and the values that sit behind a model that continues to serve the richest while neglecting the poorest.

Reflection

- You have a dream, a vision, and goals. Now is the time to turn these into a clear plan.
- You have a mentor. What does the decision to commit look like?
- A leap into the unknown. When have you done it before? What did you feel?
- What is your team? Have you identified their unique skills and qualities?
- Do they match yours?
- What risks/failures/successes can you anticipate?

11

Trials, Allies and Enemies

In this you greatly rejoice, though now for a little while
you may have had to suffer grief in all kinds of trials.
These have come so that your faith – of greater worth than
gold, which perishes even though refined by fire – may
be proved genuine and may result in praise, glory and
honour when Jesus Christ is revealed.

1 Peter 1:6–7, NIV

One thing is for sure, as soon as you do cross the line you will
be confronted with the magnitude of the trial that you have
taken on. There is no going back at this stage since you have
now left your Ordinary World and made your commitment.
You will find allies and enemies – allies who come from
nowhere to support you, and the enemy to try and break
you. In *The Lord of the Rings*, the Fellowship immediately
get behind Frodo offering their different skills in support of
his journey. This happens in real life as well, in a way that
is providential, even supernatural sometimes, but reveals a
vital part of leadership. Followers can't respond until the
leader commits. In my own journeys the right people with
the right skills have materialised just on cue whenever I
have made the commitment, and extraordinary things have
happened. As your light shines, it attracts.

For I am convinced that neither death nor life, neither
angels nor demons, neither the present nor the future, nor
any powers, neither height nor depth, nor anything else
in all creation, will be able to separate us from the love
of God that is in Christ Jesus our Lord.

Romans 8:38–39, NIV

At this time I was visiting to Shepton Mallet prison once
a month to attend chapel with the prisoners. Then Shepton
Mallet mainly housed sex offenders and those with life
sentences for murder. My finances were on a knife-edge.
We faced the prospect of having to sell our house and take
the girls out of school. On one of these Sundays at Shepton
Mallet I met Adrian for the first time. He looked familiar.
As I subsequently discovered, many of those who are sent
to guide you along the way do. We never asked why people
were in prison, but it became apparent over time that his
offence had been murder. He was studying social sciences
and another degree while in prison as well as keeping
himself fit on the cycling machine in the gym. He had been
a very gifted amateur cyclist. I told him about my vision for
Believe and we shared our frustrations about the criminal
justice system and David Blunkett, then Home Secretary.
He confirmed that *Believe* was exactly what was needed. I
shared my financial difficulties and he said that the message
was clear: you must be prepared to sacrifice everything to
discover that God won't expect you to sacrifice everything.
He reminded me of the story of Abraham and Isaac. *You
have an aura. I know you will succeed.* This was a huge
encouragement (though one cannot accept the adjective!)
At this stage in the journey, the Disciple needs people to
believe in him and what he is doing.

Friends appear from nowhere to maintain this encouragement. I still find it extraordinary that people can just turn up with a vision for your life. Rosemary, who I knew vaguely in the village where I live, came and told me that she had a clear vision of a very colourful image of me lifting young people out of a grey and colourless pit. *You will bring hope* she told me. Someone else had a picture of me with a hacksaw cutting through a thick anchor chain. That picture still resonates since the anchor chain is very thick indeed. The anchor on one hand represents the prison of self that entraps us all, but equally, on the other hand, the anchor of hope that is the foundation of our faith. Another friend, Rosalind, shared a picture of an old apple tree bearing lots of fruit. In my fifties by now, this gave me hope that it is never too late. Yvonne, a neighbour, just appeared like an angel, with regular communication that she received in prayer, specifically for me.

Enemies come in different guises. In his book *Becoming Fully Human*, Patrick Whitworth identifies the three principal enemies: the world, the flesh and the devil. The greatest enemy that will appear is temptation. Following hard on his baptism, Jesus was led by the Spirit into the desert. So it will be for the Disciple.

Then Jesus was led by the Spirit into the desert to be tempted by the devil. After fasting for forty days and forty nights, he was hungry. The tempter came to him and said, "If you are the Son of God, tell these stones to become bread."

Jesus answered, "It is written: 'Man does not live on bread alone, but on every word that comes from the mouth of God.'"

Then the devil took him to the holy city and had him stand on the highest point of the temple. "If you are the Son of God," he said, "throw yourself down. For it is written: "'He will command his angels concerning you and they will lift you up in their hands, so that you will not strike your foot against a stone'"

Jesus answered him, "It is also written: 'Do not put the Lord your God to the test."

Again, the devil took him to a very high mountain and showed him all the kingdoms of the world and their splendour. "All this I will give you," he said, "if you will bow down and worship me."

Jesus said to him, "Away from me, Satan! For it is written: 'Worship the Lord your God, and serve him only.'"

Then the devil left him, and angels came and attended him.

Luke 4:4–11, NIV

Once the trial starts in earnest, the greatest temptation is to believe that you have made a huge mistake. The Disciple becomes very conscious of what has been laid down to pursue his calling. Suddenly the possibility of what you might be achieving in the material world can seem very compelling. I am mentoring a young man who has decided to sacrifice the opportunities of a lucrative career to pursue his calling to work with the most marginalised in our society. He works in a hostel for the homeless and is confronted with the lowest form of human behaviour daily. Whether it is trying to pin down a violent alcoholic or talking down a suicidal drug addict, every day takes an emotional toll. This is tough, emotionally draining work and he has not been getting the support he should be receiving from the Christian organisation he works for. When I met him he said, *I have lost any sense of grace towards the homeless. I hate them. I have no money, my relationships with girls never go anywhere. I am just so tired. I am tempted to go and find a job where I can just make a lot of money and get away from this misery.* This highlights the reality for most disciples when they are called to operate in difficult places with challenging people. At some point you will ask whether the sacrifice is worth it. It is harder still when you look around you and see your peers realising the material benefits of the well-paid career. It is even worse when people view you critically and think that you are mad for not pursuing the paradigm of the masses. It is when we can easily be taken to the high place and told that it could be so different; we could have huge wealth if only we stepped out of God's will. This is where our support group and particularly our mentor are so important: to keep us focused and on track, but fully emotionally supported. It is a battle.

In *The Art of War*, written during the sixth-century BC, Sun Tzu said: *If you know the enemy and know yourself, you need not fear the result of a hundred battles. If you know yourself but not the enemy, for every victory gained you will also suffer a defeat. If you know neither the enemy nor yourself, you will succumb in every battle.*

Knowing ourselves and knowing our enemies is a timeless strategy. No general commits his soldiers to battle without intelligence on his enemy and a very sound understanding of his own strengths and weaknesses. During this stage of the *Disciple's Journey* our enemies start to emerge. As a young troop leader I trained in armoured reconnaissance. One of the key tasks was to move towards the enemy in order to identify and pick off his positions so that the commanding general had the information upon which he could deploy the main force. It is only through movement that you draw the enemy's fire, since by moving towards him you are presenting a threat to his position. We are constantly seeking the weakness in the enemy's defences so that we can exploit it. And the enemy is doing the same to us! If we remain in our Ordinary World the enemy remains undisturbed. So the Disciple needs to get to know his enemies.

> If a man will begin with certainties, he shall end in doubts, but if he will be content to begin with doubts he shall end in certainties. *Francis Bacon*

Our internal enemies are led by that master strategist, the killer of so many dreams, self-doubt. As you make the commitment to your journey, by crossing that line, standing directly in front of you in full armour, will be that little voice inside, saying *You can't do this; it's too big for you; you haven't got the qualifications to do this; you are going to lose all your money – you will end up bankrupt; you are going to let down all those closest to you; no-one has ever done this before, what makes you think you can?* Self-doubt is the most persistent of enemies, showing up at every stage of your journey.

It has been said that to be human is, secretly, never to be quite sure of anything. We must qualify that at once, because we can all think of plenty of examples where we feel a high degree of certitude.

> But when he asks, he must believe and not doubt, because he who doubts is like a wave of the sea, blown and tossed by the wind. That man should not think he will receive anything from the Lord....
>
> *James 1:6–7, NIV*

There are two principal reasons why we fall into self-doubt. Firstly, we haven't yet revealed our truth, discovered that inner confidence in who we are. As a result we focus on what we don't have rather than what we do have. This leads to comparison, and envy of others' gifts. I do an exercise in my workshops for entrepreneurs, in which people are asked to list what they need to have before they start to do the things that will allow them to be a successful entrepreneur. They create long lists including money, networks, know-how and people. Similarly, the Disciple – a 'spiritual entrepreneur' – may be tempted to look for the perfect set of circumstances before they commit. The secret is to turn it on its head and to 'be' (i.e. adopt the mindset of) a successful entrepreneur/ disciple, which then allows you to start doing those things that need to be done, so as to find the resources required. With this mindset, it is possible to begin dispelling self-doubt.

The second reason that we feel self-doubt is that as the trial increases and the pressure grows we become more focused on our past failures. Our attitude to failure can be a recurring theme through the *Disciple's Journey* because it does stop us in our tracks. In our thoughts we go on revisiting all those times we have messed up and failed, convincing ourselves that, because it happened before, it is bound to happen again. Yet through God's grace and mercy we have the opportunity to be released from the past. The choice is ours. Until we confront both comparison and failure, self-doubt will continue to be our constant companion.

To understand the kind of confident trust we need for a new venture in discipleship, we could consider the sort of 'believing' someone needs to be a Christian disciple – believing and trusting in Jesus. From the calling of the very first disciples, as depicted in the Gospels, there had to be a willingness on each disciple's part truly to trust the Lord personally. It went far beyond a merely intellectual belief 'that' – it was a practical belief *in* him. That had to continue, it wasn't just a beginning, important as it is to make a start! At a different level, we need that kind of ongoing trust as we embark on – and persevere in – a new venture.

My growing doubt as to the wisdom of what I was doing would not go away. I began to wonder whether I was being irresponsible in relation to my duty to provide for my family. I discovered that enemies will come in two guises: the external and the internal. Sadly one of your greatest challenges will come from those closest to you: your friends and family. To see you embarking on a journey of change will both frighten and threaten them. There will be the fear of the unknown, especially, if like me, you have a family to support. Often the *Disciple's Journey* means leaving behind financial security and a structured life – those aspects of life which help to provide stability for those around you. The fear that your journey generates with them is bound to affect you and play to your worst nightmares. Their fear of your failure can make it become a self-fulfilling prophecy, since fear can inhibit appropriate action. Furthermore, the changes you are making may sometimes be threatening for others, maybe challenging them to make changes as well.

Moreover, your changing will threaten those who don't, challenging them to change too. Others, often parents, will see your adventure as reckless rather than pioneering. The truth is that it is *your* journey, no-one else's. This makes it hard for those who are swept along in the wake, as my family has been, but for the Disciple it is unavoidable. And then there are the critics – those who sit in judgement, happily having a go at anyone who tries something new. Most people instinctively prefer to stick with what they know and are suspicious of change. It's not that the critics don't have dreams (or cannot conceive of the Disciple having a dream), they just don't believe that they are achievable – and there can be a fear of trying.

When fear strikes someone, the Disciple can encounter envy from those sitting in the safe seats in the Ordinary World who haven't had the courage to set out on their own journey. As the Disciple's light begins to shine, these people would like to extinguish it.

Another challenge the Disciple will face is impatience.

> For the revelation awaits an appointed time;
> it speaks of the end and will not prove false.
> Though it linger, wait for it;
> it will certainly come and will not delay.
>
> *Habakkuk 2:3, NIV*

We hate waiting, especially for God. But he usually has greater plans than we can conceive, and times of waiting are opportunities to understand the true nature of faith, and refining. The jigsaw piece has not had the rough edges knocked off it yet. Often the Disciple is pioneering something new that has never been done before – he is testing out his own unique contribution to the world. As with a new baby, the project will need careful nurturing as it embarks on its first wobbly steps. No one would expect a baby to be able to run a marathon, nor would an experienced marathon runner criticise him for not being able to do so. All the great social movements have unfolded over time, often taking decades to bear fruit. Whatever the dream, however challenging the quest, there will be a huge gap between the vision and the achievement. Seth Godin calls the gap between when you set out to do something and the time when you start seeing results as the 'dip'. In entrepreneurial terms we talk about the period from start up to growth as the 'hockey stick'. Both represent that time when the Disciple has to suffer adversity and challenge, hard work and investment before the fruit begins to appear. We have to persevere to the final destination with confidence and faith, and it may sometimes seem rather like 'flying blind'. We may later discover the destination we thought we were heading towards is not necessarily the place we will end up.

> So do not throw away your confidence; it will be richly rewarded. You need to persevere so that when you have done the will of God, you will receive what he has promised.
>
> *Hebrews 10:35–36, NIV*

When things are new we are still discovering the right ways to do something. At this early stage in the journey there will be a lot of mistakes, maybe even failure, offering rich pickings for the critic. We are brought up with that phrase *Sticks and stones will break my bones, but words will never hurt me*. Never has there been a less true aphorism. When you are putting your soul on the line, words of criticism can be very hurtful and can often leave permanent scars. Ask any actor, or a vulnerable child who has been bullied. As the trial unfolds, the impact of the past becomes even more focused for both bad and good. There is the constant sense that because you have failed in the past, you will fail again. But equally there is realisation that the past was just the training ground for the future.

> I felt my past life had set my destiny for this trial.
>
> *Winston Churchill*

Or as Jack Nicholson put it, *It took 20 years of hard graft and sacrifice before I became an overnight success*.

The *Disciple's Journey* is ultimately a long interior battle within the soul (by which I include mind, will and emotions, in line with the Greek word *psyche*). There is something in a person that hates being dragged out of the comfort of the Ordinary World when one embarks upon an apparently reckless adventure. There is an inner realisation that once the line has been crossed there is no going back. So what we might call the 'flesh' (which, in Christian terminology means whatever in a person is still opposing God's will) uses every weapon in its armoury to sabotage the journey. This kind of attack is subtle.

All Disciples will encounter resistance and temptation at this stage. Resistance comes in many guises. At one end of the spectrum it will manifest itself in busyness, helping you to pretend that you are doing the important things when in reality you are generating lots of emails and meetings to give the world the impression that progress is being made. The Disciple can become a world expert on displacement activity, finding every excuse for not completing the very things that will allow him to make progress. Because he is alone at this stage, with little accountability, it is easy to pick the path of least resistance. In my own walk I endured many crises of confidence, during which it was easier to pick up the phone to a friendly supportive voice than it was to make a cold call, for example. The role of the mentor becomes crucial at this stage since he is able to provide that accountability.

Robert Louis Stephenson wrote, *You cannot run away from weakness. You must fight it out or perish: and if that be so why not now and where you stand?* It is only when the journey started that my weaknesses became really apparent. On my own journey I have learnt that sometimes 'strengths' and 'virtues' which had seemed to be allies can themselves be exposed as weaknesses and enemies.

These are difficult to defeat, but you have to learn to live with it. This is a voyage into uncharted territory, and over time the Disciple will learn to become more self-aware, understanding better what is going on and dealing with it.

It is an opportunity to discover those aspects of our character that do not serve us. I have listed some of the shadows of these virtues under the Contemplation phase of the *Disciple's Journey*, but maybe I could illustrate the point with a story at this stage which picks up on that other aspect of pride: arrogance, another trap for the Disciple.

It was a well intended email. Knowing my passion for prison reform, many friends send me articles from newspapers and other publications. It was late June and I was preparing a very important presentation for a potentially big funder in Bristol. The presentation had the potential not only to lead to some very important funding but also to the adoption of my schools programme in the new academy that the potential funder was sponsoring in a very deprived part of South Bristol. The friend sent me an article from *The Guardian*, describing the tragic case of a West Country man who had been released from prison with no support. The unfolding and inevitable tragedy was not untypical of many who could not come to terms with the transition from the institutionalism of prison to the utter despair of unsupported release. I wanted the potential funder to hear the story. The day before the presentation I decided to rewrite my script to incorporate the story.

I wanted to highlight the downward spiral that so often results from a combination of poor parenting, rejection from an educational system that makes no effort to accommodate those who don't fit neatly into a curricular framework, and the curse of drugs. The life story of the individual in the article illustrated the connections in an all too typical but very human story. Not able to cope, he had ended up taking the only thing left to him after years of neglect, abuse and the carelessness of the world he lived in: his life. The story moved me greatly. But the emotion it unlocked was to be my downfall.

June 30th was a grey day. I set off early on my regular drive from Bath to Bristol along the notorious A4, which during rush hour time is an eleven mile traffic jam. Time to take in the wonderful scenery along the way and reflect on what I was going to say. The drive up and down Pennyquick Hill through meadows unchanged in centuries; Kelston Hall, a magnificent Georgian mansion sitting on a hill guarding the western approached to Bath, Saltford, Keynsham, then Brislington, the beautiful landscape increasingly replaced by the suburban sprawl of southern Bristol. I was feeling an increasing sense of injustice. Bristol built its fortune on the slave trade, a dark cloud that still sits over the city today. There was outrage that the new shopping centre was to be named Merchant's Quarter, maintaining this scar on human history. There are some who would argue that times have changed. It is 200 years since William Wilberforce finally led the abolition movement to success. But history runs deep and it was, at best, insensitive to use the name. The potential funder was being seen as the descendants of those slave traders who built the beautiful Georgian houses of Clifton with their wealth. This is probably unfair since there is little residual wealth left and few direct descendants. But they continue to symbolise injustice in a still divided city – the extremes of wealth on the hills and poverty in the council estates that surround them. Instead of seeing this wealth as an opportunity to make a difference, I was subconsciously resenting it. Already I was making unfair comparisons between the ex-offender in the article and those whom I was about to see. I collected a colleague and, because of an appalling traffic jam in the centre of Bristol, we arrived late. We were taken into a very formal dining room at which sat a collection of the great and good from Bristol. The atmosphere was very formal and there was an air of discontent at our late arrival.

Psychologically, I was moving into the wrong space. Faced with formality and what I perceived as mild disapproval, I switched into arrogant mode. We sat through a presentation given by someone else, during which I was reviewing mine. I wanted to highlight the story of the ex-offender and how his story demonstrated the need for the type of intervention that *Believe* offered. I wanted to show that we needed to start in schools to prevent young people climbing onto the conveyor belt of crime, and I wanted to highlight the need to support those coming out of prison so such deaths would be less likely to occur in the future. I wanted to stand up for those who had no chance in society, in front of those who had every chance. Looking back, I don't know how I got it so wrong. I preached for fifteen minutes on the story of the young man in the *Guardian* article. It was not what they wanted to hear, and as I was forced to end I had one of those horrible moments when you feel the bottom falling out of your world. I walked lamely out of the room knowing not only would I not get the money that I had come to ask for but wouldn't get the opportunity to put coaching at the heart of the new academy, which was a real possibility. As we stepped into the car, my colleague told me, if I needed telling, how awful, it was. I was distraught and embarrassed, but I knew that I had learned a vital but expensive lesson: I had to deal with my pride.

At this stage of the journey, your greatest shields are firstly your mentor who, in my experience shows up, just like in all the big epics, when everything seems to be falling apart and the Disciple wants to give up. A good mentor becomes the protector of the soul, reminding it of its destiny and holding it accountable to the unspoken promises it gave when one originally 'crossed the line'. The second shield is in Ephesians chapter 6, the full armour of God.

Finally, be strong in the Lord and in his mighty power. Put on the full armour of God so that you can take your stand against the devil's schemes. For our struggle is not against flesh and blood, but against the rulers, against the authorities, against the powers of this dark world and against the spiritual forces of evil in the heavenly realms. Therefore put on the full armour of God, so that when the day of evil comes, you may be able to stand your ground, and after you have done everything, to stand. Stand firm then, with the belt of truth buckled round your waist, with the breastplate of righteousness in place, and with your feet fitted with the readiness that comes from the gospel of peace. In addition to all this, take up the shield of faith, with which you can extinguish all the flaming arrows of the evil one. Take the helmet of salvation and the sword of the Spirit, which is the word of God.

Ephesians 6:10–17, NIV

I find the most powerful sentence in this well known passage is the one most overlooked, *Therefore put on the full armour of God, so that when the day of evil comes, you may be able to stand your ground, and after you have done everything, to stand.*

There needs to be that perseverance – after you think you have done everything you can, you still stand. This was to be severely tested as the journey unfolded.

Virtue

When creativity is unlocked, the creative person becomes vulnerable. There may be allies who appear from nowhere, but it is the internal and external enemies that throw the whole venture into doubt. At this point the most crucial virtue is ***integrity***. It can be very difficult to stay true to the course that you have set yourself. Even those closest to you may begin to express their doubts as things don't go according to plan – and they rarely do. Do you give up? Or do you stay true to your original plan? There are never easy answers but maintaining integrity is vital. It is tempting to give up or bend the rules in order to achieve quick success. In my experience if you stay true to yourself and your goals, extraordinary things can happen.

Until one is committed there is hesitancy, the chance to draw back, always ineffectiveness. Concerning all acts of initiative (and creation), there is one elementary truth, the ignorance of which kills countless ideas and splendid plans: that the moment one definitely commits oneself, then providence moves too. All sorts of things occur to help one that would never otherwise have occurred. A whole stream of events issues from the commitment, raising in one's favor all manner of unforeseen incidents and meetings and material assistance, which no man could have dreamt would have come his way. I have learned a deep respect for one of Goethe's couplets:
"Whatever you can do, or dream you can, begin it. Boldness has genius, power and magic in it."

W H Murray

In September 2004, when I was setting up *Believe*, I had just enough funding to start our first programme in Bristol Prison, I needed to take on another person. I met just the right person in Peter. When I interviewed him I explained that I had no means to pay him yet. He was in a secure job, so said he would discuss it with his wife over the weekend. On Monday he came back and said he was prepared to take the risk and go for it. I was staying with friends in the

Scottish borders when he rang. I accepted his offer and prayed, *'I don't know how I am going to pay him Lord, but you do'*. Looking back on what happened next, it is still difficult to remind myself it really did take place. To the rational mind it seems extraordinary. But as W H Murray says in the quotation above, at the moment one definitely commits oneself, then one sees the providence of God. It is one of the great lessons for a disciple to learn. To reinforce a point made earlier, procrastination can a hindrance to our receiving much that God has for us. As I sat on that late summer morning, looking out across the Tweed Valley, I received two phone calls. Within ten minutes of my committing to employing Peter, the chairman of my trustees phoned. He informed me that the probate on his father's will was complete and he would like to donate some money. He would give exactly the first year's salary for Peter. But when you have made a commitment and you are on the right track, things don't happen by half. Ten minutes later: another call. This time from the PA to the CEO of HSBC the second biggest bank in the world asking me for lunch. *I wondered if you might be free to come and have lunch on October 13th*. My response as I smiled quietly to myself, with my diary upstairs *Let me just check my diary…Yes that would be wonderful. Thank you.* From that lunch I received the second year's salary.

We might talk about serendipity or coincidence, but actually we should be talking about God's provision as we are true to our quest. It is easy in our rational world to dismiss these seemingly fortuitous events as random occurrences. I have learned however that there is nothing random about it. When we are on track with our destiny these things happen all the time, big and small. They are signs that we are on track. You think of someone and they just turn up; you are looking for something and it just appears when you need it. The signs are there all the time. We have to be conscious of them, walking with God, who is our provider – and we have to walk in integrity.

That word 'integrity' comes from the word 'integer', which signifies wholeness, entirety and completion. To think and act with integrity, we have to integrate the multiple dimensions of our complex world. The opposite is to compartmentalise.

This happens at a micro level when we put on different masks depending on the circumstance and who we are meeting. We separate ourselves to project ourselves in a way that people or circumstance demand. Sometimes we can't avoid it, but it is highly stressful pretending to be someone you are not. More importantly, no-one knows the real you. The masks become the prison bars to the soul, imprisoning the person you were born to be. This part of the journey is very much concerned with revealing these masks, stripping them away so that the Disciple can be released into the effortless freedom of being true to himself. This is integrity.

On a macro level one might think of the failure of government to be able to integrate itself across different departments as being analogous to a lack of 'integrity'. The structure is far from being 'integrated' (or 'joined up') and that split into many compartments can be a great enemy of social justice. Government can only fund through separate departments, each with its own ministerial leadership and set of officials, which is not only very inefficient, but can fail to address the root causes of a particular problem. Working with prisoners as I have done, one finds that so many are illiterate, homeless, unemployed, mentally ill, drug-addicted. So when we attempt to reduce their reoffending without integrity (by which I mean here structural integration in the delivery of support services), we continue to fail at huge expense to the taxpayer. Those government ministries which would hold individual accountability for the various issues – Department for Education (illiteracy), Department of Communities and Local Government (homelessness), Department of Work and Pensions (unemployment), Department of Health (mental illness and drug addiction) and the Ministry of Justice, which is responsible for the management of offenders – operate in isolation, each with its own separate administration and budget. It is hardly surprising that reoffending remains so high.

When thinking with integrity we will often encounter paradox, an inconvenient truth, which seems to contradict reason and may even seem to be absurd. The Disciple will by now have experienced something of the pain that faith brings, and on a human level will always want to avoid it. The paradox is that by avoiding the pain we deny ourselves the unfathomed joy that comes beyond the pain, as we will discover later in the journey.

On a personal level, having started to reveal the real you, integrity is remaining true to your discovery. In essence there will be no difference between who you appear to be and who you truly are. You will be the same person within whatever company you are keeping. Furthermore, integrity sometimes means that you have to take decisions that might not serve your best interests because they have a wider benefit than your own. In a television documentary following the crash of 2008, Alan Greenspan, then Director of the US Federal Reserve, was asked for his explanation of events around the credit crunch, such as the collapse of Lehmann Brothers. His reply was interesting and somewhat naïve. He said that he never expected individuals to place their own short-term interests over the long-term interests of the institutions they served. The bonus culture had corroded integrity.

True 'happiness' (or blessing) flows when there is a right relationship with God – genuine discipleship, with all the cost and sacrifice. But in the world, in many guises, often commercially driven, there are many shallow, ephemeral substitutes on offer, and we have to recognise such counterfeits for what they are. Our real happiness (and our ability to communicate the truth with passion) require inner integrity.

Discover who you really are (and that includes who you are in the sight of God) and you will discover that unhappiness is transitory.

Reflection

- **Who are you revealing yourself to be?**
- **What are your limiting beliefs?**
- **Can you be counted on to keep commitments?**
- **Are you willing to make decisions that are best for others, even though another choice might benefit you more?**
- **Are you the same no matter who you are with?**
- **How do you respond to difficulties? Do you avoid/retrench/anticipate.**
- **What drives you? Fears or hope?**
- **How do you blend skills and qualities to maximum affect?**
- **Who is your enemy? Internal and external. How do you protect yourself? (Ephesians 6:10–20)**
- **How have you done this in the past?**
- **Who did you think was your enemy but in fact wanted the best from you? Know your enemies – they are your greatest teachers.**

12

Facing the Darkness

We do not want you to be uninformed, brothers, about the
hardships we suffered in the province of Asia. We were
under great pressure, far beyond our ability to endure, so
that we despaired even of life. Indeed, in our hearts we
felt the sentence of death. But this happened that we might
not rely on ourselves but on God, who raises the dead.

2 Corinthians 1:8–9, NIV

In order to build your faith, God will give you a dream.
Then, he'll urge you to make a decision. But then he'll allow
a delay, because in the delay he matures you and prepares
you for what is to come. The truth is, you'll have difficulties
while God delays. This isn't because he doesn't care about
you or that he's forgotten your circumstances; rather, it's
one of the ways he pushes you toward the deep end of
faith. As God delays, you'll face two types of difficulties:
circumstances and critics. This is a natural part of life. God
designed it this way because he knows we grow stronger
when facing adversity and opposition. It is when we really
begin to face up to our own compulsions and how they don't
serve us. Until this point, we have faced challenges and
thought this was just part of the journey, the overcoming of

which we can feel virtuous about. This is where God gets real. *OK, so you really want to call yourself a Christian. Well this is what its about! I can use you but not as you are. You will only upset yourself at your ability to mess things up if you continue as you are. This is a chance to get close and really understand that what I see in you is so much greater than what you see in yourself. Then you can be of service in the world.*

Facing the darkness is another world away from the syrupy warm glow you can get from going to church. I once thought that was what faith was all about; a self-indulgent way of justifying my way of life with the opportunity to confess my sin and receive forgiveness; to sing because singing makes us feel better about ourselves especially in harmony with others; and giving money in penance for what we have done.

When Moses led the children of Israel out of Egypt into the desert toward the Promised Land, he had one problem after another. First there was no water. Then there was no food. Then there were a bunch of complainers. Then there were poisonous snakes. Moses was doing what God wanted him to do, but he still had problems. When Moses died, Joshua was appointed the new leader. Moses led the people across the desert, and then Joshua led them into the Promised Land. Did he get the easy part? Even in the Promised Land there were problems! God does this because he is building our faith and character. When we finally come to a place where the difficulties become so bad, where we've reached our limit, where we've tried everything and exhausted all our options, it is then that God begins a mighty work through us. Moses learned the lesson that we can only really achieve when we let go of the need to be the one who gets the credit. He never had the credit of getting everyone back to the Promised Land. That fell to Joshua. But Moses had created the possibility of it happening and was himself a mentor to Joshua. While we all want our lives to feel significant, if we are driven by the need to receive all the glory, we will fail. The glory is never ours and the deeply human desire to have it becomes our greatest enemy. It is an enemy that is often faced at this stage in the journey when we realise that alone we are incapable of achieving great things.

I have not met a Disciple, in whatever guise, who has not at some point faced the darkness or, as I call it, the dark night of the soul. At this point it appears that the 'flesh' has won the battle. This is the point when everything seems to be falling apart and life seems hopeless. Fear is overwhelming and can in the extreme lead to suicidal thoughts. Enduring it is hell. But I came to realise over time that these are the moments where you are forced to dig deep and lean on God. For me, it is my Christian faith which has been a constant source of inspiration and comfort.

Just occasionally I get a real sense that God is at work within me, in the sense that he is truly present, leading, helping and guiding me as I face so many battles. As we go on being filled with the Holy Spirit, we become aware that we are not alone. We do need to draw close to God, and we rediscover (if we have lost sight of this) that he is close to us. We have already seen how the Disciple has to battle against the forces of the of the flesh, the world and the devil. He may have become quite accomplished as a fighter in different seasons and on many fronts, but nothing fully prepares him for this stage. This is a dark place which can seem hellish when you are in the midst of it. And the irony is that the only way to endure it is through praise and gratitude while blessing and forgiving those who may have caused us to be here. We will return to humility, but this is where the Disciple begins to understand its full nature and where, kicking and screaming maybe, he learns to depend utterly on God. Curiously, it may be that we discover that these dark times and places become the moments when healing or restoration or a fresh start become noticeable to us.

> For sudden the worst turns the best to the brave.
> The black minute's at end,
> And the elements' rage, the fiend voices that rave,
> Shall dwindle, shall blend,
> Shall change, shall become first a peace out of pain.
> Then a light, then thy breat,
> O thou soul of my soul! I shall clasp thee again,
> And with God be the rest!

In this extract from Robert Browning's poem *Prospice*, especially the line used by Ernest Shackeleton 'For sudden the worst turns to the best for the brave', we begin to reveal the truth to this stage of the journey.

I have worked with some very prolific offenders, many of whom were drug addicts. Their offending behaviour is driven by their need to buy the next fix. Those who are brave enough submit themselves to Narcotics Anonymous, run on the same lines as Alcoholics Anonymous. Recovery from addiction is one of the toughest journeys you can go on. At the heart of the recovery process is what has been termed "submission to a 'higher power'". Christians would want to encourage dependence explicitly on God – the Father, Son and Holy Spirit. People can certainly be released from harmful addiction and much more.

There is a clear understanding that there is a limit to what a human being can achieve and that we have to search outside ourselves for help. This is the unequivocal realisation that hits you when facing the darkness. Since the Age of Reason and the industrial age, the belief system of many has been that the mind can create a solution to every challenge. So we live in an intellectual age where human behaviour is driven by law, science, process and the belief that money can solve everything. When you are in the pit of despair, none of these are of service. It is only by repenting toward God and believing and trusting in Jesus that we discover the gift of humility and our true selves. For those who are brave enough to confront their demons and pray for release from them, opportunities then come unexpectedly to get you back on track. If you want things to progress, if you want real, meaningful, positive change to come to your life, one thing you have to do is concede that there are many things you do not know enough about. Simply by acknowledging this you start to become a real expert in the art of living a successful life.

Archbishop Rowan Williams in his book *The Indwelling of Light* wrote:

"As [Christ's] hand grasps the hands of Adam and Eve... we are reminded that he goes fully into the depths of human agony. He reaches back to and beyond where human memory begins: 'Adam and Eve' stand for wherever it is in the human story that fear and refusal of God began – not a moment we can date in ordinary history, any more than we can date in the history of each one of us where we began to forget God. But we are always dealing with the after-effects of that moment, both as a human race and as particular persons. The icon declares that wherever that lost moment is or was, Christ has been there, to implant the possibility, never destroyed, of another turning, another future...."

In December 2007 I faced the biggest obstacle to my own journey. By then *Believe* had grown substantially and we were operating in eight prisons from Bristol to Belmarsh as well as establishing a successful engagement project for NEETs (a rather bureaucratic acronym to describe those Not Engaged in Employment, Education or Training), largely young males who had left school with nothing, a living testimony to a failed education system.

At this time *Believe* was at the latter stage of negotiations with a government capacity building body to raise substantial funds to expand our operations. Our application had been accepted in principle, but for internal bureaucratic reasons beyond our control, had become stalled. This placed a huge strain on the finances of the charity. On the back of this funding, *Believe* was expanding both operationally and in terms of staff. I mentioned earlier that an understanding which should develop on the *Disciple's Journey* concerns the humility needed to realise that, however we convince ourselves otherwise, we are not individually the full package. We are good at some things and not others. I realised that while I was good at creating things, I was not a great manager. So in 2006 I stepped down as CEO and handed over to someone who was good at deal making and getting things set into a process. I had worked with him and trusted him. It is the hardest thing a creator does, handing over their baby for another to nurture, but it is a healthy thing to do. Every organisation, especially charities, will tell you about the problem of 'founder syndrome'. Inevitably we become very emotionally attached to what we create, and this can inhibit objectivity and poison relationships. So it was time to let go, and by letting go, create the space for the next stage to emerge. Letting go of the familiar is another challenge the Disciple has to get used to but, hard though this is, it is the only way we can grow. It is back to that word faith spelt RISK.

At first all was well and the charity grew quite rapidly. We expanded into more prisons and started other new projects. People were beginning to understand what it was we had to offer. There comes a time in our lives, however, when our intuition begins to suggest that not all is well. It is that gut feeling that we are unwise to ignore. It starts with a sense that you are maybe hearing what you want to hear rather than the truth. I only discovered that there was a problem in August 2007 after I had received a fine from Bristol County Court for non-appearance in a case involving this new CEO, where an attachment of earnings had been made against him. He was declared bankrupt. The court had sent seven letters addressed to me to the *Believe* address in Bristol. When they weren't responded to, they sent a bailiff who personally handed a letter to our administrator. The CEO took it from her and destroyed it. I was able to prove my innocence in the matter and had the fine rescinded. Events unfolded at a pace thereafter. It became clear subsequently that he had fraudulently set up at least three direct debits in favour of two finance companies to fund three expensive Audis.

We dismissed the CEO and passed his case to the police and appointed an interim to try and rescue the situation. We had to inform the capacity building organisation of the situation and let them know that the accounts that had been submitted to support the application had proved to be inaccurate despite significant due diligence by them. It became clear that the survival strategy would depend on laying off a number of staff and closing some operations. By early December we had things back on track and the signs from the capacity building fund were promising. The account manager informed me that at the meeting on 19th December there would be a recommendation to resume funding us. It was a nervous time. I can remember the time and place, 11.07 on 20th December 2007, sitting in Bordeaux Quay in Bristol with my mentor. My mobile phone rang and it was the account manager informing me that the Board had decided that they needed two more months before they could make a decision to release the funding. I knew then that the game was up.

It was the week before Christmas. I had no money. We had exhausted all our savings, remortgaged the house twice to pursue my dream and there seemed to be nowhere else to turn. I can't remember going home that night, but I do remember trying to sleep. But sleep was impossible. It is difficult to describe how painful this stage of the *Disciple's Journey* is. You feel totally alone; not even those closest to you can help. I was facing the darkness, my dark night of the soul. I tried listening to the radio, but the depressing theme of Up All Night on Radio 5 Live, which to this day remains a musical reminder of that dark night, forced me out of bed. I decided to walk, since walking and running has always helped me think things through. It was a glorious moonlit frosty night. The moon was full and, with the deep frost, visibility was excellent. Everything was silent and white. There is something about silence that, for some reason, many of us try to avoid, but it is a gift. To be lost in a world where all we are conscious of is our breathing that tells us we are alive, allows us to reflect in a way that the normal noise of life prevents. I walked down across the Monkton Combe valley close to Bath, where I live. I started beating myself up for ever starting on this journey. How irresponsible I had been to risk everything on setting up a charity when I had four daughters to bring up. How arrogant I had been to think that I could change the prison system. I had lost everything and I only had myself to blame. The words from the Lord's Prayer, 'Thy will be done' kept running through my mind as I prayed for a solution. I was reminded of the importance of perspective. Earlier that evening I had attended the carol service at Shepton Mallett prison. After the service I had a long chat with Keith, who had been sentenced to three years imprisonment twenty-two years ago! When his release was reversed, the year before, he had contemplated committing suicide. He revealed that his mother had committed suicide when he was ten. No one had ever helped him with that. My problems seemed insignificant in comparison.

Of course the solution that I prayed for was the survival of *Believe*, but as I know you rarely get the outcome from prayer you seek with your limited perspective. I walked for about four hours, returning home just before dawn. I fell exhausted into a short, deep sleep. When I woke and went downstairs, I noticed that there was an envelope lying on the doormat. I opened it. It is difficult to explain to a rational mind what I found inside it, but the truth is I removed not one but two substantial cheques. They were for us as a family. At least we would have a wonderful Christmas, knowing that our financial needs for the months ahead had been looked after. God has an amazing knack of turning up when you most need him. He knows what he is trying to achieve and what he wants from you and he never lets you down, whatever your worst fears may be. It didn't solve the problem of *Believe*, since the trustees were forced to close the charity a month later, but it was an encouragement to continue the journey. That journey that was to take a different twist in the new year. At the time it looked like failure, but what the Disciple learns is that failure is our greatest teacher and that every time we fail we have the opportunity to grow.

Achievers (Disciples) do not take failure as a moral judgement on themselves. They see it merely as a passing event, a transitory setback...achievers are by definition those who do not give up. No one learns to walk who does not learn to try again after falling over.

Stephen Cherry *The Barefoot Disciple*

When I was younger I sailed across the Atlantic on a brigantine, The Eye of the Wind. I remember setting sail from Southampton and sailing through the Bay of Biscay in an autumn gale. None of us knew each other. We had to climb the rigging with the hull of the boat tossing around in the wild seas below. Never good with heights, I was beginning to wonder what on earth I was doing. Violent sea-sickness followed and, for those who haven't experienced it, literally stepping out of the boat seems preferable to enduring another moment of the misery. In a real sense I was facing the darkness and I began to accept that all I could do was find the inner resilience to stand and trust. And this is what it is like for the Disciple. Be encouraged; we all find ourselves at sea or in a desert despairing in the darkness. We soon understand that there are limits to our self-sufficiency and that it is time to burn off some pride and turn to God.

It is a place where the masks of false identity are stripped away and the person you were born to be can emerge like the butterfly from a chrysalis. We may need to find our wilderness to find our true selves. It can be at the bottom of the pit where we begin discovering who we are and what we are to do. We are sometimes broken to be blessed and to be made ready to be a blessing to others.

Having endured a personal struggle that is at its most challenging, I now had to move on to a place of deep contemplation.

Virtue

Something else that I see holding back so many people is their inability to deal with failure and loss, both of which we encounter at some stage. I am always humbled by those who can treat personal tragedy as just that – a tragic moment, but not something to go on being oppressed by in the long term. One key can be *forgiveness*. We need to forgive whatever personal wrongs have been done to us. Another key (having first repented toward God) is to truly accept that we ourselves have really been forgiven: self blame can continue and that can be corrosive. Once we recognise that none of us is perfect, no situation is perfect and the present is just that, we can learn to grow and treat everything as a growing opportunity.

As Jesus teaches his disciples, we have to go on forgiving those who sin against us, indeed to do so is a condition for being forgiven by God ourselves (see Matthew 6:14-15).

One of the greatest privileges of my life was to provide the coaching for a retreat for the parents of children who had had their lives taken from them in the most tragic (and often gruesome) circumstances: most had been murdered. As a father myself, I could only empathise with the depth of their pain. Two of them, both extraordinary women from Manchester, were still trapped in the moment when the police arrived on their doorstep to tell them that their child had been found murdered. For one this was ten years earlier; for the other nine. Their grief was still palpable. This was their first opportunity to break through their grief and come to terms with their loss. I remember the first night sitting with Mandy and hearing the whole saga, and it began to dawn on me how hopeless we are as a society in helping people like her. From the moment she was told, the dead bureaucratic hand of the state took over. Invited to identify the body of her daughter, she was only allowed to view it through a glass panel. Her little girl had ceased to be her daughter in the eyes of officials – she was now evidence. So no opportunities to say goodbye; no last hug; just a cursory look through a screen and a nod to confirm that it was her. And in an era when people seek counselling for trivial reasons or seek compensation for hurt feelings, nothing was offered. Mandy's feelings were never considered in the build up to the trial, nor was she offered the chance to contribute in any way. Just lots of well-meaning but crass people telling her it was time to move on. Yet we don't create a space where people like Mandy can move on. News cuttings fade and the newspapers move on to the next gruesome story. But the Mandys of this world are left trapped in their grief – trapped in the moment when the police knocked on the door.

Sarah was cooking supper for her three boys when she was vaguely aware of a helicopter circling nearby. She thought nothing of it. And then the knock on the door; the two policemen on her doorstep; the police car parked outside. Those precious seconds before life as she knew it was no more. That easy life with all the day-to-day pressures and silly rows that every household with children is so familiar with. Sarah had had lunch with John only hours before. He was 17 with life unfolding before him. He was a devoted cyclist and could play tricks on his bike that only a 17-year old boy can. He had gone out on an errand on his bike at the same time that another 17-year old boy decided to do a bit of joyriding. Their destinies combined in a moment of speed and horror, leaving John dead by the side of the road. Those precious seconds, when this reality did not have to be confronted, before those words that no parent wants to hear: *I think you had better sit down. I am so sorry....* When

I met her, Sarah and her husband, Chris, had been trapped in this moment for fifteen months. I spent four hours with Chris, whose sense of failure as a father in letting his eldest son die was so painful. He described his family since as being four people on four different islands in a lake, each unable to swim to another. They coexisted in the same house but were unable to communicate their innermost feelings to each other. They ate and slept separately. The dining table regularly used for family meals had not been used since John died. Each day they separately made their lonely vigil at the grave, the only tenuous contact they still had with him. Chris was so angry – with himself, with his family, with the world beyond, and most of all with the boy who had killed his son. But there was no way for him to unlock that anger and find a focus for it and so he could only direct it at himself and his own feeling of inadequacy as a father. Never before had I witnessed in the flesh that life of quiet desperation which so many men apparently lead. He asked me if I would talk to Sarah. I agreed to speak to her the following day.

It was a perfect summer's afternoon in the beautiful gardens of a country house in Buckinghamshire. The sun shone and the ground was dappled by the leaves of the apple tree we sat beneath, as Sarah told me her story. Sarah is one of those people for whom the word 'rock' could be used. Her life was one of service to her family and friends and the community beyond. She is one of life's givers. Since the moment that her son was taken from her, she had done all she could to keep her family together. Despite her aching grief for the boy she called her soulmate, she knew that she had to try and maintain some level of normality for the sake of the rest of the family, but the act was now too stressful to keep up and the mask was slipping. We had been talking for what seemed hours, when she quietly looked at me and said, *But it is going to be OK now. I have worked out what I am going to do. In fact I nearly did it last week, but Chris came home early.* It dawned on me that Sarah was letting me know of her impending suicide. *I have given everything and there just isn't anything left to give. I am empty.* This was no cry for help – it was a statement of fact. Never before in my life had the response I was to make carried such responsibility. I can remember that moment so clearly, a bee landing on a nearby pale pink rose. The response was divinely inspired: *Sarah, at the moment John's memory is pure. If you take your life now, Chris and the boys will blame John for the rest of their lives for your death. Is that what you really want?* Sarah broke down. It was as though a line had been crossed.

Subsequently Sarah was released from the prison of grief and took up the offer to participate in a restorative justice programme run by the local Youth Offending Team. She had to do it behind Chris's back because he would not have been able to accept it. Restorative justice allows the victim and offender to come together, the former to explain the impact on their lives of the crime, the latter to explain the circumstances that led it being committed. One morning she was driven to the Young Offender's Institution where the boy who had killed her son was imprisoned. Knowing that she would almost certainly be too emotional to make her statement verbally, she had written it out carefully to be read by someone else. In fact she managed to deliver it herself and talked about the pain of a mother's son and soulmate ripped away from her, about the devastation that this had wreaked upon her family and their utter inability to come to terms with it. The offender, the same age has her son, stood there facing her, tears rolling down his cheeks at first, then sobbing uncontrollably. He had never had a mother who loved him so unconditionally. He had no idea who his real father was. He had a series of 'uncles' who at best ignored him, at worst abused him. He had no idea what real family life was. Love was foreign territory. He had stolen the car for a laugh, something to do, something to take him out of the day-to-day pain of his existence. He didn't even see the cyclist, let alone realise the loss he had inflicted. Just another avatar on his Gameboy destroyed. Only in this moment did he encounter the power of a true love – the love of a mother which he had never received. Only in this moment did he have a sense of loss of something that he should have had but never did. Only in this moment did the dreadful consequences of his actions hit him in a place he had never felt before. As he sobbed, utterly alone in his misery, a remarkable thing happened: a grieving mother stepped out of her own grief and stepped into his. Confronted with his tears Sarah did the one thing that came naturally to her. She crossed the room, took him in her arms and embraced him. They hung onto each other, eternally linked in their grief, for what seemed an age their only connection being a dead boy. There was not a dry eye in the house. Out of it all came healing. Sarah was able to forgive; he was able to repent and start the slow journey to rehabilitation.

I tell the story just to illustrate the contrast between the mechanistic and the human approach. I do not diminish the need for punishment. Loss of freedom is punishment, but it doesn't address the needs of either the victim or the perpetrator. The victim remains locked in the effects of the crime; the perpetrator remains locked in a system that doesn't allow repentance or forgiveness and fails to address the factors which led to the criminal behaviour in the first place or to reduce their influence. This represents such a missed opportunity.

We always have a choice as to how we deal with failure, hurt or betrayal. We can either mask and bury them and allow them to steal from us the very things we cherish, or we accept the healing that comes from forgiveness. Forgiveness necessitates letting go of the possibility of changing the past. Whatever we cling to controls us. When we forgive others we release ourselves from the chains of resentment that can overwhelm our lives. It can be a helpful reminder if we use the two syllables in the word 'forgive': for and give. By letting go of what went *before*, we are *given* back our future. But it was by facing up to my past and acknowledging my own shortcomings that contributed to the demise of *Believe*, that I was able to remind myself that I had been forgiven at the cross once and for all time. As I had been forgiven, so I could forgive others.

At some point the Disciple will have to do the same. Otherwise, more often than not, the journey ends here. The Disciple is not immune from making mistakes. Indeed he will make more than his fair share. But he has a God of grace who is ready to forgive those who repent, and as the father in the Prodigal Son illustrated earlier, will always be there to welcome us back to the true way. Progress requires us to confront the issue, accept our responsibility, repent, forgive others and receive God's forgiveness ourselves. And solace during these often terrifying times are found in the following passage:

Do not be anxious about anything, but in everything, by prayer and petition, with thanksgiving, present your requests to God.

Philippians 4:6, NIV

Reflection

- When have you faced the darkness? What might it be this time?
- What is keeping you awake at night?
- Who do you talk to about your most difficult decisions?
- What are your three most critical threats?
- What have you/will you have to leave behind?
- What events have wounded you before? How did you crawl out of the pit? Trials can inspire creativity. What am I meant to learn from this one and how can I deploy that knowledge in the future?
- What aspects of your character are being brought to the surface?

13

Contemplation —
Continuing the Journey

"'If you can'?" said Jesus. "Everything is possible for him who believes."

Mark 9:23, NIV

For those who emerge from the darkness, there will be a time of contemplation before the journey continues. The Disciple emerges battered and bruised from his ordeal and needs the time, as any soldier will know, to regroup. He begins to understand that if you go with your faith, the place of your greatest failure can become the place of your greatest success. We begin to understand that the early stages of the *Disciple's Journey* were a quest to discover our own identity. The *Disciple's Journey* is one of growing faith. It begins with the greatest step of faith as we leave behind our comfortable known world for one that is full of uncertainty. We have responded to a voice that calls us to take the next step, without our really having a clue where it all ends. As we launch on our quest we have been joined by friends and attacked by enemies until finally we have ended up in our dark night of the soul. Why does God allow this to happen? Why does he allow suffering?

It sounds ridiculous to the rational mind, but he allows

it because he loves us. God the Father watched his only-begotten Son suffer and die upon the cross. Did the Father stop loving the Son? No, of course not. He just knew the end of the story. He knew that on the third day Jesus would walk free from he prison of his grave. His death and resurrection would open up an opportunity for us to be changed and have life, rather than die in our sins. By so doing we can become a 'new creation' living in him. The only good Man had to die so that all of us bad people could become everything that we were created to be. The journey we have to take as Jesus' disciples calls for ongoing faithfulness to him as well as perseverance.

The whole account of the resurrection of Jesus is supernatural, but not contrary to reason. There are varied accounts from many eyewitnesses who saw the risen Jesus. The evidence for the resurrection is there. It is easy in our sceptical and rational world to dismiss all supernatural claims, no matter how strong the evidence. A rejecting mindset is the greatest obstacle to coming to faith.

It is during periods of contemplation that the Disciple can look back and see how far he has come and to reflect on those moments when events can only be explained supernaturally. I can feel from my own experience that this is true for me and if it is true for me it has to be true for others too. The historical testimony of witnesses, as recorded in the New Testament, provides solid evidence that the resurrection occurred. The early Christians would scarcely have been willing to be martyred for their faith if they thought the message they were preaching concerning the resurrection was a pack of lies! Moreover, it is the experience of countless Christians that we know Jesus is alive now and relates to us. We are aware of his living presence through the Holy Spirit. We are conscious of what pleases him and what grieves him; we are given all this in direct experience and in practical ways in our lives, as extraordinary things happen. Why else would I be writing this book?

What I do know is that it was only through suffering that I was able to strip off all those masks that really haven't served me, and God, through Christ, has revealed the man he wanted me to be. When we really repent, believe and trust in him, we start to discover and explore in a new way our own true identity. We find that we are compelled to enter periods of contemplation where we may be shown the significance of things we have gone through and are still battling with. We are specifically called to enter his rest so that we can be free to begin the journey of 'Be—ing'.

In early January 2008, I was taking one of my daughters back to university in Newcastle. As I often did on this journey, I stayed with a friend in North Yorkshire on my way home. He works at Ampleforth College and, as it was a Sunday night, he asked if I would like to join him in the Abbey for Compline, the final service of the day before the monks retire for the night. After a deeply moving service, the monks silently dispersed. As we left, we were stopped by the Abbot, who was keen to meet the new visitor. We talked for a short time and as we parted he looked me in the eye and said, *When you need to come here, know that you are welcome and that we will look after you*.

I was reminded of these words two weeks later when the trustees were forced to close *Believe*. The internal despair I felt as I proposed the motion to close the charity was matched by the sense that although this chapter was drawing to a close, this was not the end of the journey. I knew that I needed to withdraw into the desert to contemplate, taking time to think and to be alone with God. I needed that time of reflection and so it was that I drove back to Ampleforth to spend some time on retreat with the monks.

For me, it seemed that there was something extraordinary

happening in my life, spiritually, during my stay in that monastery. There exists a routine unchanged in centuries. There are the services throughout the day starting at five o'clock in the morning and ending at nine in the evening; there is the glorious food eaten in silence as a book is read aloud; on feast days there was wine and wonderfully enriching conversation; there is a sense of unhurriedness and peace. For me there were long walks around the beautiful Yorkshire countryside, which provided many opportunities for prayer and reflection. The end of *Believe* had created a personal crisis for me. It was not meant to be this way. But this time forced me to confront those parts of myself that contributed to its downfall. I began by feeling a strong sense of shame for all those that I had let down, not least my family. I discovered that all my perceived virtues have a flip side, a 'shadow' or set of temptations and pitfalls. Here are a few I discovered:

- Care for others .... To avoid confronting myself
- Confidence .... Sense of infallibility and feeding off praise
- Courage .... Foolhardiness
- Commitment .... Reluctance to test and confirm
- Charm .... Manipulation
- Control ... Inflexibility
- Dedication ... Busyness
- Drive ... Impatience and lack of attention to detail
- Energy ... Overpowering
- Inspiration ... To avoid perspiration
- Leadership ... Unwillingness to include others
- Optimism ... Unrealism
- Perseverance ... Resistance to change
- Pride ... Vainglory and arrogance
- Relationships ... Lack of focus
- Self-motivated ... Inconsiderate of others

- Thriftiness   ...   False economy
- Trusting   ...   Laziness
- Vision   ...   To avoid detail

When you put all this together it is not surprising that things ended up as they did. Within all these shadows was a hardwired need for self-sufficiency. This was my vision and I had felt that I had to realise it on my own. Combined with my pride around money and my sense of worthlessness in terms of deserving it, it is not surprising that *Believe* always struggled financially in the same way that I do personally. Part of my reasoning in handing over *Believe* to a new CEO was that I realised that my strength did not lie in management. I was more of a creator. But for too long I had failed to deal with my pride which convinced me that I could do everything, despite the prompts and opportunities to do so. One of the Disciple's tasks is to ruthlessly cut loose those elements that are not strengths, and learn to prioritise and delegate. At some stage it might mean sacking yourself!

As I have described in Facing the Darkness it is easy to get trapped into a sense of hopelessness. But God doesn't let us dwell there. This is where the ability to seek forgiveness and to remind ourselves that our sins were forgiven at the cross is crucial, and being with the monks was the right place to experience this. Knowing that we are forgiven and accepted not only releases us from our mistakes and failures, it sets us free from self-sufficiency with an inner confidence that no longer needs to envy and compete. Then we are able to move towards collaboration with others. It is interesting to note that while Jesus frequently took himself away to be on his own with his Father, most of his ministry was done in collaboration with his disciples. We don't know how Jesus' team worked but a team they were, made up of individuals with different gifts. This made them highly effective, not only as witnesses to his ministry but as the foundation for a faith that resonates across the world to this day.

Maybe one of the reasons why Christians are not as effective today as they might be is that so many, like me, are still trying to fulfil their vision in their own strength. I have come to learn (but have not yet fully succeeded in always acting on!) that when God wants to do something he calls different people to a similar vision. So what do we do in our human frailty? We think that our vision is unique to us and that all of those who have similarly been called are our competitors. We want to own the monopoly in caring. *The world needs changing and only I can do what's needed.* Competition is what we have learned in our world. It begins at school where we are compelled to compete for academic excellence. It doesn't reflect the real world where we have to learn to collaborate – share our unique set of gifts and skills – in order to achieve anything. So the competition has to be defeated and the very people who God wants us to work collaboratively with to achieve his ends, we resist and avoid. I see this symptom across the charitable sector with individuals fighting for supremacy.

It is a common human weakness to start to help others in order to help ourselves. Needy people need needy people. I occasionally turn people down as mentors, because it is plain that their motives are driven by their own needs, not because they genuinely want to help another. None of us is squeaky clean. We all seek the warm satisfaction of helping another person, but we have to be conscious of this so as not to corrupt the relationship. Sadly, this phenomenon is all too prevalent in the voluntary sector. Charities are there to meet the needs of the needy. It follows that there must exist a sufficiently large group of needy people to justify the existence of the charity. And of course the world is not short of needy people. However it becomes a problem when the existence of needy people (some would say victims) becomes essential to the survival of the £35 billion industry that charity has become. On one hand you have charities fighting for an ever decreasing pool of resources; on the other hand there is an in built requirement to ensure sufficient victims to justify the survival of the industry.

I was only at Ampleforth for five days. I arrived a broken man and emerged lighter – a huge psychological burden lifted from my shoulders. I was ready to face the next stage on the journey, which was to appear as soon as I got home.

Virtue

Forgiveness requires the next virtue and is the gift that comes from it: *humility*.

Learning humility involves learning at the level that causes us to adjust our sense of who we are and what the world is really like. We cannot become humble by dint of effort, but we can 'opt' for a way of living that might lead us in the direction of becoming more humble.

Christian learning is of the essence of what we rightly call discipleship. There is something circular here: we need humility in order to be able to learn, yet one of the things we need to learn is humility.

Stephen Cherry *The Barefoot Disciple*

This is the essence of the *Disciple's Journey*. While it is essential to have a degree of humility to start the journey, the true nature of humility only emerges as the journey unfolds. There are no rewards for humility, but it is essential to the *Disciple's Journey*. It begins with offering our lives to God and beginning the process of understanding what is getting in the way of us fulfilling God's purpose for our lives. Humility is not just facing up to some of these unpalatable truths about what is within us, it is also realising that we are just a very small piece in a very large jigsaw. It is where we learn the truth of the maxim that there is no limit to what can be achieved if you don't care who gets the credit. We begin to move from 'me' to 'us'. While we start out on the journey with a level of humility, because it is so central to discipleship, the reality is that we don't really understand it until this stage, when we have been through the refining fire of the darkness. Self-pity is the servant of the devil.

So the closer I get to God the more imperfect 'I' feels. Not just the more imperfect I feel as his light shines onto my sin, but the more imperfect the concept of 'I' feels. I now realise that I am connected to a wider whole that encompasses the whole body of Christ. When the Disciple sets out he believes, as he must, that his journey is unique and that no one else can possibly share his vision. As I have said, naivety is often his best friend at the outset. But, as the journey unfolds, he discovers that there are some on similar journeys with a shared vision and others who have been there before. It is easy to become disheartened and think that it has all been a waste. But the world has conditioned us to be individualistic. It is why humility is key to leadership. It is easy to be tempted by the advantages that come with the elevation of leadership. Only through understanding that it is about service to others that we remain grounded and continue to have the humility to be self-aware of those faults and character flaws that get in our way.

My hero is William Wilberforce because he saw a fundamental human injustice – slavery – and dedicated his life to eradicating it. On reflection, the part of me that was holding him up as a hero sought the place in history that he has achieved – that old sin so rarely mentioned today – vainglory. Yet when you read the history of the abolition of slavery, Wilberforce was just one man among many who dedicated their lives to it. Indeed the prophetic soul who first considered that slavery was wrong is lost in the mists of time. But without him planting a seed, Wilberforce would not have his place in history. The Disciple will learn that his part may be just a small one, but nonetheless significant for that. He may never see the outcome this side of eternity.

So humility is one of the greatest gifts that the Disciple will bring back from his journey. Humility stems from the experience of the 'failures' which so often seem to occur when the Disciple steps out in faith. When you have experienced failure you become less judgmental and more sympathetic. You know the pain of failure and this makes you a better friend and mentor. Humility creates a sense of worth, but, crucially, without a sense of self-importance.

On another level, meeting soldiers who have fought in Iraq and Afghanistan I witnessed individual acceptance of intense hardship and bravery in the most frightening of circumstances. For those seeking leadership roles it is worth recalling that motto for young officers at Sandhurst, Serve to Lead. All leaders need to understand that they are servants to those they lead and this requires humility. We cannot help being humbled by the stories of our young servicemen in Afghanistan. I recall sitting in the comfort of my armchair watching a BBC documentary called Wounded about two soldiers who had lost four legs and one arm between them. Hard to imagine and yet hundreds of young men are returning from Afghanistan like this. There were no complaints, no demands for compensation, just concern for their mates. And I wondered how on earth they could be so philosophical in the face of such loss. The answer is simple. They had the humility to recognize a cause greater than themselves and in setting out to achieve it they did not want to let down their fellow man. *No greater love has a man than to lay his life down for his friend.*

In discussing the nature of courage in combat with a group of soldiers and businessmen, the conclusion was that it stemmed from a deep love that is not acknowledged, but is nonetheless powerful for that. In interviewing soldiers returning from Afghanistan who are now, due to injury or defence cuts, having to leave, the emotion they talk about is bereavement. It is that sense of loss that all ex servicemen feel when they leave. It is the failure to discover such strong bonds in civilian life that sows the seeds of problems later.

In a small way mentoring is giving individuals the opportunity to give up a part of themselves for the benefit of others and discover something deeper, profound and loving in the process. And so we change the world two by two.

Reflection

- Do you need to revisit the plan? When have you had to focus on detail?
- What happened when you didn't?
- What do you need to let go of?
- We can't fight on all fronts – are you choosing the right ones and prioritising?
- What risks are you prepare to take? Calculated or uncalculated?
- When have you given up? What are the fruits of persistence?

14

A New Perspective

Once, having been asked by the Pharisees when the kingdom of God would come, Jesus replied, "The kingdom of God does not come with your careful observation, nor will people say, 'Here it is,' or, 'There it is,' because the kingdom of God is within you."

Luke 17:20–22 NIV

Our individual journeys are long or short – continuing, or culminating in a climax. Having got this far and endured so much, the Disciple is able to view life from a new perspective. Not only is he able to discover that life is not just about surviving the storm, it is about learning to dance in the rain. The object of the journey may well have been changed or taken to a new level, but he will have acquired a new level of insight. It is a time to recognise achievement but also to review the goals that underpinned the original plan. It is the stage when we begin to embrace the virtues listed in Colossians 3:12 – mercy, kindness (compassion), humility, gentleness and peace, forgiveness and, above all, love. It is also where we learn the importance of transparency. We are proud people who like to put on a brave face to the world. But when you have struggled with great personal battles you are able to talk openly about your doubts, fears and failures. When you do, others are able to share theirs with you too.

Jesus was not afraid to be transparent. He even uncovered himself and washed his disciples' feet, thereby giving his disciples permission to do the same.

With this new gift of self-awareness and transparency we begin to realise that our existence is no more than a single wave crashing on a beach – no less significant for that, and no less useful in the world. But it places our lives in a context. One is a small part of God's created order. In one moment we make an impact, salty water crashing on a sandy shore, a single wave, maybe grabbed by some surfer to carry him thrillingly to the shore, or maybe just a gentle splash, hardly discernible.

I have not been a great believer in those who say that by imagining your future you create it. But I was about to be proved wrong. For two years or more I had this nagging idea of travelling to some poorer parts of the world, taking with me graduates of the *Believe* programmes to give them the chance of putting something back from what they have gained – or 'paying it forward', as some people put it. It would also offer them a new perspective of life. On return from my period of contemplation at Ampleforth, I received a call from my mentor – who says the mentor doesn't show up when you need him? He had recently received an email from an old school friend who had sent out a round robin seeking someone who knew anything about mentoring to help him set up a new charity. This simple connection was to open up a completely new perspective on my life, which itself gave me a new perspective on me and my purpose. In accepting this new challenge I received an invitation to Dubai, by no means one of the poorest parts of the world, at least financially, to meet an inspired and very successful entrepreneur, who had a vision for an international mentoring programme for entrepreneurs in developing countries. He and I were to found a new charity, *The Mowgli Foundation*, which is designed to provide a new approach to alleviating poverty in the non-industrialised world by identifying and mentoring the entrepreneurs who would create wealth and jobs.

A new chapter in my life had opened up, and I dedicate a chapter to describing how the charity developed and the new challenges I faced. But I was beginning to learn that we have such a small vision for the possibility of our lives, especially when we see it through the self-sufficient lens of *self*. I realize in retrospect that in letting go of what had happened in the past with the demise of *Believe*, I opened up the possibility of a new future. In surrendering the belief that I alone could change the world single-handedly, I gave myself the opportunity to create something far greater along with somebody else. The extraordinary thing was that as I stepped into this new phase I began to realise that the quest was not just about releasing people from physical prisons, it was about releasing people from the prisons of themselves.

Virtue

'I have no goals that are not the goals of this community; I have no well-being, no happiness, that is not the well-being of the community. What will make me content or happy is what makes for the good of this particular part of the human family.'

Dr Rowan Williams Archbishop of Canterbury 2003–
2012 at the Diamond Jubilee Service in St Paul's

The virtue that our servicemen demonstrate daily is one that has powerful connotations, but a surprising meaning. It is the word *sacrifice*. The word contains a recognition that in life there is always something greater than we are, and this requires the humility to give up ourselves (using the familiar analogy, our piece of the jigsaw) for a whole greater than ourselves. Despite the fact that the word 'sacrifice' is not particularly fashionable in our individualistic society, we see evidence of it everywhere – obviously in the lives that are laid down in Afghanistan and Iraq, but less obviously in those who forgo opportunities for personal wealth, instead trying to make a difference to the world, as a number of young friends have done, eschewing the riches of the City for something of far greater value.

Another one of my heroes was a young man, Rob, I was introduced to in the Royal United Hospital in Bath. His life story typified that of hundreds I have worked with. He never knew his father. Rob ended up being excluded from school at the age of 14 since they could not deal with him. Drug dealers love excluded kids, since they are looking for an escape from the grim reality of their lives and the pain of the abuse, while also seeking a way of maintaining a livelihood. Rob was no exception and was soon hooked on cannabis. In order to maintain the habit he started stealing just to survive. He soon ended up in prison and was introduced to heroin there, which took away the pain. His addiction drove his crime for many years.

Rob arrived at this point and found the courage to seek drug rehabilitation. He slowly came off drugs and found a new life, a girlfriend, a vision for a hairdressing business and somewhere to live. At the age of 32 he had life sorted. Until he went for a check at the hospital and discovered he had leukaemia and six days to live without treatment. He was offered a trial drug instead of chemo. The stakes were high. He told me of the dilemma he faced: an extension to life through chemotherapy against the possibility of either full recovery or death through the trial drug. His choice; no one could make it for him. But he has found faith and through that faith he was able to choose. *I have decided to take the trial drug,* he told me, *because even if it doesn't work on me, the doctors will have had one more body to try it out on and get closer to the point when it will work for everyone.* He was prepared to lay down his life for his fellow man. That is sacrifice.

> Therefore, I urge you, brothers, in view of God's mercy, to offer your bodies as living sacrifices, holy and pleasing to God – this is your spiritual act of worship.
>
> *Romans 12:1 NIV*

So to achieve fulfilment it is essential to use our gifts not just for personal gain but as a contribution to the whole, your single jigsaw piece linking up with others to create a complete picture: the kingdom of God. Sacrifice becomes both the means and the end. As my journey has progressed, I have found that my deeply inbred self-sufficiency does not serve me well. True richness is found in sacrificing to God what one thought was one's individual purpose. For, as John Donne famously wrote, *No man is an island.*

Look at the words 'sin' and 'sacrifice'. Our sin has 'I' at its heart, whether that is our greed in wanting more and hanging onto what we have got, our envy in wanting what others have, our pride, arrogance and self-pity, our lust that pervades and corrupts everything today, our gluttony, our laziness, and apathy about doing something to change things, and the anger that sits just beneath the surface, waiting to be triggered by the slightest cue. 'I' is at the heart of all this. And the objective and the solution is sacrifice. But it is an awesome challenge, because individually we have to sacrifice that letter – 'I'. What Jesus did on the cross was to show us the way. He died to save us from our sins. He was perfect – without any sin – and he teaches us how to sacrifice ourselves – our 'I' – to a greater purpose – *his* purpose.

In the passage from Romans above, Paul links sacrifice to worship. Through our sacrifice we discover the fulfilment of worship of him. There can be escape from the prison of *self* to a world marked by love, compassion and freedom.

The words that describe Jesus' human pain (*"My God, my God, why have you forsaken me?"*) are followed by the release into the peace of: *"Father, into your hands I commit my spirit."*

As a young man I had the enormous privilege of playing Jesus in a mystery play. In hanging on that cross for fifteen minutes, while of course not suffering the pain of so many kinds that Jesus would have endured, I experienced in some small way the vulnerability of that position. Now I knew why for some the cross can represent an 'I' crossed out.

Reflection

- **What did you really want?**
- **Did it give you all you wanted or did you lose something along the way?**
- **Was it all self-motivation or did you do it for others?**
- **Take an opportunity to reflect on and review your life.**
- **Have you now found your life's purpose?**
- **Are you I prepared to sacrifice your life to Jesus Christ?**

15

The Return

All of us also lived among them at one time, gratifying the cravings of our sinful nature and following its desires and thoughts. Like the rest, we were objects of wrath. But because of his great love for us, God, who is rich in mercy, made us alive with Christ even when we were dead in transgressions – it is by grace you have been saved.

Ephesians 2:3–5 NIV

It was never about us as individuals except to discover the grace of God so that we can take our place in his kingdom (and always remember that the kingdom is where he is obeyed). The final stage to the *Disciple's Journey* is the return to the Ordinary World with this understanding. The Disciple has changed. It is the Disciple's imperative that he returns to his Ordinary World to share his story and perhaps become a mentor too, thereby inspiring and giving tacit permission to others to set out on their journey. This is the gift that all who step out in faith can bring to those who have yet to start. It is the opportunity to give your testimony to encourage those you may have left behind.

I found this letter I wrote to a friend who was enduring the struggle of embarking on his own *Disciple's Journey* as he tried to get a new organisation to achieve his vision off the ground.

We are both in similar places. We are leading organisations that have little or no infrastructure or support and this can be a lonely business. We are both carrying the heavy load of responsibility and other people's expectations of us. It is easy to slip into fear. Do I think that fear is a negative feeling? A certain amount of fear and stress keeps us motivated and focused. But when fear becomes overwhelming, it can cripple us. The world we live in is dominated by fear and this affects the way we are and the way we respond. The only antidote to fear is love. Through love we can respect and value ourselves and thereby each other. You must believe, that whatever the weight of responsibility, you are doing the job you do for something noble and greater than yourself. The irony is that the closer you get to achieving the noble goal the more doubt and fear you feel. This is normal. The course of human history is full of people who have changed things and made a difference. What you don't see are the doubts and fears they felt while doing it. When we are trying to do good there are forces that will try and stop us. Once you know that you can arm yourself against these forces. It is how we grow in inner strength.

If you are like me, you will have a clear vision of where you want to go, but get frustrated by the amount of detailed work it takes to get there. Because we can see where we want to be, it is easy to get frustrated and impatient. But look out of your window. The flower growing in your garden didn't just appear overnight. It grew over time through a natural process that you can't change. It is the same with your vision. It will grow in its own time and there is nothing you can do to change that. We have to remember nature, since we are all part of it. All you can do is your best to make it happen, by constantly nurturing your vision, and most importantly yourself. Those moments when things aren't going well or you are under pressure are your greatest gifts, since it is in those moments that you will learn most about yourself and get closest to God. That is how we truly grow as human beings.

*So have no fear. You are a good man who has been put where you are for a pur*pose*. We are in it together.*

It is often through others that we find moments of new insight for ourselves. I find this one of the joys of mentoring. It is in deep relationship with another that we can view the world in a different way. This new perspective that we have found may clarify our own purpose or it may take one in a different and unexpected direction, as this extract from my diary illustrates:

I am sitting on an Airbus A380–800, a magnificent new aeroplane with a seating capacity of 800, en route to Dubai to speak at the Arab Scientific and Technical Foundation conference, listening to my favourite piece of music, the Adagio from Mozart's Clarinet Concerto. I have just watched the truly inspiring Invictus about how Francois Pienaar and Nelson Mandela plotted successfully to win the 1994 Rugby World Cup as a means of uniting the South African nation. It is a reminder of the power of inspiration to understand that whatever our ethnicity we are all connected. Yesterday I listened to a talk about vision – that we have all been born with a God-given vision. Our sole purpose in life is to find that vision and then live it out, seeking out those who share connecting parts to our jigsaw piece. I now realise that the vision for my life is to:

1. Help release people from the prison of fear by knowing Christ;
2. Identify their piece of the jigsaw, their inner confidence/ truth;
3. Help them to find assurance of forgiveness themselves and to help others to do so too – in so doing, their jigsaw piece becomes smoothly rounded, so that they can seek out those pieces with which it fits;
4. Sacrifice their own piece in God's service.

It is interesting to note that when I embarked upon my journey my vision was clearly directed towards prisons. My compassion for those many young people who end up in society's dustbin, having not stood a chance since they were conceived, is undimmed. My desire for reform is still strong and I still try and contribute in a small way to campaigning for reform but, more importantly, to continue to pioneer new solutions to preventing and reducing re-offending. I also enjoy encouraging and mentoring those who are themselves trying to address the problem. I am working with others, including those ex-servicemen who have returned from war with mental and physical injuries, to set up a non-military national service that is specifically targeted at the hardest to reach in our society: the unemployable, the ex-offenders and the gangs. It will give them the opportunity to find themselves through service to others and find something within them from which to build their lives. Combining service with the tough reality of their experience will create powerful agents of sustainable change. It is the start of another journey, with all the uncertainty that brings.

I believe that one of the key lessons we learn on the journey is our ability to deal with uncertainty. In a world that demands certainty and predictability, we plan and we design processes to minimise the risk of failure. But as all those who have served in the army know, no plan survives the crossing of the start line. The Disciple soon learns to be flexible, driven by inner values that are unchanging, not circumstance, which is constantly changing. As I start a new 'circuit' of the *Disciple's Journey*, my quest is less about helping individuals through the transition of release from physical prisons, but more about us all being released from the prisons of ourselves. This is the ultimate purpose of the cross: to release us from the limitations of self into the freedom to serve God in his kingdom. How often do we recite the words from the Lord's Prayer, 'Thy kingdom come, thy will be done on earth, as it is in heaven'? This is not a vision that we earn through good behaviour. Within each of us, it all starts with our response to God's call.

In his book *Surprised by Hope*, Tom Wright reminds us that God intends to save the whole of creation. He talks about the relationship between the kingdom and the Cross. We have come to believe that the kingdom will not come before the return of Christ. Yet he argues that the the process of creating the kingdom began with the resurrection, which frees us from the sin that prevents us from being a manifestation of kingdom values here today, through social transformation. Thus the role of the church is not simply about saving souls. It can anticipate renewal by working for God's kingdom today. By facilitating its followers to become 'masters of themselves' and encouraging service within our communities, the church can begin to serve the wider world in a way which brings healing and hope. By so doing the church can be seen to be relevant to a world that is becoming more secular while, paradoxically, searching for meaning.

For me, this has become my passion and purpose. The awful irony is that the resurrection sets people free from the prison of sin, but we have become so accustomed to our cells that we are afraid to leave. The cell has become the Ordinary World for humanity. I knew a young man who released from a Young Offenders' Institute. He had no family, having been brought up in care. The only 'family' he had was the similarly lost souls he encountered along the way. Walking away from prison with £46 in his back pocket, he made his way to the B&B accommodation allocated to him. A sparsely furnished room, a bed with a thin mattress covered with sheets suspiciously appearing to be secondhand. There was an old TV in the corner, but there only for decoration since it had long ago ceased to function. At least the one in his cell had worked. Imagine the misery that young lonely 18-year old felt. He slipped out to the local corner shop and spent most of his money and beer and cigarettes, small comfort for the aching loneliness and terrifying future. The beer consumed, the young man checked to see how much money he had left. Waiting for the first bus, he used what was left to travel back to the Young Offenders' Institution, the only home he knew, that he had paid farewell to the day before. Walking up to gatehouse, he approached the security guard on the door and asked *Please can you let me back in*. Tragic and true though that story is, that young man is no different to us. Prison had become his security.

And we all crave that security. We prefer being locked in prison rather than being free to take full responsibility for our lives. We love to have others to blame when things go wrong (where would lawyers be without this?) But security only exists in our minds; it doesn't exist in reality. Stand in any security checkpoint at any airport in the world. We have created a massive industry to make us think that we are more secure, but the reality is that we are not. At best we close stable doors after the horse has bolted, but even a half creative mind could conceive of many different ways of by-passing the systems. And successful terrorists tend to be very creative, determined, and often sacrificial too. It is the same with children. We no longer trust anyone, even teachers. Every other human being is a potential abuser. Ask yourself what this does for communal trust. There are rich pickings for those in the security business, and if those are ever threatened we can be sure that new fears will be generated. It is a great big lie that we have bought into.

Security is mostly a superstition. It does not exist in nature. Nor do the children of men as a whole experience it. Avoiding danger is no safer in the long run than outright exposure. The fearful are caught as often as the bold. Life is either a daring adventure – or nothing. *Helen Keller*

So, although we have been released from prison, we just don't understand how to deal with true freedom. We cower in the corner of our cells, afraid of what may be outside. It has been said that until we realise that we are in prison no escape is possible. Freedom is innately uncertain and, if we are honest, slightly threatening. In stepping out of the boat, as Peter did, walking away from his mates and towards Jesus, he was exercising his freedom. But how soon he loses faith; he cannot believe that he is doing something as irrational as walking on water and begins to sink. We are just the same. Offered the freedom to step out of the prison of the fallen human condition, we refuse, since the offer offends our sense of reason and looks so unsafe. Why would you give up all you know for something that you don't? Why threaten all that you have worked towards creating, that sense of security demanded by our modern world? We still don't get it. We allow our financial services industry to kid us into parting with our hard-earned money in exchange for future financial security that is at best ephemeral. Look into the eyes of those who do this work and see the pain. They know they are selling you a pup, but hope, despite all the evidence to the contrary, that you will continue to fall for it.

And we do, because of course the intellect is thought to have all the answers. Ask Richard Dawkins, A C Grayling and a string of other academics who continue to produce their soulless propaganda. These are the prison guards of our modern world, convincing us that life in our limited cells is preferable to the total freedom found in Christ. It is they who stand in the way of human potential, believing that only the intellect can be the arbiter of potential. After all, we have allowed the academics, in a tradition based on Ancient Greece, to design our education system. Is it surprising that it has continued to condemn half our population to lives of under-achievement and failure? As governments continue to wrestle with generational poverty and unemployment, has it ever occurred to them to abandon the philosophies of the gilded towers of Oxford and Cambridge that are only interested in 'excellence', whatever that is. Where does that leave those who are not excellent? In prison? Certainly metaphorically speaking, since the only acknowledged route out of poverty involves the academic. It is a modern curse.

The 'prison' of self is utterly defeated by the Cross, where we find ourselves truly of worth, with our unique set of qualities, gifts and talents, each a contribution to the kingdom. By stepping outside the prison of our Ordinary World, we begin the journey within which these qualities, gifts and talents are revealed.

It may sound that (in some inverted snobbery), I am having a go at the academics, but I am not. I am simply flagging up the fact that we lay too much stress on the intellect in our world and, by so doing, deny the value of the other parts of our make up. As human beings we are body, soul (including mind, will, emotions) and spirit.

The 'religions' of the world have revealed their human

flaws, making them easy meat for the sneering academics who want nothing to do with such uncertain concepts as the soul and 'religion'. Much in the world that has the label 'religious' is mere outward regulation, ritual and even idolatry, but this book is not a study of comparative religion.

Jesus Christ can set us free, but the idea of 'freedom' has been badly abused by some modern churches. Christian leaders will talk about freedom in Christ, while doing all they can to hang on to to the reins of power. How patronising is it to suggest that my only route to God is through the hierarchy of the church. The glorious thing about a personal, living relationship with God is that it is a real relationship which is available to all people, diverse as they are, regardless of their ethnic and cultural origins. Nothing can obscure the connection with the Christ I read about and am deeply conscious of within me. Countless millions can testify to this for themselves.

Life itself is God-given, and so is new life in Christ. Our Lord releases us into discovery of the extraordinary potential that he puts within us.

I have found the words of Marianne Williamson, made famous by Nelson Mandela, to be helpful:

Our deepest fear is not that we are inadequate. Our deepest fear is that we are powerful beyond measure. It is our light, not our darkness that most frightens us. We ask ourselves, Who am I to be brilliant, gorgeous, talented, fabulous? Actually, who are you not to be? You are a child of God. Your playing small does not serve the world. There is nothing enlightened about shrinking so that other people won't feel insecure around you. We are all meant to shine, as children do. We were born to make manifest the glory of God that is within us. It's not just in some of us; it's in everyone. And as we let our own light shine, we unconsciously give other people permission to do the same. As we are liberated from our own fear, our presence automatically liberates others.

That passage focuses on potential. Maybe it would be better to say that God has a will and purpose for everyone, with all the potential that implies. What is in everyone is that all human beings are made in the image of God, but that image is marred in us by our tendency to sin, and by actual sins too, as we see in every culture on earth when humans show such cruelty and wickedness of every kind, directed against others. We are all imperfect, and we all need to know and believe in Jesus Christ – his forgiveness, and the kind of abundant life he wills for us. There are life-changing opportunities, and, when they happen, we are free to respond and receive or to go our own way instead. Jesus himself allowed people to reject him and walk away.

I have recently led programmes in North Africa to empower young entrepreneurs though mentoring. I was running a workshop for micro-entrepreneurs in rather seedy offices in the back streets of Alexandria. What is fascinating is the easy connection they make between mind and soul. Initially the mentors we were preparing stayed in their heads and resisted the process, but very soon they were beginning to get it. One, Ahmed, was particularly resistant. He spoke a little English and during the break I touched his heart and said that this was what we were trying to open. Like so many in the intellectual world we live in, he thought that the solution to every problem lay in the mind, through careful calculation and clear process. I let him know that he was only using half the tool kit available to him. By using heart as well as head he would be able to inspire, empower and guide the entrepreneurs he was supporting to much higher levels of performance, and thereby maximise the chances of the loan being repaid.

When the entrepreneurs arrived, the fear was palpable. They were suspicious that there was some trick, but after two hours they realized that the loan officers had a completely different attitude towards them and genuinely conveyed belief, encouragement and support. One loan officer said *I felt like I was dealing with a human being for the first time so I was able to understand my client's needs.* Another said, *We have better communication and through that we achieved higher levels of understanding. Everyone is more open and this leads to high levels of trust.* As someone said: *You have started a virus that will not be stopped.* The virus is a spirit of kindness, even love, in which individuals are set free from the paradigm that has trapped them for years. It is the paradigm of fear prevalent in all authoritarian societies. It is a fear of creativity and a fear of getting it wrong; it leaves people disempowered and profoundly unhappy. In a short space of time, through an experience of mentoring, we were able to set people free. Something is unleashed which will grow and develop. Very often in mentoring I discover that individual purpose is hidden to the person I am mentoring – they can't see what gift it is that they so obviously have! In other words, our greatest gifts seem so natural to us, so effortless in delivery, that we assume everyone has them and are thereby unconscious of their value. As believers we are so familiar with the great truths revealed in the death and resurrection of Jesus, but we may be much less aware of the meaning that has in terms of the purpose and value and potential of human lives today. We may have allowed a secular mindset to imprison us. The *Disciple's Journey* is our long road to freedom. As we have seen, it is not a picnic, but it was never designed to be so.

In the same way that it is difficult to leave the Ordinary

World to embark on the journey, it is equally difficult to return to it at the end. The Disciple becomes very attached to the journey and to what has been revealed. It is easy to reject what was, and to avoid returning to it. Inevitably, because we are conditioned to do so, we want to rationalise what has happened to us. In my case, my journey has left me, as a father, conflicted. On the one hand I want my children to be free to embark on their personal journeys, but the protector within me wants to shield them from the dark times and challenges along the way. But I know that no parent can hold their children back, nor should they try to shield them from the experiences that will allow them to become all they were meant to be. The joyful reality is that life can be quite unpredictable.

There is a sense in which quite a bit in this book is autobiographical, and it would be lovely to be able to report that in this earthly journey one arrives at a point when you can relax and bask in the glory of success! I meet so many middle-aged men who worked all their lives to achieve what they would term 'success'. This may be to climb to the height of promotion, or to achieve material wealth way beyond their needs. Rockefeller, when asked what else he had to achieve in life having accumulated great wealth, said *Just a little bit more?* I have a very wealthy friend who buys only the best, and is always highly critical of anything short of perfection. I once asked him what would make him happy and I still await the reply. A wiser wealthy friend admitted to me that he had done the material bit – the Ferraris, the yachts, the expensive holidays – and had concluded that there was nothing there. He now uses his wealth to make a difference to the lives of those without his advantages. Through that he has found happiness. For myself, the *Disciple's Journey* is the gift I bring on my return from my travels, with the fervent hope that others may be inspired to walk out of the open prison door and embark upon their own.

When asked the greatest of the commandments, Jesus replied in this way:

> "The most important one," answered Jesus, "is this: 'Hear, O Israel, the Lord our God, the Lord is one. Love the Lord your God with all your heart and with all your soul and with all your mind and with all your strength. The second is this: Love your neighbour as yourself.' There is no commandment greater than these."
>
> *Mark 12:29–31, NIV*

The Disciple knows the reality of God's love, and desires to put into practice that teaching of Jesus. Our love for neighbour means giving to those who seem to have little or nothing to give back, challenging the selfish concept of 'I'. Never has there been a time more important than *today* to obey Jesus' summary of the Law in those two great commandments. The world faces its biggest crisis ever. Many have become prisoners of the man-made 'world system'.

> The world is too much with us; late and soon
> Getting and spending we waste our powers
> Little we see in nature that is ours
> *William Wordsworth*

It could have been written of our world today. As Christians we have been given the gift of freedom, and by releasing ourselves as leaders into a world that is crying out for what we have been given, maybe – just maybe – we can begin the creation of the kingdom here and now.

The Ultimate Virtues

The ultimate virtues brought back from the journey, and the virtues that can change the world are: love, compassion and wisdom.

> Who is wise and understanding among you? Let him show it by his good life, by deeds done in humility that comes from wisdom.
>
> *James 3:13, NIV*

I recall in the early days I opened up a Bible at the Epistle of James and my eyes fell on that passage. It has been my observation that there are a lot of people writing about, speaking out and campaigning for change but little of this is converted into action. This is my point about us living in an intellectual age as opposed to the kingdom that is driven by a combination of love, compassion and wisdom. The thing about true compassion is that I can't just *talk* about it. I can't just walk by on the other side. I have to do something. 'Inspiration' is simply in spirit, the Holy Spirit at work in me. I see many in the Evangelical movement who truly believe that bringing people to Christ represents the truth of faith. I wouldn't knock this, but it is only the beginning, not the end. Filling up the car does not represent the journey. The journey starts here. We are all called to do something. It isn't because God doesn't care that people suffer; it is because we aren't fulfilling the needs of others. We are called to be a bridge between God and our fellow human beings. Mother Theresa was asked if she was a saint. '*Yes*', she said, '*and so are you. Sainthood is simply living the life you were meant to live, with love.*'

And here is the key. Who am I? Who are you? Why are

you here? It is in our suffering and sorrow that we have the opportunity to move through our pain and shame and discover our true selves. Furthermore, it is often in the midst of suffering that we find compassion. It is through compassion and wisdom that we can be involved in making the world a better place for others. But we have to take the risk of stepping into what is often painful, despite living in a world where we are encouraged to avoid that through busyness, alcohol, drugs, entertainment, television, and other strategies (there is a long list). Christians can be the worst culprits, turning up for church each week to feel better about themselves. We can confess our sins, sing stirring hymns or worship songs, meet nice people and walk away in the confident knowledge that our sins are forgiven. John Stott, an Evangelical, highlighted the problem with evangelism. He said that evangelists are so convinced of the Second Coming that they don't need to do anything about it today. How are those who truly suffer in our world today served by this? Often it is easier to judge and condemn, because that lets us off the hook of actually doing something to address it. Many are prone to jump to condemnation and judgement. For a Christian it is perilous and wrong to look down on others, and we have to be careful not to fall into that trap. Yes, Jesus and his apostles did warn sinners of the need to change their ways and "stop sinning". But such warnings came from a compassionate heart that desires the best for the other, who may be trapped in patterns that harm themselves and others, and which they would love to be released from.

The Bible does condemn sin, but there is more to be said. God's grace in opening a way for forgiveness, giving mankind opportunities to repent and find peace with God through Jesus Christ, means that the church has to be true in its proclamation of the authentic gospel of righteousness (not self-righteousness!) whereby bad people are enabled to become good, with the help of the Holy Spirit. So it is that, for two thousand years, despite its many failings, at its best the church has taught that sinners can repent, find forgiveness and peace with God. At the level of personal contact and witness, the Disciple needs a deep compassion for all who are failing, and who so need to know for themselves a real relationship with the living God, so that they can find true peace and real purpose in their lives. If our attitude is not compassionate from the outset, our ministry isn't going to get very far!

Jesus' earthly life demonstrated perfect compassion, sacrifice and service. We discover compassion in caring for those who suffer, unity with all who know and love Jesus, and real love when we realise what he did for us and seek to obey those two great commandments he gave us.

I believe that we hold a piece of the kingdom in our hearts. Our life's purpose is to discern what that is, whether it is to teach, to preach, or to be good at making money. Life's meaning is then fulfilled by bringing that knowledge to the whole. In my case, my mission is not just to release people from the prison of self, although this is important. It is to fulfil God's purpose for me, enabling others to do likewise, finding *their* real purpose and fulfilling it. That is a creative process, and it is the fuel that allows me to survive the daily doubts and fears, the crippling financial insecurity and the horror of letting down my family.

Here is is the secret. We are all born to a cause greater than ourselves. As a Christian, I know that cause involves a unity in love that is the Lord's will. In us (often locked away) there is the *potential* to respond to God's call to mission, that piece of the jigsaw we are meant to fulfil. But how do we find it? Well, there is a sense in which we have to *lose* life to *find* new life. The sacrifice of Jesus on the cross – and his resurrection – are key to our faith. Dying to save us from the penalty due for our sins, he then allowed us to participate in *his* eternal life, and we can begin living *in* him – and, as he instructed the first disciples, we need to *go on* abiding in him. There follows for the Disciple a battle against our sinful nature, but no longer are we alone in that struggle.

Jesus was radical, and by so being he gave us permission to be radical too – and now the time has come when we need to be. The British 28th Social Attitudes survey, published in December 2011, indicates a hardening of attitudes towards those less fortunate than ourselves. As we become more self-interested, by default we become less compassionate. Since, as we have seen, suffering is often the midwife of compassion, it allows us to empathise at a deep level with those who are suffering too. It is only when we have faced the dark night of our own souls that we are able to see into the souls of others who are enduring their own. Compassion is an expression of love for our fellow human beings and recognition of our shared vulnerability and connectedness. It is an active expression of the universal golden rule that we treat others as we would do ourselves or, more colloquially: *do as you would be done by*. It is an active virtue and very different from sympathy, because compassion can be a catalyst for action. We can walk along any high street and sympathise with the homeless people we see sheltering in the doorway... and walk on. If we are acting compassionately we will acknowledge the suffering and do something to alleviate it. Giving money is often not the most effective thing to do, but buying a coffee and a sandwich might be; even just acknowledgement of their existence as a fellow human being is better than passing by on the other side. As a mentor, I know that I am more effective by being able to place myself in the shoes of the person I am mentoring. Without compassion, mentoring can be an intellectual exercise without that soul connection that creates enduring relationships. It is only when we feel securely held in a compassionate relationship that we are able to express our innermost needs. In short, compassion for others increases the happiness of yourself and the world around you.

Wisdom is oft-times nearer when we stoop than when we soar. *William Wordsworth*

The reason that I link compassion with wisdom is that, as suggested here by Wordsworth, one follows from the other. In the same way that we only really understand compassion through personal challenge and suffering, so we discover wisdom when we 'stoop'. I have only learned whatever wisdom I now have through the trial of the quest that started the moment I walked through a prison gate. Christ had divine wisdom and great compassion towards the poor, the sick and the suffering – those who are trapped in the prison of self and circumstance. The resurrection set us free to embark on our own journey towards wisdom. Wisdom is wrought from the experiences of life and the ability to reflect and learn from those experiences. It gives us a deep understanding of human nature, and the ability to understand what is true and right, and the ability, with God's guidance, to judge how best to act in any situation. The *Disciple's Journey* provides the experiences, the highs and lows of life, that allow us to face any situation with a sense of proportion and a longer-term perspective. Knowing that we are going to face challenges when embarking on something new, we are aware that so everyone else has who stepped out in faith

Blessed is the man who finds wisdom,
the man who gains understanding....
Proverbs 3:13, NIV

My understanding of both wisdom and compassion has been heightened in one of my favourite places in the world: Feynan Eco lodge in the heart of the Jordanian desert, not far from Petra. It is a place of uncommon beauty, where the word 'peace' takes on new meaning – a perfect retreat. It was built as part of a sustainable project to preserve the Bedouin culture by creating markets for their produce and jobs. They are charming people with warm hearts and a deeply human connection that is so rare these days. I was sitting having breakfast on my own, having returned from a mountain climb to watch the sunrise after saying my farewell to the mentors from the latest *Mowgli* programme. I watched a couple of young Bedouin men walking past, hand in hand, deep in conversation. There was a simplicity and a beauty to their friendship that had none of the sexual connotations we would have given it in our culture. It is difficult to come to Feynan and not reconnect with the environment. The beauty of the oleander growing in the wadi against the backdrop of mountains carved out of limestone, sandstone and granite, with the different colours they bring, is breathtaking. An area that has a history going back to the origins of time, it has changed little in millennia, goat herds driven by Bedouin carving out narrow tracks in the side of the hill. It is a place where lie the earliest remains of mankind in the world. It is a reminder that this is our future, to remember the true nature of man and to start living out lives of compassion and wisdom in service to others. There was something world has forgotten but the Bedouin are aware of. We are all deeply connected.

Feynan is surrounded by mountains. I tried to climb a different one each morning. It is no coincidence that Jesus, when he needed time to be alone with his Father, climbed a mountain on his own. I find sitting on a mountain an extraordinary place to reflect.

Here are some of my reflections on climbing mountains in Feynan, Jordan, and how it applies to discipleship and life:

• To start you need a lot of energy and momentum to gain height.
• If you hesitate, you fall back – so keep going.
• Sometimes you discover you are climbing the wrong mountain so you need to come down and start again.
• As you climb you get a new perspective on the world.
• You often don't know precisely where you are heading – you just have to follow a general direction until you can focus.
• Sometimes you go around in circles before you find your way.
• You never see the end at the beginning – you travel from one small peak to another.
• Keep your eyes up.
• There is often a trail where someone has been before. You can either follow that and make it better or you can take the road less travelled.
• When you realise how high you have got it is easy to wobble.
• You need to consider every step.
• You can always go higher than you think you can.
• The last climb to the peak is often the hardest. Sometimes you have to get down on your hands and knees to get there.
• There are always mountains higher than the one you have climbed.
• You can see how far you have come when you get to the top.

We can't choose the times we live in, but we are responsible for the time given to us. So we need to create a new paradigm based on the foundations of human relationship and interdependence – a world that is living in harmony with its environment; a world where we truly value compassion and wisdom. We need to invest in the diversity of human talent, not in conformity. We have to work together to create a world where all individuals are valued, and where everyone is fulfilling their true talent – and using it not just for selfish gain but for the good of all. It will focus on well-being, sustainability and social justice. It will be about collaboration, not competition. Collaboration seeks long-term solutions while competition is short-term and creates conflict. As the world faces its many challenges it is important that we retain our humanity. Nobody has to wait a moment before starting to improve the world. And by so doing we bring hope. 'Thy kingdom come, thy will be done on earth, as it is in heaven.'

Reflection

- **What wisdom did you learn to pass on to others?**
- **What did you reveal about yourself of which you were previously unconscious?**
- **What are you going to do with this knowledge? Who can you help to start their journey?**

Those qualities again: *inspiration* – literally, in spirit; *confidence* – reveal the truth within yourself – identify that jigsaw piece; *courage* – to take a risk because without it we'll never experience the failure from which we grow; *trust* – through relationship through which we realise ourselves; *creativity* that is unlocked through risk; *integrity* remaining true to yourself; *forgiveness* – allow yourself to fail and let go of the possibility of changing the past so that your jigsaw piece doesn't get so damaged that it no longer fits; *humility*

– to understand that you are part of something greater than yourself; *sacrifice* – to make whole, seeking out the pieces of the jigsaw that fit with yours; *love, compassion and wisdom* – valuing our fellow human beings above everything and recognising that we are all in this together. As you face the choices about your own future, ask yourself the question, *It is not a case of what do I need from life, it is what does life need from me.* Having completed the *Disciple's Journey* you will become self-disciplined under Christ, so that you may be a servant to others.

Andy Busfield
A Disciple's Perspective

From a young age through my relationship with God I wanted to work with the homeless in some way. I think I was 14 when I first had an awareness of the poverty that existed and wanted to respond.... Unsure how to proceed I just started talking to and buying some lunch for a few homeless people in my town. I learnt a bit about drugs and was fortunate enough to attend a local day group for those who had a whole range of addictions.

I never confronted the idea of actually using this love for people in a career until after leaving university when I decided I wanted to obtain a doctorate studying addiction and offending behaviour.

A year after graduating from university I started working for a charity that supported ex-offenders, providing them with a mentor through the prison gate. I was deeply challenged during this time and quickly learnt about the common needs and stigma that faced many of this population, including housing needs.

God challenged me on my choice to pursue a doctorate and showed me that most of my motives were selfish to serve myself. From this moment a desire and dream was birthed in me to create a sense of family and community housing for men and women coming out of prison. I could not shake this dream and passion and my mind was consumed by it until I mustered up the confidence to share it with my mentor. I was quite nervous telling my mentor as I didn't want to sound fickle about my ambitions, but on telling him he gave me a little punch on the arm and smiled. I felt immediately affirmed, believed and supported in my dream.

Not knowing how to proceed in this dream, my mentor helped me to establish the important themes and values in the dream and asked questions to begin putting a short term plan of action in place. I have always felt safe devising my goals and actions with my mentor, I have never felt that my mentor's opinion or slant has been imposed on me, but rather that this is my dream and that the ideas that are being discovered are mine which is incredibly empowering

Soon after devising a plan of action I was offered a job in another city working in supported housing but for less money and where I (thought) knew no one. This was a big step and I remember a sense of thinking there is no turning back now if I accept this! I remember having such confidence about it all except leaving all my friends and current job and stepping into a place of uncertainty and taking a step of faith. After several conversations with my mentor I soon realised that I had the faith to take this leap and that this might require sacrifice if I wanted to step toward my dream but this was superseded by the belief in the pursuit of the dream.

Along the way there have been huge challenges and I feel like I have come up against a handful of enemies along the way. At times it has felt like the world has been against me and that I could pack it all in. I have thought about pursuing a more glamorous job and with better pay, however this isn't what I really want and my mentor helps keep me aligned with *my heart and passion. There have been other times when I have failed in either my role or other people in my job. This has caused me a great deal of upset. I have found these times the hardest and I have spent much time doubting my ability, skills, character, and this has left me feeling foolish for ever having the dream in the first place. This has possibly been one of the most important times for me having a mentor to talk this through with. There has been an element of pride in me that has needed undoing, but also I learnt ... that I am not the first person to fail. Many of the seemingly competent people out there are going to have failed at one point or another – we are human.*

Even in writing this now I am very much in the midst of a trial as funding cuts, housing uncertainty, thefts and no certain role to step into looms in the not too distant future and I am coming out of a period of hopelessness. Challenges like these and worse are hard work and can take their toll, but I realise I am on a journey and in each challenge I learn more about myself. I am not doing this alone though, but am reminded by my mentor what enthused me for this in the first place. I recently met with my mentor who affirmed me in character and ability by asking me about someone who inspires me and what I have been proud about in past achievements and why. It demonstrated that my qualities are right for this dream and that I have already demonstrated the skills in various contexts to drive this dream forward.

Having someone keeping you accountable to your dream is essential. It is not the easiest journey to step into but it is incredibly fulfilling, it reflects your image (in God) and it brings purpose, meaning and it is something you can wholeheartedly pursue.

16

Mowgli

It is not the critic who counts, nor the man who points out how the strong man stumbles or where the doer of deeds could have done better. The credit belongs to a man who is actually in the arena, whose face is marred in dust and sweat and blood; who knows great enthusiasm, great triumph of achievement and who, at the worst, if he fails, fails whilst daring greatly so that his place shall never be with those odd and timid souls who know neither victory nor defeat. You have never lived until you have almost died. For those who have had to fight for it, life has truly a flavour the protected shall never know.

*Theodore Roosevel*t

Driving across the desert hanging onto the roof of a 4x4 is one of life's simple pleasures. On this late May morning with sun rising above the breathtaking scenery behind, it is time to reflect on my visit to Feynan Eco Lodge set in a wadi at the foot of the Dana Nature Park in South West Jordan. Feynan lies surrounded by mountains, pink in the light of the awakening sun, in the heart of the desert. Built by the Jordanian Royal Society for the Conservation of Nature, it is unique. There is no electricity. Solar panels heat the water and the lodge is candlelit in the evening. The view from the roof at night is breathtaking. With no ambient light, the stars are stunning, with a depth that you do not get in Western Europe. Inside, the rooms are comfortable, the food is a superb example of how vegetarian food can be created, and a log fire roars in the sitting room. The nearest neighbours are tent dwelling Bedouin, living the simple life that has served them well for centuries. They have nothing and yet they have everything – a connection to the earth and each other that humbles the visitor who is busy worrying whether they have the right shirt on.

As part of his welcome, and to emphasise our common humanity, the Bedouin manager, Hussein, greets arriving guests with the following words, *We all have the same blood and the same heart* – a great lesson for someone arriving from a different culture. As a setting for escaping from the outside world and the busyness of our everyday lives it would be harder to find a better place. That the only humanity living in the area is Bedouin adds richness to the experience. The Bedouin have an understanding of the simplicity of life in a way that more 'enlightened cultures' have forgotten. They understand the interdependence between each other and with the environment. Their sense of family is so strong that children will take responsibility for their parents until they die. As my Bedouin friend Ali Ammarin (with whose family I have been honourably included) says: *I will not leave here. My parents have given me the gift of life and everything I have. I owe it to them to look after them in their old age.* My Bedouin friend has nothing yet he has everything. He has the humility to be grateful for what he has: his family, his friends, the beautiful desert he lives in, food, shelter, work and purpose. In the West we have so much, but we take it for granted. We live our lives fearing the loss of all that we have accumulated. We build gated communities to keep the world at arm's length, because we can. We put our heads down in the street to avoid eye contact with others, because we are afraid.

Yet we remind ourselves of Jesus two great commandments. We are to both to love the Lord God and to love our neighbour as ourselves. How can we love that neighbour if we hate ourselves? And why do we learn to hate ourselves? Because we live lives that are out of alignment God's best will and purpose for us. The gulf opens up and we become unhappier. As we become even more unhappy, pride kicks in to convince us in one moment that we are not good enough and that life is futile, and in another that we have the self-sufficiency to sort it all out for ourselves. Either way we cut out those to whom we are connected. Then we get stuck – we fail to move on from whatever is holding us back. The Bedouin, by contrast, live lives of simplicity in harmony with time and the seasons, moving on when they need to find pastures new.

I do not wish to leave the reader with the impression that the Bedouin culture is perfect. Like any culture it has its imperfections. But it does provide a stark contrast to the lives we live in the post industrial West and provided me with a very new perspective on the benefits of the simple life lived out in humility.

It was a lesson that I began to learn when destiny took me to the Levant, the Holy Land, to establish the work of the *Mowgli Foundation*. While my own *Disciple's Journey* had taken many different directions, few of which I had envisaged or intended, one important lesson is to understand when we have to move on to pastures new. Again this means leaving behind the familiar and those things we learn to love. The call to change is always there and the art of discipleship is to be tuned into this and to follow the promptings from God that at first don't seem to make sense in relation to the overall direction we think we understand.

As the 4x4 drives across the desert landscape, the Bedouin encampments are coming to life. The cock crows, the goats in their pens get restless, and the smell of newly lit wood fires drift across the road as the morning chai (tea) is brewed and the flat bread is baked on a metal sphere above the fire. The children get ready for the walk along the valley to the school that, apart from the eco lodge and the small mosque, is the only solid building around. No breakfast television blandly imparting the morning's news; no emails pressing urgently for an answer; no mobile phones disturbing the simple peace of another beautiful day. It is a reminder of the stress we create for ourselves maintaining a busyness which prevents us from experiencing the inconvenience of confronting ourselves and discovering the raw humanity, which the Bedouin have and we have lost. I asked Ali what he wanted from life. He said that he was very happy with the 100 Jordanian Dinars (about £100) he earns each month and wouldn't swap his life for JD 1 million, since that would bring him stress and upset the simple equilibrium of his life.

Above Feynan is an archaeological dig where the earliest evidence of humanity has been discovered. There is a beautiful irony that we bring people here to reconnect with the humanity that we have lost or forgotten. There is something extraordinarily humbling about drawing together a group of complete strangers from different continents, cultures, faiths and colour and together connecting in a profoundly deep way that could only be described as love. What linked the individuals who had travelled to Jordan from different parts of the world was a desire to cut off from the world to reconnect with themselves. One of the key factors in the success of the programmes I lead is the environment. Whether it is walking through the desert or watching the sunset together, sipping sweetened wild thyme tea, or sitting around a log fire exchanging stories and songs, this is where we meet each other as human beings. This is where so much learning can be acquired. And this is where so much learning is needed.

There is also something about living in the desert with its wide vistas and huge skies. You can see for miles with uninterrupted vision. Leaders create vision and a culture of safety, predictability, and trust in which their followers can thrive. As we have seen, to be effective, a leader needs to be authentic. I learned so much about authenticity from the simple lives of the Bedouin, for whom day to day reality allows them to span the bridge between survival and service without resorting to the masks we seem to need in our apparently more civilised world. In the desert, survival depends upon mutual support. Great leaders concentrate on the highest good, rather than "I win, you lose" scenarios. They appreciate that individual success need not occur at the expense of others. Those that are least confident in themselves tend to be the most competitive and, whether consciously or not, need to get the better of others. The Bedouin teach us about the paradigm of collaboration, which is based on a purity of motive essential for growth and sustainability. Leaders cannot establish thriving partnerships with others unless they are playing to their strengths and allowing others to do the same. Within the tribe, individuals discover their strengths and use them in service of the tribe.

This is a region full of paradox and opportunity. Anne Leslie, the distinguished foreign correspondent, wrote this:

I feel so desperately sorry for 21st Century Arab men. Told by their mothers that they are princes of the universe, told by their teachers that their culture is history's finest flower, told by the Koran that they are God's chosen warriors, told by their Imams that they are torch bearers of the divine light, told by their political leaders that theirs are the greatest nations on Earth and they emerge as young men imagining that everything lies before them. And then what awaits them? Emptiness, unemployment, corruption, broken countries, broken economies and no sex. Nothing has turned out like they were promised. It must be profoundly bewildering.

Which is why entrepreneurship is so important to this region, and overcoming the obstacles of starting businesses that create jobs for those young me and women is a vital part of maintaining security. The challenges of the region and the vision for the *Mowgli Foundation* are best summarised in a speech I gave at the launch of the charity in January 2009 in Dubai:

Our strapline is *mentoring a changing world*. And we live in a changing world. It is a cliché to suggest that the world is at a crossroads. But the truth is that we really are. As a generation we have the huge privilege of being given the opportunity to change it for the better. Indeed Barack Obama has spelt out the vision, *to choose our better history* but a vision without action from all of us soon fades. In this part of the world his words are particularly poignant, *We cannot help but believe that the old hatreds shall someday pass; that the lines of tribe shall soon dissolve; that as the world grows smaller, our common humanity shall reveal itself.* And that is why it is so important for individuals to reach out across cultural, ethnic and religious divides to break down ignorance and allow our common humanity to be revealed. There is a gripping poem by the American poet Drew Bellinger which opens with these words:

It's 3.23 in the morning and I can't sleep
Because my great great grandchildren wake me to ask
what I was doing as the world unravelled

What can we do? More importantly what can you do?
We can't solve problems with the same level of thinking
that created them. It is easy to live life thinking that
the problems of the world are always someone else's.
'Something must be done' is the universal cry with no
sense that we carry a responsibility to contributing to the
solution. Take world poverty. People have traditionally
responded to the world's poor through generosity. The
20th century paradigm was to support them through aid:
an act of financial generosity. But this is not sustainable.
From government aid to Live Aid there has never been a
challenge in raising huge amounts of money. Collectively
we can salve our consciences by seeing a tiny proportion
of our taxes spent on overseas aid or making an online
payment or dropping coins in a collection tin – job done.
Others can work out how to spend it. Nothing changes.
People remain poor and suffering continues. Another
expensive elastoplast over an ever gaping wound. But aid
levels are dropping with the world economy and anyway
it needn't be like this.

Mohammed Yunnus the pioneer of micro-finance put
it this way:

My observations amongst the poorest people in the
world suggest that entrepreneurial ability is practically
universal. Almost everyone has the talent to recognize
the opportunities around them. And when they are
given the tools to transform those opportunities into
reality almost everyone is eager to do so... All that is
required to get poor people out of poverty is for us to

create an enabling environment for them

And the need is pressing. Asma Assad is the wife of President Assad of Syria. In an article in the Sunday Times recently she said the following,

Take a second to ask yourself . . . Where would the extremist preach if poverty did not provide the audience? Where would a terrorist recruit if poverty did not line up those in despair?

"The reason why alleviating poverty is so important is because it affects us all. When people are poor they have no hope and when they have no hope, they become desperate and desperation can breed some bad, bad things...." (Please note the bitter irony in this viewed through the prism of subsequent events in Syria.)

Youth unemployment – one of the great challenges of the 21st century – devastates the social and economic fabric of society, cheating countries, particularly in this region, of their greatest potential. For young people, being unable to find a job often means not having the means to get married, have a family or plan a future. Chronic unemployment can lead young people to feel excluded, frustrated, and angry at a world that has failed them.

So the world must now create a new model for the 21st century based on empowerment and co-operation. True generosity stems from a generosity of spirit: a giving of ourselves with no expectation of return. What if it were possible to create successful businesses which delivered both a return on investment and began to alleviate poverty? Through nourishing entrepreneurship, economic, social and political change can be driven in a way that could achieve this. Let us inspire a new generation of leaders. This is where the *Mowgli Foundation* will make a difference: matching skilled and experienced mentors with budding entrepreneurs in developing countries, beginning to unleash the extraordinary potential that remains largely untapped. In addition to providing opportunities for visionary entrepreneurs, small businesses become important drivers for economic and social growth in these communities: providing jobs, capital, and an improved economic outlook and future for many bringing hope where there is none. And what is *Mowgli* mentoring? Our definition: *A long-term relationship within which an experienced individual inspires, guides, and empowers another in achieving business and personal potential.*

Let me bring that alive with a story. One of our participants in the pilot to take place in Jordan is Rula. Rula comes from a very poor background. Her future security lay in her marriage...until her husband left her. Faced with no income and two young children to support, she took a risk. She followed her heart doing the only thing she was good at and the one thing she loved: cooking. With a small loan from a micro-finance organisation, she set up a catering business which now employs seven people, all women deserted by their husbands. Her vision is simple: she wants to open a factory employing 1,000 women who have been similarly deserted. And do you know I think she just might. It is people like Rula who will make a big impact on their communities that *Mowgli* want to support.

To be or not to be? Being an entrepreneur is tough. We never anticipate the end at the beginning. We are full of hope, possibilities, optimism, potential and it has to be said naivety. If a baby was able to see its death while still in the womb, would it go through the trauma of birth? If any of the great inventors, creators, entrepreneurs knew the pain they would endure taking an idea from conception to implementation, with the high risk of failure, would they ever bother to start? But we do. For life is an adventure. In the old cliché it is better to travel than to arrive and we determine how exciting the journey will be. For anyone inspired enough to create their journey it won't be easy, but it won't be dull. And we can create our own journey. We need to unlock creativity. We live in a fatalistic society where stuff happens, apparently beyond our control. But if you believe that destiny sits waiting to be grabbed, you can create the life you were born to lead. As Carlos Ruiz Zafon says in his book *The Shadow of the Wind*: *Destiny is just around the corner like a thief, but what destiny doesn't do is home visits*. You have to go out and grab it. Pity those who get to the end of the journey with the words 'if only' on their lips. Or 'I could have', but didn't have the courage to try. Or even in the great Peggy Lee song, *Is that all there is?* As I was to learn, it is not the end but the journey which is important, since this is when you meet that stranger inside all of us – our true selves. That is the gift of risk: if you can step through the pain that risk entails, you will discover the pure gold that is you on the other side. That pure gold is the person you were meant to be. And through living authentically it is possible to unleash the creativity within.

I have created both a business and a charity. Would I have carried on if I knew the challenges I would face? Would I have allowed myself to be inspired if I knew the despair I would feel, the utter helplessness, the dark nights of the soul? Would my family have supported me if they knew the sacrifices they would have to endure, while I pursued my dream? If we knew what was to come, who would have the courage to start? And yet we do. The course of history is defined by those who have taken risks in order to make a difference, leave their mark, pursue their dream.... *Better to have tried and failed than never to have tried at all*. And better to have tried with a mentor, a trusted guide alongside us, who can help us navigate the huge challenges of creating something new.

This why supporting entrepreneurism is so important. This why we believe that mentoring entrepreneurs is one of the keys to change. We need to empower a new generation of leaders who make change happen. Give them a fishing rod rather than a fish.

But mentoring must never be one way traffic. Travelling to some of the poorest parts of the world, I am struck by the number of smiling faces in what we would view as the most abject poverty. They have nothing in material terms; they battle to survive from day to day. They cannot rely on the basics of food, water and shelter. How can they be so happy? I have come to appreciate that the reason is simple. Their lives aren't filled with busyness and doing. They aren't attached to stuff and they aren't bombarded with advertising reinforcing a lack of self-esteem. They simply are, and in that connection to themselves and the world around them they find true happiness.

Furthermore, it is now in the direct interest of business to engage with the world's poorest. It is time for business to be socially responsible, not just to fill the CSR box in the annual report, but because it should become second nature to them. And there are opportunities in what is termed the Bottom of the Pyramid. The business models highlighted by C K Prahalad are based on affordability and sustainability. As the world economy as we have known it unravels we can learn from these business models. They are primarily driven by fulfilling need, not to satisfy the demands of shareholders. The market amongst those earning less than $2 a day is huge – calculated at $13 trillion. So I believe that we have as much to learn from the people we aim to help as they do from us. If our mentors can discover a new perspective of the developing world and how to do business there, if they can discover what is really important in life, if they can discover something new within themselves, then they will return to their normal working lives as more authentic and creative leaders and thereby more valuable assets to their companies, as well as having contributed to the process of a transformed world. So sponsoring companies can make a difference and get a real return on their investment in the development of their staff. So, in conclusion, I believe we have created something that can work for everyone: companies, their employees, individuals who want to make a difference and, most importantly, our budding entrepreneurs and those living in poverty.

I want to thank all of those who have volunteered to be mentors for our pilot in Jordan. Not only are they taking a risk, a step into the unknown, but they are paying for the privilege. But I particularly want to thank Tony. It is not only his incredible vision, but he has made a huge personal investment into *Mowgli*. He is a successful entrepreneur who has put his money where his mouth is. I fervently hope that as a result of tonight, he will find others to share that investment so that his vision can achieve its full realisation. The world wants to end poverty, but it is only by getting behind practical, ground-breaking initiatives like this that we can start turning hope into reality.

And there is hope. It exists within each of us. For that hope to mean anything, we all have to do something. *'Another world is on its way. On a quiet day I can hear her breathing.'* Nobody has to wait a moment before starting to improve the world. To be or not to be? Only you can answer.'

Since that speech, *The Mowgli Foundation* has been

pioneering an international mentoring programme in the Levant: Jordan, Syria, Lebanon and Palestine/Israel and more recently in North Africa – Egypt and Algeria. Recently, Comic Relief marked its 25th anniversary by raising over £75m to alleviate poverty and ease suffering worldwide. Most would celebrate its success. But equally it reflects failure, for little has been done to empower people to take responsibility and create the wealth that will take them out of aid. It is that old cliché *Give a man a fish and you feed him for a day; give him a fishing rod and he can feed himself forever.* Perhaps the greatest testimony for what has been achieved came from one of our mentors as expressed in Forbes magazine:

The secret kernel of Mowgli's success is in having realized that without engaging passionate and seasoned mentors one can hardly add any meaningful value to the journey of entrepreneurs and mentees.

Mowgli is light years ahead of other programmes. The most amazing element perhaps is the seemingly serendipitous but thoroughly thought over and well analysed methodology of matching mentors and those whom they mentor.

You may be asking why the name 'Mowgli'? When we were first setting up the charity in 2008, Tony Bury and I mapped out a strategy, but couldn't find a name. One morning, as the sun was beginning to rise over the desert, I was awoken with the name 'Mowgli' in my head. It wouldn't go away. I got up and checked it on Google, knowing where it came from but searching for its significance. The first item I came across was a description of the character 'Mowgli' in *The Jungle Book* on the Disney website. It contained the following: 'Mowgli is a classic tale of mentoring as a young man discovers his true identity by being mentored by different animals in the jungle'. Then the words so true about mentoring: 'A mentor will tell you what you need to hear not what you want to hear.' Later, over breakfast, I offered the name to Tony for the new charity. He laughed and told me that *The Jungle Book* was his favourite film.

Ultimately it allowed me to develop a model of mentoring that allows those who participate to remember the power of human relationship.

Having launched a mentoring programme in Syria in 2010, the unfolding situation is in stark contrast to the optimism felt by the entrepreneurs at the time. One of them was a young woman from a very conservative background. Huda was only able to join the programme with her mother accompanying her as her chaperone. On the last day, just after the group photograph, Huda's mother appeared on the balcony above and was also recording the moment. She sent down a note, which Huda translated: *I am happy and proud to see such a day that gathers the good people who give us the hope of the future we have always dreamed of.*

Sadly, the dream is on hold. For a Syrian woman, being an entrepreneur is like the flower in the desert, struggling against the culture of her tradition. The dream of entrepreneurship along with the dream of freedom has been cruelly crushed by the very regime that for a moment, offered new hope. The Arab Spring has bypassed summer and autumn to become the Arab Winter for those in Syria. It is an irony that, in a world where religious extremism is blamed for all its woes, Syria was a nation of great religious tolerance where three monotheistic faiths lived alongside each other in perfect harmony. Visiting the historic Old City of Damascus and its wonderful souk, the visitor is struck by the fact that the Grand Mosque, containing the tomb of John the Baptist, and the Cathedral, sit alongside each other in the heart of the Jewish quarter. Hearing the call to prayer melding with the bells of the cathedral is a remarkable sound which touches all but the most spiritually unconscious.

My journey continued as I travelled to visit the West Bank. This was my first trip to Israel/Palestine; the part of the world where Jesus lived out his earthly ministry. It is a place of perpetual conflict where the human face of religions has involved pursuit of sole ownership and control of this tiny, blessed place. On a visit to Jerusalem, as I stood by the Wailing Wall, I eavesdropped as a guide was taking a group of tourists around: "You are standing on the point where the three great world faiths have their roots and the point at which the Third World War will start." We can only pray that this will not be realised, but the reality is that we all know it could be. If my journey so far was beginning to change my perspective of life, my experience of coming here was to embed this shift forever.

They say it is better to travel hopefully than to arrive. Not if you are travelling from Jordan to the West Bank, believe me. It was not an auspicious day; it was grey and cold in Amman, with remnants of the snow, not as unusual as one would imagine in this part of the world. The words of the carol *In the bleak mid winter,* so familiar at Christmas in England, seem so inapposite when celebrating the birth of Jesus in Bethlehem. Yet it is perfectly possible that, to coin the words of another carol, ...*the snow lay round about, deep and crisp and even*! It does get very cold here.

The Jordan Valley is impressive. You get the real sense of its part in the Great Rift Valley sinking below sea level to a fertile plain that runs into the Dead Sea, the lowest part on earth. Equidistant from the northern tip of the Dead Sea, east and west are the cities of Amman and Jerusalem, sitting high up and sharing a similar climate. As the crow flies they are quite close, but it is just not the steep climb to both of them that sets them further apart. It is easy to forget that the border between Jordan and Jerusalem until 1967 lay between East and West Jerusalem. The sharp eyed will notice an unfinished palace built for King Hussein of Jordan sitting on a hill in the eastern outskirts of the holy city, a reminder of how close the two nations were. From the taxi we are transferred to a bus when we cross the River Jordan. An American travelling with us told me to keep my eyes glued to the window or I would miss it. He was right. The river crossing is disappointing. No raging torrent; just a gentle stream. The crossing point is only a couple of miles from the point where Jesus was baptised, and I for one have had to change my mental picture of that scene. But gazing into the river is the last sense of peace that we will feel this day. The fact that it is also the border between Jordan and Israel/ Palestine – the West Bank – does not register at this point. I was about to be offered a new perspective of the whole Arab/Israeli issue that has been a constant challenge for the world during my lifetime. It is easy to forget the key lesson that the Jews learned from the Holocaust: that even in fleeing from Nazism, there was never a safe place to live. Israel is the creation of that safe place and, although the impact it has on its neighbours and its visitors may seem unjust, they have been forced by experience to create a place within which the most basic human need for secure survival is assured.

Crossing the border you become a product in a process. While it provides a barrier to the outside world, it provides a reminder of the fine balance that exists between security and humanity. It is easy to gain the impression that the process has less to do with security and more to do with intimidation. The underlying question seems to be *Why are you wasting your time visiting Palestinians?* Perhaps I made the mistake of telling the truth – that I ran a NGO, which was working with Palestinians to create jobs. I was to learn what this process feels like for a local through the eyes of Jibril. I am not telling the story to have a go at one protagonist or another in what is a hugely complex political situation. Jibril is a Palestinian Christian living in East Jerusalem. He was born in Nablus in 1966. Soon after his birth he contracted polio. He travelled from the West Bank to Shobuk in Southern Jordan to participate in a *Mowgli* mentoring programme for entrepreneurs that I was leading. He described the reality of living in Palestine, a life of daily oppression and humiliation. I have always been struck by the stoic humour of those living on the West Bank. Jibril lives in East Jerusalem and works in Ramallah, a journey no greater than that between Bath and Bristol. But each day he has to drive through the wall that surrounds East Jerusalem and the checkpoints that feature on every road on the West Bank. To join us, Jibril had travelled across the King Hussein Bridge, which spans the River Jordan, just as I had done. From there he joined the group travelling down to Shobuk. He arrived on crutches with his withered limbs and crutches in stark contrast to the beatific smile on his face.

In the midst of the horror of his day to day reality, he shared with us his dream for inspiring young Palestinians to embrace IT, for this is an industry, as across the Levant, that provides a route to future peace and prosperity. He told us of the many challenges he faces running a business on the West Bank, but what made most impact on us was his description of his anticipated return journey from Jordan. Because of his disability, he knew that he would be stripped naked. His calipers would be removed and he would be left helpless and stranded in this condition for up to two hours. He is just another potential terrorist. Jibril sent me an email after his return journey:

You have also inspired me to stand up for the Israeli security officers on the Israeli side of king Hussein's bridge who asked me to take off my pants and my leg brace. I have challenged them to give me a written document of these orders, at first, they refused and threatened to send me back to Jordan or take me to jail for refusing to obey the orders. After more than two hours of tough negotiations, they compromised to make me take my pants off only without the brace. I made a police report and complain of this behavior (which means that the incident is now documented and archived in the Israeli police department). I have accepted this compromise to make sure that it was documented, however, I have promised my family and myself that this is the last time that I will accept such humiliation, even if I have to go to jail.

I know that our group is not involved in politics, I am not involved in any political activities, and I am not asking for sympathy, nevertheless, I think that we owe the Palestinian disabled men and women who get such a humiliating treatment and keep their silence of this "psychological rape". I will contact the human right organizations to follow up on this matter....

Jibril's story is both an inspirational witness to the power of one man who has had enough and a reminder how easy it is to forget our innate humanity as we fall out of relationship with one another. An absence of relationship breeds ignorance which generates fear .... and so the cycle continues. Jibril's witness is one of patience, endurance of the day to day humiliation he experiences, but this is now matched by his determination to challenge the status quo, not just to accept things as they are. He is an example to us faint-hearted souls who accept the world as it is without ever believing that we could do something to change it. Jibril has decided that his situation, and that of his fellow Palestinians, has to change. Others have decided or been persuaded that violence is the only way to bring about change. But Jibril, as with many of his generation, prefer a more subtle and long-term approach. Quiet resistance can be very effective in tackling injustice. The fact that I am writing about Jibril is indicative of how human story is so powerful in creating change. Jibril is an exemplar of the modern leader. He is a humble man who is no longer prepared to accept *humiliating treatment and keep silent of this psychological rape*. He is prepared to stand up for fairness and justice, even being willing to go to jail to ensure that his children don't have to endure the same.

On a later visit I found myself standing next to a Roman Catholic priest from Dunfermline, who advised me strongly to say that I was a pilgrim visiting Jerusalem. *But that would be lying*, I responded, highly conscious of who he was and not wanting to make a confession on the far side! *No it won't because you are coming with me and I am priest in charge of a church in Jerusalem. If you decide to change your plans en route to Jerusalem, I would be happy to give you a lift to Ramallah*. We passed through the entire security process in less than ten minutes and, hand on the heart, there was no lying. His driver dropped me outside my hotel in Ramallah and one day I will be that pilgrim.

The drive up to Ramallah is dominated by the views of Jewish settlements built on top of all the hills. Quite apart from the political implications, the environmental consequences of building ugly tower blocks in what was once the beautiful hills of the Holy Land, is another example of the tragedy of this situation. For it is not just about the settlements themselves, it is about securing the water supply, 90% of which is now controlled by the Israelis in a region where water supply will become more crucial than energy. We pass by East Jerusalem. My first image of this beautiful city, which is so symbolic for so many people, is of an ugly wall that is reminiscent of the Berlin Wall. Surely we have learned that human progress is not advanced by walls? Look what happened when the Berlin Wall came down. The physical represents the psychological. Basic human rights have flourished when walls have been brought down, whether real as in these or walls or legal as in apartheid. It is a reminder of why I am here: supporting the entrepreneurs who will create the jobs for the many young people, particularly men, who are unemployed. Jobs keep idle hands occupied; jobs reduce terrorism. This is not to excuse the terrorism of some Palestinians, nor to condemn the Israelis who feel understandably threatened by it, but as I pass that wall I am reminded of the protest song of the 1960s *Where have all the flowers gone?* which concludes with the words *When will they ever learn, when will they ever learn?*

Further on up to Ramallah, a small city built on top of a series of hills. The city centre is bustling with activity. Shops spill out onto the pavements with wonderful looking breads, fruits and vegetables. A barrow of strawberries wheels past us at the lights, every large and delicious looking strawberry carefully laid out to create a pyramid of fruit. It is impossible to come to the West Bank and not talk about politics. They are not optimistic about the future. At best they see themselves moving from crisis to crisis management. Peace is still a distant dream along with the vision of their own nation state. Some talk still of the possibility of a two nation solution; others say that the only possible outcome now is a one nation state with both Israeli and Palestinian coexisting peacefully under one democratic government. It is difficult to see the Israelis buying this solution since the demographics work against them – the Palestinian population is rising faster than theirs.

I met Mazen, a former government minister and one of Palestine's most successful businessmen. He is charming and we have the long statutory political discussion before addressing the purpose of my visit – a project whereby the *Mowgli Foundation* would provide mentoring for local farmers who were trying to sell their produce to leading British supermarkets. The quality of their fruit, vegetables and olive oil is excellent with the added bonus that their main harvest in the Jordan valley is between November and March, neatly filling the winter months when local produce is not available in UK. Mazen had negotiated a route out of the West Bank with the Israelis that allows his produce to be in London within 10 hours. This is a significant advance since it normally takes up to 24 hours just to get out, but he had had to negotiate for many years to get this dispensation. For the majority, export is not financially viable. The Palestinians are natural business people but entrepreneurship is difficult because of the inability to access markets. This is slowly beginning to change, but it is a brave Palestinian who puts everything on the line to start a business.

It does seem to me that an essential ingredient in achieving the goal of peace is to work from the bottom up. Levels of high unemployment with a young population are sowing the seeds of worse problems in the future. Young men, particularly, without purpose, with no job, no income and no hope soon become desperate. Terrorist organisations have never found it difficult to recruit such young men. I reflect, and I know that Baroness Jenny Tonge has got into trouble for saying so, but placed within a set of circumstances where I had no hope, could I become a terrorist? My hard-wired belief that killing is never a solution to anything is very strong, but would it be strong enough in desperate circumstances. Could I find myself at the base of a rocket launcher? I don't know and I suspect that no one does until presented with the circumstances, but at least we should learn to step into the shoes of those that do and understand why they are doing it, for there lies the root of the solution.

On the journey down from Ramallah via Jericho to the border, the traveller passes the site of the story of the Good Samaritan, a reminder of how easy it is for us in the West to pass by the wounded soul of this divided country. What I have learned in the heart of the Holy Land is that things that really matter in life – love, wisdom, compassion, kindness, generosity, courage – transcend borders and different cultures. Yet we waste so much energy in politicising every aspect of our lives, to the extent that these human qualities get lost somewhere along the way. Politics, while on one level converging, is at the same time becoming more remote from real life. Political leadership is essentially shallow as the reality of it becomes more exposed. Why haven't we been able to resolve some of the world's great challenges – poverty, climate change, shortage of resources, the Israel Palestine issue? Maybe because the ability of those that we elect to take a lead is diminished by the greater power blocs who pull the strings, maybe because we just don't care enough.

I began to realise that while the *Mowgli Foundation* is dedicated to entrepreneurship, the principles can be applied to any context. Entrepreneurs are by definition leaders; disciples are spiritual entrepreneurs and thereby leaders too. They are not satisfied by the status quo and see opportunities to change it. Unlike the majority they have the courage to put their head above the parapet and their money on the line. Sometimes all we need is the right inspiration and permission to do so. It was through the eyes of my own entrepreneurship and those of others that the idea for the *Disciple's Journey* began to emerge. Maybe instead of waiting futilely for politicians to sort out the world's ills, we, as Christians, should take the lead.

Sami Awad is such a man. A Palestinian Christian from

a family that was forced to escape their home in Bethlehem when his grandfather was shot by Israelis in 1948, he was born and brought up in the US. A comfortable and fulfilling life beckoned as his family lived the American dream. Yet he couldn't sit back and see his heritage being destroyed by the violence that now pervades his former land. So he returned to Bethlehem and set up the Holy Land Trust to try and provide a new answer to the intractable problem – an answer based on non-violence. He has inspired those from across the religious divides to work together to achieve a united nation at peace with itself. I attended a weekend retreat in Jericho where young leaders were brought together to seek new solutions. Not one of them saw a two state solution. In an inspiring afternoon of presentations each young Palestinian shared a vision of a united country where Jew, Muslim and Christian live contentedly side by side. It would be a proud nation providing a beacon of hope to the world. One group even envisioned that this new state would host the World Cup in 2026.

What I have learned from Sami is the power of a non-violent approach. As an ex soldier who is now working with the casualties of war, I am challenged by the contradiction that exists between my faith which is based on the tenets of 'love your neighbour as yourself' and, indeed, 'love your enemy', and our fixation with warfare as a means of solving political differences. The new perspective that is achieved from the *Disciple's Journey* is about the equal value and integrity of everything. Continuing the jigsaw puzzle analogy, it is impossible to compete the picture if the individual parts believe that their particular piece is more important than another and end up fighting to resolve this. While there will always be the principle of the just war, it seems that we are more inclined use warfare as the weapon of first rather than last resort. So traumatising were the effects of two world wars in the 20th century that a generation of politicians attempted to create a world that could be free of war. Institutions like the United Nations and the European Union, whatever their perceived shortcomings now, were the fruit of this. With the direct experience of war now gone for the current generation of politicians, it has become too easy to believe that it can be a short cut to achieving political ends. Indeed, with the rapid advances in technology it is now possible to conduct war remotely with no connection to the consequences. Thus, by illustration, it is possible for a young technician in California, to have breakfast with his children, drop them off at school, go to work to sit behind his computer screen, from which he is able to fly a remote drone that is capable of killing hundreds of people while he sips on his cappuccino chewing his muffin, then later collect his children from school, help them with their homework before preparing the barbecue. I might exaggerate slightly to make the point, but once we are able to conduct warfare in this way with no connection to the moral consequences of our actions, we cease to become a civilised society. It is a sobering thought that at any moment in time there are on average 68 million people in the world playing war games on their computer, where killing is the only objective. It is a small step from doing this virtually to doing it for real, although the effect on the 'player' is pretty much the same.

O God help us to achieve what in our hearts we most earnestly desire – peace on earth, good will among men. Help us to realise that the horrors of war and suffering of mankind came for neglect of your will. Rouse us from our apathy, give us confidence in our task, energy and vision, and may we have the moral courage of our convictions. Grant that we may live in obedience to you, that we may be united in true and lasting peace, and that your will may be done on earth as it is in heaven. Through Jesus Christ our Lord. Amen.

As I wrote this chapter, Israeli missiles were raining down on Gaza in response to missiles landing on Israel. Pictures of children burned to death filled the television screen. Not a week passes without our seeing more casualties of the war in Afghanistan now in its eleventh year – young men and women with bodies and minds shattered by the brutality of war. Across the Middle East the Arab Spring, so keen to turn over what was, is now struggling to articulate what will be. Syria continues to tear itself apart. The threat of nuclear conflict between Israel and Iran is never far away. At home, every institution we took for granted displays its moral deficit as the spotlight of transparency is turned upon them. Frankly, it could be any normal week in current world history. How much longer are we prepared to sit back and watch the world fall apart? 'So what?' you may be asking? Where are the institutions that can offer a better narrative? Where are the great leaders? What is leadership?

17

Leadership —
from Survival to Service

I am two men: one is filled with a longing to serve; the
other is afraid. *Anon.*

The aim of the *Disciple's Journey* is to show the relevance
of Jesus Christ as we unleash a cascade of good leadership
to create an impact on the world. Leadership can be a great
expression of love. It begins within each of us. Being filled
with God's love helps us to see ourselves in the right way
and be equipped to serve others. What does that mean for
you? It means that, as with the *Disciple's Journey*, a flame
is lit which allows us to begin the process of finding our
purpose, stepping into the truth, with God-given authenticity.
Leadership begins with self-leadership. How can we lead
others if we don't know how to govern ourselves? How can
we expect others to follow, if we don't know where we are
going? How can we love others if we don't know that we
are loved? And how can that love come together to make
the impact on the world that the world is yearning for? The
first disciples had a world-changing impact as they preached
and lived out the gospel, and we should apply that same
message today.

I would love to report that the *Disciple's Journey* is a short
way to fulfilment. But sadly it is not. So how do we achieve
the transformational change the world so desires? I have a

vision of a *chain reaction* of leaders, like a cascade of grace. These will be people who pass on the benefits they have received to others who similarly 'pay it forward' – where relationship defines leadership; where authentic relationship feeds personal responsibility; where being all you were created to be allows others to be all they were created to be; where our common humanity is discovered and enjoyed; where wisdom and compassion work in perfect harmony.

The vision was summed up rather well for me in the words 'I am so you can be', surely the foundation for all good leadership. Within this short phrase is articulated the sense that through our being we create the environment within which others can step into their being too.

The means of achieving this is linking the qualities learned through the *Disciple's Journey* to personal leadership, the foundation for team, organisational and social leadership. Amongst other things there lies an opportunity for the older generation to inspire and empower the young, since the young are the generation upon whom the burden of leadership now falls

Do not wait for leaders, do it alone person by person.
Mother Theresa

Again we recall that the most commonly used prayer around the world each day is the Lord's Prayer. We all know the words and within it is very profound petition: 'Thy kingdom come, thy will be done on earth, as it is in heaven.' This is partly looking forward to a future in which Jesus will be seen to reign over all. But it is also about relationships in the *present*. God empowers us to make a difference here and now, bringing the kingdom (rule, authority of God) to situations in which we find ourselves. That is part of discipleship.

Empowerment requires a response. Indeed the word responsibility defines our response-ability. There is no part of it that stresses passivity in our human journey. We have been created to exercise creativity through our own unique set of gifts, skills and passions. It for us to discover them and then use them in service of the kingdom. The greatest service that we can bring is playing our full part in making known and allowing God to use us to bring a foretaste of the kingdom here on earth today.

The inspiration comes from my own journey and a number of books by Tom Wright, particularly *Surprised by Hope* in which he talks about creating the kingdom on earth today and *The New Conspirators* by Tom Sine, which is all about us 'conspiring' to start building heaven on earth.

In his book *Surprised by Hope*, Tom Wright reminds us that God intends to save the whole of creation. He talks about the relationship between the kingdom and the Cross. We have come to believe that the kingdom will not come before the return of Christ. Yet he argues that the the process of creating the kingdom began with the resurrection, which frees us from the sin that prevents us from being a manifestation of kingdom values here today, through social transformation. Thus the role of the church is not simply about saving souls. It can anticipate renewal by working for God's kingdom today. By facilitating its followers to become 'masters of themselves' and encouraging service within our communities, the church can begin to serve the wider world in a way which brings healing and hope. By so doing the church can be seen to be relevant to a world that is becoming more secular while, paradoxically, searching for meaning.

A constant theme is that heaven is here right now. Our job as Christians is to work together towards drawing it ever closer to us. The world is both dying to its old ways and seeking something better. That is why there is so much New

Age activity currently. There are many ways that Christians could be putting good biblical teaching about the kingdom into practice, rooted in love. We are living in times, as ever, when Christians need to be Christlike witnesses out in the world. As we have seen, God often sends us into some dark places, and that is where you find him in a deep and moving way. The *Disciple's Journey* teaches us that you won't discover the nature of God until you step out in faith. And this takes humility, huge courage and encouragement. It often requires leadership without authority – in other words following the promptings of the Holy Spirit rather than any human prompting.

It follows that the role of a church leader is principally to create the environment within which individuals can use their faith to become disciples, creating the leadership that can impact communities. So helping others to find the courage to step out in faith and become more authentic is the first challenge. We have seen how we hide behind a series of masks, which prevent us from building relationships based on trust. This is unhealthy in life, but particularly unhealthy in a leader. A leader is constantly seeking to help people discover their true gifts and their purpose in life/calling, and giving them the opportunity to step outside their self-interest and serve others. The *Disciple's Journey* creates the framework for leaders to use to encourage individuals to step out in faith on a journey of self-discovery. With this knowledge it is then possible to step beyond self to a place where we move from independence to interdependence. The Alpha initiative has brought many individuals to independence in faith, but it poses the question 'So what?' If Alpha signposts people to Jesus, the *Disciple's Journey* will give people the opportunity of discovering and fulfilling the purpose for which they were created by God and establishing the interdependence through which the kingdom can begin to be seen. By becoming a Disciple, individuals, by default, become leaders.

'May another take his place of leadership' (Acts 1:20). Little did I know as a young Officer Cadet at Sandhurst, as I read out the words of the Academy's Collect, that the words spoken so lightly actually carried the secret to leadership in the world as it is today. So much is studied and written about leadership, but I have come to realise that it all starts within each of us. You may be asking: what do we actually mean by leadership? In the corporate world, where the MBA has become the passport to success, we have allowed management to overwhelm the whole concept of leadership in our desperation to be able to account for every penny and every aspect of our lives. Management is a tool for leaders, not the end in itself, as expressed by Field Marshall Slim, as we saw earlier. When we rely on management only, we end up with the corruption quoted in the report on the Mid Staffordshire NHS Trust. My experience in the Army, and then working in schools and prisons, is simply that the most effective officers, head-teachers and prison governors were those who were the best leaders. They understood that the business of leaders is human beings. *The leader must be practical and a realist yet must talk the language of the visionary and the idealist.*

Leaders have vision. They inspire individuals to follow, to do the impossible – and they build teams that can achieve the seemingly impossible. They provide the moral framework within which individuals can prosper and create the cultures that encourage the best in human behaviour. Many modern leaders are actually managers who just don't get any of this. We should hardly be surprised therefore at the failure of all our major institutions.

Many current corporate leaders don't understand the simple connection between leadership and behaviour.

Because they, understandably, have no knowledge of what individuals employed by them are up to, this does not, as a leader, excuse them.

The leader creates the culture and the values by which behaviour is informed. As a leader it is essential to have a moral compass since without it we are rudderless and prone to being tossed around on the stormy seas of life. It is therefore incumbent on the leader to first become *masters of ourselves*.

Thus personal leadership is the first quest of the *Disciple's Journey*. I am grateful to Richard Barrett who has studied and facilitated the art of leadership throughout his adult life, the accumulation of which is his recent book *The New Leadership Paradigm*. This offers to me an intellectual rigour to what has been for me a journey of the soul. In it he describes what is becoming a crisis of leadership in a world that is facing a level of complexity combined with challenges that threaten its continued survival. The pace of change, whether it is related to the environment, the financial system, energy needs, global terrorism or population growth and the need for employment, is so fast that it demands a new level of leadership. Barrett uses the significant evidence and research found in *Leadership Agility: Five Levels of Mastery for Anticipating Change* by Bill Joiner and Stephen Joseph. In it they state: *To develop organisations that are effective in anticipating and responding to change and complexity, we need agile leaders – not just at the top but at all organisational levels. Yet we face a significant leadership gap.*

Richard Barrett has developed a clear understanding of true leadership available in the world today. In *The New Leadership Paradigm* he describes the 'seven levels of leadership consciousness'. It is manifestly clear, as has already been stated, that we cannot achieve what is needed with the current mindset. He says that next generation leaders must embody the key qualities of trust, empathy and compassion, qualities that would resonate with any follower of Christ. These are qualities that emerge over time, often through the experience of perseverance and tough realities. This is why the *Disciple's Journey* is so critical. It presents Christians with the opportunity to reveal them and other qualities key to leadership. Both represent journeys from 'I' to 'We'.

I am grateful to Mark Bailey the Lead Pastor of Trinity Cheltenham for the following quote on leadership: *'The pathway to leadership is strewn with complexity, and only those who manage to negotiate that complexity can pass on to the next level of leadership, for which their reward is yet more complexity!'* It sums up the seven levels rather neatly, ensuring that leadership is placed into the context of a lifetime's quest, not a single destination. As we become masters of ourselves, we realise that leadership requires even greater humility as we uncover the complexities that lie within us all. We become far less than we thought we were.

The seven levels loosely match the stages in the *Disciple's Journey*, beginning with the Ordinary World of survival through the transformational stage of Crossing the Line to the internal cohesion that comes through Facing the Darkness to the New Perspective of service to others. But more significantly, the *Disciple's Journey*, while seeming to be a single circuit, is not. In my experience you can be at different stages in different aspects of your life but, more importantly, each circuit can take the individual to a different trajectory on the Seven Levels of Leadership – rather like a spiral.

Let us look at the seven levels in more detail.

1. Survival

Survival is our start point. From the moment we are born

and utter our first breath, we embark upon a lifetime's second by second mission to survive. As babies we are reliant upon our mothers but, as we grow, we learn to be self-sufficient. As we grow older, our survival strategies become ever more sophisticated as we move from our basic needs for food and shelter to an ever-growing acquisition of perceived material necessity. Ask a starving African and a multi-millionaire what their survival needs are and they will give you very different answers. The fact is that as our societies become more sophisticated and wealthier the definition of survival changes. In UK now, for example, possession of a television set is seen as a basic human right and would now be considered a survival need. Notwithstanding the differences in definition, we can agree that survival includes our ability to earn an income, feed and house ourselves and our children.

Beyond this individual survival is the creation of a safe and secure psychological environment. The responsibility for this has in the industrial age been assumed more and more by the state. While within a simple community an individual might assume the role of night watchman to keep guard at night, as we have been able to afford it the state has invested in police forces, security cameras, surveillance, defence, for example, to create safety and security for its citizens. These have become so much a fabric of our societies that, when any is threatened by cuts, those that have a stake in their survival invoke fear, thereby destabilising the safe and secure psychological environment. The struggle to meet basic survival needs will be a constant theme for the Disciple, while discernment of what is essential to life as opposed to what is desirable will be an ongoing challenge. As we hang onto what we want we deny ourselves what we need: continual grace from a God who wants us to trust him for our survival.

2. Relationships

Having met our basic survival needs, we begin to search for our place within the world. Our relationships become a medium through which we begin to discover who we are. As has already been highlighted, this begins with the relationship between the infant and the birth mother, a crucial stage in the brain's development during which we begin to understand social interaction and emotional intelligence. It is where we begin to satisfy our need for belonging and feeling loved and accepted by those with whom we interact on a daily basis. As a child grows up and begins to take on relationships beyond the immediate family – as, for example – going to school, the nature of our relationship with the world becomes an ever more sophisticated search for a sense of belonging and a reinforcement that we are affirmed. We are inherently tribal and need to feel a sense of belonging to something greater than ourselves. This starts with friendship groups at school and develops into the need for national identity. Whether consciously or not we are constantly seeking out tribes to which to belong. This could be as straightforward as becoming a supporter of a football club (Arsenal, in my case) or something less apparent such as political affiliations.

But the most important of our relationships is that we have with God. There is much we can be said and could be said in criticism of many of man's religious traditions. Too often, the great truth about faith in Christ as *relational* and, in the best sense *personal* is missed. This reinforces the point that what we 'belong to' defines us in a way that fulfils that need for security. If our basic survival needs are underpinned by the need for a safe and secure psychological environment, so are our relationships increasingly underpinned by the law, which has served to separate ourselves from each other.

(Though we need an appropriate framework of just laws in societies, since the opposite, anarchy, provides no freedom for anyone.) In a world without a great deal of love (in the sense of selfless caring) in evidence, or where love has been perverted by lust, we have failed so often to get the matter of relationships right and humane. It is only through the love is revealed in our relationship with God that we, individually and collectively, rediscover the nature of true relationship with each other.

3. Self-esteem

As we begin to understand our relationship with the world, we begin to question whether or not we measure up. We seek out benchmarks to test this. We want to feel good in ourselves and to have a sense of pride in our existence. It is where we begin to acquire the masks that allow us to survive in whatever tribe or tribes we have ended up in. While we seek our place in the world, the paradox is that, for most of us, we have to go through a lot of pretence in order to survive in our tribe. We see what we believe is expected of us and adopt the behaviour most likely to meet others' expectations of us. This begins within the family, as parent tend to set the conditions for ongoing membership of the tribe, and moves to global corporations, who create sophisticated rules and values for all their staff. We are expected to conform, and in so doing we usually lose the essence of ourselves, but it allows us to survive. I have lost track of the number of masks that I have worn in my many different lives, but I have learned that they are heavy burdens to bear. It is only as we step into our *Disciple's Journey* that we begin the process of revealing the people we were born to be. This is the step into transformation.

4. Transformation

It is at this stage where the action really begins. This is where the quest for truth becomes unquenchable as we first seek our authentic identity and our reason for living before seeing where we fit in for our service in the world. The transformation stage for the Disciple usually begins at the point they hear the call to change and come to faith. It is when they receive the Holy Spirit and begin to realise that what has served them in the past is unlikely to be of use in the future. As we build up experience of life in relationship with God we begin to understand that we can be unique and clearly defined. It is at this stage that we search for the means to achieve this. It is where we begin to embrace our individuality – so you can become a fully self-actualised, authentic individual taking your place within a group that affirms and celebrates uniqueness. The masks melt away as the need to conform to the expectations of others evaporates. You can become the person you were born to be. This in itself can be a lifetime's work for many as we come to terms with our past in a way that can make sense of the future. As we have seen, true transformation is only possible after facing the darkness since it is here that those false parts of our being are burnt off. Someone once asked me whether it is possible to truly find ourselves without entering this pit of despair. My answer was that for most mere mortals it was impossible.

5. Internal cohesion

As the real 'me' emerges, this stage is about identifying purpose and creating a vision for the future you want to create. It is where the jigsaw piece becomes defined and we begin to seek out those pieces with which it fits in order to give our life real meaning. If the transformational stage through facing the darkness begins the process of burning off those parts that no longer serve us, this stage offers the chance to reflect on what is left and integrate what is authentic to us into a meaningful whole. Only then are we fully equipped for the next stage.

6. Making a difference

At this stage we are able to fully actualise our sense of purpose by collaborating with others to make a difference in the world. In a highly competitive world, as we have seen, it is very difficult to achieve true collaboration. It is only when we have resolved our past and fully integrated our present, letting go of that self-centred need for significance, that we have the inner confidence to truly collaborate in a way that makes a sustainable difference. When we have done so we are able to seek out those with whom we can align with shared values and objectives in a way that can really change the world. I have had many opportunities to reflect, for example, how difficult it is for charities to make a sustainable difference, since they are competing with each other for other people's money. True collaboration is an uphill struggle since few have discovered their true identity and have the confidence to reach out to those who might have identities complementary to theirs. So it is with us as individuals. In every organisation we witness this played out – in politics large and small. Collaboration, if it is ever even considered, remains a distant dream.

7. Service

'Serve to Lead' – the Sandhurst motto, the pinnacle of leadership. It is at this level where we can truly serve the world in pursuit of a big vision. As disciples this is the ultimate destination where we can fulfil the calling on our lives in harmony with others. This is truly where we can experience something of the kingdom on earth today. It is our destiny as disciples, although the fulfilment of it is unlikely in our short life span. But in embarking on our *Disciple's Journey* we are conscious of our own purpose and we seek to help others to pursue their journey.

'So what?' you may be asking. What does this mean in our lives at this point in history? Soldiers understand the concept of 'mission'. Of course the overall mission of Christians is given in Christ's Great Commission. Within that, there will be those called to give various kinds of leadership, which is all about service – and that sense of service comes from deep within our souls. If you believe, as I do, that we are all born on purpose for a purpose, our life's journey is to discover what that is, and to fulfil God's call to each one of us.

The link half guessed, the gift half understood, is incarnation. *Anon*

Having embarked on and described my own *Disciple's Journey*, I am extending an invitation for others to do the same and to step into the new kind of serving leadership that the world needs. The *Disciple's Journey* highlights the importance of experience. In the Politics of Conscience, the late Vaclav Havel talks about *the inner discipline of truth*. By truth, he meant the truth to experience the confrontation with the world of life. During my journey I have had the opportunity of confronting the world of life at many different levels (and often at its most conservative), which has provided the inspiration to write this book. As we confront change, the lessons of our faith teach us that true change comes through something much deeper and inspirational, which Christians would describe as the power of the Holy Spirit. Through it we learn to understand our part in the great story that underpins all our lives. People ask *You use this term the 'Holy Spirit'. What does it mean?* I can't give you a complete answer to that, but quite simply Jesus promised disciples that this person, the Holy Spirit (a person of the godhead, so not an 'it', not an impersonal 'force'). John the Baptist had foretold that Jesus would baptise (immerse) in the Spirit, and that is what happened at Pentecost, as recorded in Acts Chapter 2. Jesus' promises remain as true as when he uttered them, and this same Holy Spirit keeps coming, imapcting, empowering, helping and guiding. We are also told that it is God the Holy Spirit who convicts the world of sin, righteousness and judgement. Far from being something gloomy and unpleasant, this is a great, liberating truth, that Christians believe in a God who didn't just start things off, like a watchmaker who winds up a watch, but he is involved, and he prompts us to become aware of our true need to come face to face with what is wrong in us, acknowledge that before our Maker, and find and receive forgiveness. What a wonderful release from guilt, shame and the wrong kind of autonomy that would say "I did it my way'. The Christian's aim in life is to do it in Jesus' way, not necessarily in our way.

The Holy Spirit sets us free to be all that we were born to be, to be fully content in whom we are. We should not focus on what we *don't* have; we must use what we *do* have. The Bible teaches us that we are to *go on being filled with the Spirit*, and it is a very joyful thing for Christians that we know and experience the living presence of the living God. Gathering together to pray and worship, believers are in a special way conscious that the risen, ascended Lord is active in their midst.

For where two or three come together in my name, there am I with them.

Matthew 18:20, NIV

That well-known verse and the Lord's Summary of the Law that we considered earlier in this book are keys to unlocking the human condition.

Let us now turn again to some practical issues flowing from our life in society. During the last thirty years there has been a political battle between the power of the individual and the power of the state. As we have become more individualistic, and as government has fallen into disrespect, it is very easy to fall into the trap of saying, 'I know how to spend my money far more effectively than the state – so why should I pay tax?' Of course, that is only about our role in life in economic terms as consumers. Why should I have to take responsibility for those less fortunate? After all they have the same chances as I do so why should I have to sacrifice my hard earned cash to fund their laziness? This misses the point entirely. We are individuals living in community. We might think of a familiar line from Shakespeare: *The world is but a stage and we are merely players*. The play only makes sense if we all play our part. Discerning what our part is, we are able to play it to the full and make sense of the whole. But most of us drift through life unaware of what part we are playing, and even those who do have some inkling of what that part is may end up fluffing their lines. Only God can enable us to we discern our part. We only need to ask, and that calling will be revealed. It is pointless to play our part in isolation. We may have to withdraw to learn our lines, but once we are performing we need to co-operate with others.

Good communities can help to protect from sin and temptation. When we isolate ourselves we are much more easily tempted. Hotels know this, which is why every hotel room has a mini-bar and easy access to porn. Men left alone can easily be tempted. Living in community provides a means to create a degree of accountability.

The truth is that in working in harmony with others we are better able to realise our potential. All the most effective teams are made up of a complementary set of skills where each individual is able to play his or her part without the need to compete with others in the team. What would any play be like if each of the actors were competing for each other's lines? What would any football match be like if individual team members tried to win on their own? But this is what happens in so many organisations because the individuals within are insecure about their particular contribution. Churches only work effectively when individuals are playing in harmony with others the parts to which God called them.

We thought about fear and how it holds us back from living the lives we are meant to live. Fear tends to hinder us spiritually in many ways. It makes it harder for faith to operate. God is love, but we fall far short of his love, whatever label we may carry. Clearly we need to see and know what his love is like, what that word really means in his own self-revelation. To really know what it is, you have to allow God to do something for you rather than thinking you can do everything necessary for yourself. The Hebrews looked back to a time when they were rescued from slavery in Egypt. Christian believers think of when they were rescued from slavery to sin and self, first found that could rely on the righteousness of their Lord rather than any innate goodness they might have imagined they possessed.

We have already mentioned that it is not for us to judge others. If others are ever to be touched by the best that God has for them, we have to have compassion on those who we can see are heading down a route where they are harming themselves, harming others and doing what God's self-revelation has shown is contrary to his will.

The only way forward is in relationship with each other and in beginning to understand each other. Understanding, like love, is an antidote to fear. As I have already said, bringing together a room full of strangers from different cultures and then helping them to understand that there is much that connects them, even though they are from disparate cultures and backgrounds, is one of the most rewarding aspects of what I now do.

If there is much ignorance about other people, the same is true of the future. We do not what is going to happen to us individually or collectively from one day to the next. This creates uncertainty, and uncertainty leads to fear and, as we have noted before, fear freezes action. As disciples it is our role to be an example to the world by overcoming that fear and acting to do what is right anyway. Faith doesn't eliminate uncertainty but it does allow us to live with it.

The greatest fear is of death, although for some without faith the fear of living can be so overwhelming that it overrides even the fear of death. We often fear what we don't understand. Because we don't understand death or the eternity that follows, it is easy to reject the love of God. The love that I am describing is rooted in the Greek word 'agape', which means doing something for someone else: caring service with no expectation of return. Think again of the Good Samaritan, for example. Not only did he pick up the wounded person and give them first aid, he ensured that all his needs could be met over time, even though that person in distress was beyond helping himself. In the same way Jesus, in 'agape' love, gave his life selflessly. He did for us what was needed; something we could not have done for ourselves.

It is a basic misunderstanding, sadly perpetuated by the world's religions, that we can 'earn' the right to heaven by sheer effort of being good. This generates fear, because we know that we will continue to fall short and mess things up. Surely the real message of the Cross – that God himself, in the person of Jesus Christ – did what was needed to release us from fear, so that we can live lives of complete freedom. With faith, forgiveness and trust, I can know that I am loved by God, depending on his strength rather than my own. That is the freedom that leads me to really *want* to love him and love my neighbour.

With freedom comes responsibility. We all have a conscience, which is there to help us make the right choices so that we can flourish as individuals within our communities. Yet history is littered with examples of the mess people and societies make. The positive message of this book is that, released from fear, and the growing awareness of those characteristics within that mess things up, we can make a difference to others: as a leader, beginning with personal leadership learning to develop mastership of ourselves. Only then do we have a foundation from which we can lead others. A great entry point for leadership is mentoring (and thereby being a role model to others). We may progress to more substantial leadership, but wherever we find ourselves we will be a manifestation of a life that is all about that selfless 'agape' kind of love: the perfect antidote to the selfishness that is so prevalent in our world.

When we attempt to do things in our own strength, then the enemy of crippling fear can be the sad result. Liberation from that is a by-product of knowing personally that God has released us from fear, and is living and active and within us as we set about pursuing our calling. Many people today shy away from all forms of religion, often because they have been hurt by people representing that religion in a way that hasn't borne witness to a loving God, whose will is to give them the freedom that comes through dependence on him. The word 'faith' has as much to do with trust as it does in belief. It is far more than just assenting to a set of propositions; it is about being a living witness to those propositions in a way that allows others to believe in their truth. So, for some people who have suffered and have caused others to suffer, existence becomes a prison without hope. The door is open but those imprisoned don't realise it. It was only when I started to work in prisons that it began slowly to dawn on me that my work was not just about helping individuals make a transition into crime-free living, important though that was. It was about releasing individuals from the prison of fear that got them there in the first place. This is grace: simply an undeserved gift of God available to all those who seek it.

All we have is each other now. So we have to set out on our *Disciple's Journey* to reconnect ourselves with the people we were born to be, and to be free of fear. The true, living God can release us from unhealthy fear. It is only in relationship with God that we begin to realize the limitations of what we can achieve in our own strength. It is only in relationship with God that we begin to understand how to relate to others. It is only, as disciples, with others that we can fulfil the body of Christ. Those who go it alone soon get burnt out in one way or another. In human terms, when we are born, we are entirely dependent upon our mothers. They provide all the essentials needed for survival and growth. We are nurtured to break that dependence so that we can stand on our own two feet and find our way in the world. We become independent and self-sufficient in control of our lives. And that is where most people stay: independent and proud of it. But as we have discovered there is another stage: interdependence. And we are not only interdependent of each other we are also interdependent with our environment, together the essence of creation. While this is not a book about political systems, we can see how they often fail at a level of simple humanity. The politicians to whom we have sub-contracted so much responsibility are just a reflection of us. Like people in other walks of life, they are driven by a variety of motives. For some it is the need to be re-elected or the need for affirmation or the desire to create a legacy. Some are motivated by great ideals, some truly want to serve but all have the same shortcomings as us and will fail too.

So if we want to be part of the change that the world is aching for, we need to find our own path. As we do so our own God-given purpose will unfold, allowing us to deploy our own unique gifts in our own time. Beneficial change can begin to emerge. We can then bring something of that 'agape' love in lives of service others in the name of Christ, not through any sense of duty but as the fruit of the love we have received: a simple act of paying forward. We can then return to a world that truly values humanity, a world where we meet our emotional needs not through the consumption of material goods, but through human relationships. A world where we measure our progress not through how much stuff we produce, but through our quality of life. In the UK we are only just beginning to grasp the concept of well-being as a measure of quality of life. We boast of the National Health Service yet politicians always seek greater 'value for money', and we end up with the aberration of the Mid Staffs NHS Trust. Money is the driving factor. We have a world where in order to place a value on human beings we try to measure too much in money terms instead of using money for what it is – a means of exchange. What is beginning to emerge from some contemporary philanthropists is a sense that money has value because it can make human lives better, rather than being an end in itself. It was a lesson that the Victorians learned and acted upon, laying the foundations for much of the welfare state that we now take for granted. We should not forget that many of the valiant social reformers were motivated by the 'agape love' in the Christian gospel. We are at a similarly pivotal point in history so maybe it is a good time for a history lesson.

18

Reclaiming the Lost —
Tackling Social Exclusion

*If this were the first time that this wail of hopeless misery
had sounded on our ears the matter would have been
less serious. It is because we have heard it so often that
the case is so desperate. The exceeding bitter cry of the
disinherited has become to be as familiar in the ears of
men as the dull roar of the streets or as the moaning of
the wind through the trees. And so it rises unceasing,
year in and year out, and we are too busy or too idle, too
indifferent or too selfish, to spare it a thought. Only now
and then, on rare occasions, when some clear voice is
heard giving more articulate utterance to the miseries of
the miserable men, do we pause in the regular routine of
our daily duties, and shudder as we realise for one brief
moment what life means to the inmates of the Slums. But
one of the grimmest social problems of our time should be
sternly faced, not with a view to the generation of profitless
emotion, but with a view to its solution.*

*Is it not time? There is, it is true, an audacity in the
mere suggestion that the problem is not insoluble that is
enough to take away the breath. But can nothing be done?
If, after full and exhaustive consideration, we come to the
deliberate conclusion that nothing can be done, and that
it is the inevitable and inexorable destiny of thousands*

of Englishmen to be brutalised into worse than beasts by the condition of their environment, so be it. But if, on the contrary, we are unable to believe that this "awful slough," which engulfs the manhood and womanhood of generation after generation is incapable of removal; and if the heart and intellect of mankind alike revolt against the fatalism of despair, then, indeed, it is time, and high time, that the question were faced in no mere dilettante spirit, but with a resolute determination to make an end of the crying scandal of our age.

What a satire it is upon our Christianity and our civilisation that the existence of these colonies of heathens and savages in the heart of our capital should attract so little attention! It is no better than a ghastly mockery – theologians might use a stronger word – to call by the name of One who came to seek and to save that which was lost those churches which in the midst of lost multitudes either sleep in apathy or display a fitful interest in a chasuble. Why all this apparatus of temples and meeting-houses to save men from perdition in a world which is to come, while never a helping hand is stretched out to save them from the inferno of their present life? Is it not time that, forgetting for a moment their wranglings about the infinitely little or infinitely obscure, they should concentrate all their energies on a united effort to break this terrible perpetuity of perdition, and to rescue some at least of those for whom they profess to believe their Founder came to die?

Before venturing to define the remedy, I begin by describing the malady. But even when presenting the dreary picture of our social ills, and describing the difficulties which confront us, I speak not in despondency but in hope. "I know in whom I have believed." I know, therefore do I speak. Darker England is but a fractional part of "Greater England." There is wealth enough abundantly to minister to its social regeneration so far as wealth can, if there be but heart enough to set about the work in earnest. And I hope and believe that the heart will not be lacking when once the problem is manfully faced, and the method of its solution plainly pointed out.

This Submerged Tenth — is it, then, beyond the reach of the nine-tenths in the midst of whom they live, and around whose homes they rot and die? No doubt, in every large mass of human beings there will be some incurably diseased in morals and in body, some for whom nothing can be done, some of whom even the optimist must despair, and for whom he can prescribe nothing but the beneficently stern restraints of an asylum or a gaol.

But is not one in ten a proportion scandalously high? The Israelites of old set apart one tribe in twelve to minister to the Lord in the service of the Temple; but must we doom one in ten of "God's Englishmen" to the service of the great Twin Devils — Destitution and Despair?

Cut through the Victorian language and the words of William Booth written in the 1860s could have been written about our society today. While this set the scene for the founding of the Salvation Army, to this day a force for good in our world, we have still failed to eliminate the poverty of both survival and spirit that exists within our most disenfranchised communities. For too long we have accepted that there will always be an underclass. For generations we have buried it beneath a system of benefits that provided just enough to keep them suppressed. As long as the 10% of those that make up this underclass don't bubble through this and affect the 90%, life can continue as normal. But whether you take objection to this on moral grounds or wake up and smell the coffee of our current reality this is not sustainable. For too long we have been prepared to pay the enormous cost of living with what we had long ago deemed as unacceptable.

2012 was the 200th anniversary of the birth of Charles Dickens, who brought Victorian Britain to a greater understanding of the underclass of his day. On the back of his writing rose a new age of welfare, philanthropy and Christian revival. I would suggest that we could be on the verge of a similar revival today and the *Disciple's Journey* is designed to contribute to this. So what do we do? The Coalition Government has made benefits reform a central pillar of policy. But a rationalisation of benefits must walk hand in hand with a radical attempt to transform the circumstances in which this underclass lives. Neither left or right has been able to transform the lives of those on the margins, but this is where the focus should be. If we view people as beings of potential, then that potential is there in everyone. Through my experience I have witnessed this potential and have great faith in it. Because of the tough reality they have faced, those who have struggled with life have a gift for those who have not. But we need to believe in this collectively and create the means of drawing it out, because it's from the margins of society that social transformation can be achieved.

It has long been recognised that wise leadership of change requires that who are to be its agents should be willing to live among and build on what is good in communities. Those who may benefit should be engaged in the process in order for progress to happen. They need to 'own' the change if it is to be real and lasting.

Yet again, it all starts with relationship. Jesus called twelve disciples and built a deep relationship with them which was to enable them to become all that the Father wanted them to be – and they created a change so profound that it still resonates today. Twelve men – eleven of whom stayed the course. So we have been shown what such a small number of individuals coming together in deep relationship with Jesus and each other can achieve today. What if churches and their leaders simply became facilitators of these groups so that they could step into the world and make an impact in whatever area they felt compelled to be? What a cascade of grace they would unleash.

So what is the contribution of the Disciple? It can be big or small: maybe setting up a charity to meet a particular need or building relationships where you live or work or study. Get to know people, listen to their needs, build them up so that they too can find something within themselves to serve others, let them feel valued. We are relational beings who discover ourselves in relationship with others. In the past we expressed this within our communities through church and pub, both of which created networks of neighbourliness, the means of bringing us together while allowing us to moderate our behaviour for the greater good of others. I recently stayed with an American friend who lives in a suburb of North London. He was reflecting on the fact that it was a safe place to live because the sense of community was so strong. I asked him, which came first: community or safety? *Community*, he replied, *People talk to each other and know each other*. And this is the basis of feeling safe, because by communicating we seek to understand each other and thereby reduce the fear that pervades those places where people hide behind locked doors and in gated communities, demanding higher levels of safety from the police. The root of fear is simple ignorance. *There happens to be a big police station just down the road*, my friend said, *but we don't really need it, because the levels of crime are so low.* Strong communities communicate and understand the power of human connectivity, which generates a spirit of generosity and service. And we all crave it.

Keep on loving each other as brothers. Do not forget to entertain strangers, for by doing so some people have entertained angels without knowing it. Remember those in prison as if you were their fellow prisoners, and those who are ill-treated as if you yourselves were suffering.

Hebrews 13:1–2, NIV

It is through conversation that we explore our own sense of being in relationship to others. In our pursuit of individualism we have abandoned many of the structures that provided the means for communities to come together and provide the glue to hold us together. We have retreated behind closed doors to a life of television and ready meals where, even within families, there are rare opportunities to commune. There should be opportunities at home and in communities to bring individuals together to learn from each other and allow the passage of wisdom to pass down the generations, building confidence through generating debate. Young people stretch their learning as they have the opportunity of testing newfound knowledge and opinion within a safe environment. It is, again, an opportunity to unlock purpose as we test our own preferences within a loving and supportive environment. So many young people now arrive in their first employment without the interactive skills needed in order to be effective. The innate desire for community continues to exist, but in the rather sterile setting of the internet where we receive status by the number of online 'friends' we have.

As Christians we should understand the power of community better than anyone. The 'church' is not a building, much as we still like to invest in them. We are foremost a community of people who are able to individually and collectively express the love that underpins our faith. It is in our relationship with God that we understand the transformational power of love, and it is through our deeds that we can express this in a way that illuminates a dark world. Allowing the light of Christ to shine in and through us, we draw others in and in doing so provide beacons of hope.

> What we have to be is what we are
> *Thomas Merton*

To complete my *Disciple's Journey* I have developed a vision that draws on the overlapping areas of my experience thus far, and I hope that this book may be an inspiration to the reader to become involved in some way or, by bringing together groups of like-minded people, create an even greater impact. Christians hold much of the social fabric of this country together as it is, and the country would notice if we all downed tools. So many voluntary organisations, whether overtly Christian or not, are reflections of people giving tangible expression to their faith. Equally, there are the individual acts of kindness like the man who quietly paid for the supermarket shop for a family who could not make ends meet; or the teams who cook meals for the newly bereaved, or those who just pick up a piece of litter in the street – simple acts of kindness that are an expression of love for others around us. I don't want any of that to stop, but I am inviting the reader to reflect on whether through simple acts of kindness they may be avoiding the big one, the real reason why they are here. Neither is mutually exclusive, but I have a sense that we are being called to make a big impact in the world in a way that the world will notice, and in so doing begin the process of creating the kingdom here on earth today. Each reader will have his or her own 'thing' so I apologise if yours doesn't appear below. What does appear is simply the fruit of my own journey.

So where better to start than where this book began, in prisons. The UK prison system remains a scar on our civilisation. We continue to lock up a larger proportion of our population than any country in Europe. Only the USA is more vengeful to its criminals. Politicians see the prison system as some macho totem, where being seen to be tough is essential to political survival. Those that weaken are soon reminded of their responsibility to be tough – through the editorial of the *Daily Mail*. The Coalition government showed all the early signs of changing this and there was hope that they would start implementing policy that was genuinely going to tackle the Cinderella of rehabilitation, indeed they even talked of the 'rehabilitation revolution'. Having been inspired by Jonathan Aitken to go into prisons, I ended up in 2008 being a member of a group chaired by him that published the report *Locked Up Potential* published by the Centre of Social Justice, a think tank set up by Iain Duncan Smith. This report did much to inspire the rehabilitation revolution, and some of its recommendations, especially around mentoring, are beginning to see the light of day. Since I started taking an interest in prisons in 2001, I have come across so many initiatives, which had the capacity to transform lives, now neglected and lying in the gutter, often just wanting a little extra investment. We continue to set up those in prison to fail, almost, as a cynic might suggest, as though a whole industry depended upon it. Solutions lie in really understanding the nature of the average prisoner.

In Tom's story at the beginning of the book I attempted to offer some insight into the typical back story of a prolific offender. But there is another factor, most notably in our inner cities. The word 'sacrifice' was a quality that emerges at a key stage in the *Disciple's Journey*. Despite the fact that the word is not particularly fashionable in our individualistic society, we see evidence of it everywhere – obviously in the lives that are laid down in Afghanistan and Iraq, but less obviously the same concept appears in the lives of young criminals, particularly in the gang culture. The individual is subsumed into the greater cause of the gang. Individuality is sacrificed to achieve a sense of belonging. Indeed we condemn them for doing what is as natural to them as menstruation is to women. We fear them, demonise them, criminalise them and write them off before their lives have really started. Combine these natural instincts with poor parenting, lack of male role models, bullying, abuse, drugs and an educational system that is obsessed with academic performance, you have a combination of factors which lead inevitably to high levels of crime by young men.

The top down approach to social policy can miss the true nature of the problem and serves to further isolate communities which already feel marginalised from mainstream society. A long-term approach to gangs will require the empowerment of affected communities: we must work with them rather than continuing to do things to them.
(Dying to Belong Report, Centre for Social Justice, 2009)

The rise in gangs is partly driven by a hard wired need of young men particularly, to belong to something greater than themselves with a purpose beyond themselves. They are seeking a rite of passage, still used in many tribal traditions, where the men of the community take the young man away from the nurturing feminised environment and put them through some sort of initiation that marks their passage from childhood to manhood.

Let us unpack that a bit. There is strong evidence now that the roots of behaviour start in the womb. As a species we are unusual in that our brain is only 50% developed at birth. The right brain, where our emotional and creative intelligences reside, is less well formed at birth. Its development is determined by the nurturing the baby receives by the birth mother. The first eighteen months are vital. Without this nurture the baby is immediately handicapped in its development. The next twelve years are determined by the boy's relationship with his father, who he will see as a role model, beginning to copy the same behavioural traits. Many young men who end up in the criminal justice system grow up without fathers. This void not only creates a lack of a male role model, it places huge pressure, both emotional and financial, onto the mother. Her nurturing role evaporates in the relentlessness of stress. There is another more sinister consequence as we saw in Tom's story, not widespread, but significant in those that end up in the criminal justice system and swept under the carpet by a society that would rather deny its existence: abuse, often sexual abuse at a young age. There is an inevitable cycle to the whole process. Young women brought up in loveless families yearn for unconditional love. They also often crave independence from their families. The solution to both is a baby, which at once provides the unconditional love and qualifies the mother for social housing. The father, his orgasmic contribution quickly forgotten, is probably unaware of the existence of his child. Faced with the loneliness of bringing up an infant with all its human needs, the mother seeks the companionship and support that is only natural. Unfortunately this results in a series of relationships more driven by lust than love. As the child grows up, a series of 'uncles' come and go – literally. Sadly, the child is often the recipient of the emotional fallout of this.

So on the verge of adulthood the young man has neither been nurtured by his mother nor had the role model of a father to copy. The only community he can find to offer him a rite of passage into adulthood are those other young men who have similarly lacked the foundations for responsible living. Hence the popularity of gangs. There is an urgent need to create alternative 'gangs' motivated to provide the needs of the nascent young man. One of the objectives of *Believe* was to create a supportive environment within which young men can find these male role models through mentoring and a community that allows them to make sense of their lives. The *Believe* strapline was *Respect Relationship Responsibility*. It remains true today, since the key to successful rehabilitation lies in respecting the circumstances of life that brought the individual to this point, then offering a relationship through mentoring that encourages personal responsibility. Building relationships is key since it is only through this that we can understand the individual and, even more importantly, the individual can start to understand themselves and begin to work out who they are and what they want to do with their lives. Only then can they accept responsibility for themselves.

The ability to accept responsibility is a measure of the character and maturity that leadership based on the example of Christ can offer. Imagine churches around the country offering this. With this change in behaviour and attitude, the practical needs of the individual can also be addressed, so that when the individual walks out through the prison gate the chances of re-offending are significantly reduced.

We talk about *the golden hour* in medical terms: that hour that can make the difference between life and death if you can get medical treatment. I observed and coined the phrase *golden day* for those leaving prison. The reality is that for many prisoners, and all those serving sentences of less than twelve months, there is little preparation or support for those making this emotionally and practically challenging transition, although the government is now seeking to address this by contracting the problem out to the private and voluntary sectors on a payment by results basis. While this seems to be a positive step and something that I have been campaigning for, the reality is that it is driven by money rather than relationship, and, as we have seen with other public sector activities that have been privatised, the risk is that companies driven by the profit motive will only handle the easy cases.

So the ex-offender walks out of the prison gate with £46 in his back pocket, that must last until his benefits kick in some six weeks later! Typically the £46 doesn't last the day, since the first port of call is the pub to fully partake of the alcohol previously unavailable to them. In Bristol, conveniently, there is a pub just beyond the prison gate! While drugs are still sadly very available within prison, for those addicted there will be a pressing need to top up from one of the local dealers who know the score. So the prospects don't look great and when the money runs out, survival instincts kick in and it is back to what they know best: theft.

Transition is an opportunity for transformation or failure. The stubborn re-offending figures suggest the latter. Many will commit greater crimes just to get back into the relative 'security' of the prison. *Believe* used mentoring as a framework of support during transition. It was based on the four pillars of motivation, stability, opportunity and support. An early observation during my time in prison was the sense of resignation many had to their fate. Many prisoners' lives had been a litany of failure since they were born, so why should it be any different now. They had been sent down in every sense. Before any rehabilitation was possible, the inner motivation to change needs to be unlocked. This was at the heart of the name *Believe*. Believing in another is a self-fulfilling transaction, which allows that person to begin to believe in themselves, believe in the possibility of going straight and building the foundation of self-esteem.

Furthermore we need to believe in something greater than ourselves in order to fully find ourselves. One of the major factors in offending behaviour is, in a literal sense, carelessness. Many in prison don't believe they have any stake in society, nor that society has any care for their lives, so why should they care?

The start point for those we worked with was to help them find something good within themselves, something upon which they could rebuild their lives and begin to think how they could make a difference. Everyone has something: a gift a talent. It is just a question of finding it. In my experience this releases motivation, essential to thinking that the effort to change your life is worthwhile. The experience of so many offenders, and indeed others on the margins of society, is of others doing things for them. The motivation is driven externally, often with a carrot and stick approach. Yet motivation, to be sustainable has to come from within. As Christians we know this, although we don't necessarily live it. We use the same framework as the *Disciple's Journey* to help individual offenders, while they are still in prison, to discover their inner motivation through finding something good within themselves. This lays a foundation for their future. Some decided the time had come to change. What is interesting about prolific offenders is that at some point, usually in their late twenties, a switch is flicked inside which creates a strong desire to reform. Having spoken to many, it seems that they suddenly wake up to the life that they are missing out on. Their peers and siblings are settling down with jobs and families. During one of the exercises we completed during the programme *Believe* ran in prison, participants were invited to articulate a vision for their future. Almost without exception the vision was *I just want to be normal*. When asked what this meant to them, the response usually revolved around a job, a wife and kids and a mortgage! So some arrived at this point of motivation and found the courage to seek help.

The second stage is to achieve a framework of stability. This requires an honest assessment of the factors that led to prison and the barriers to successful rehabilitation. The National Offender Management Service (NOMS), an unwieldy and failed attempt to amalgamate Prison and Probation Services, identified seven pathways to underpin the rehabilitation journey, providing a framework of stability: accommodation and support; education; training and employment; health, drugs and alcohol; finance; children and families; and attitudes thinking and behaviour. The stability is only achieved when these become personalised for the individual they apply to. The key to those being released is having stable accommodation to move into, the foundation of survival. But it has to be fully supported accommodation – many local hostels used as 'first homes' for ex-offenders are rife with drugs, so any attempt to come off them stands no chance from the outset, and the cycle of crime continues.

With motivation and stability comes the possibility of opportunity. When we understand who we are and what our goals are, we begin to seek the means of achieving them. There is no shortage of opportunities for ex-offenders. I have already described how surprised business leaders are at the talent that exists within our prisons, when they are motivated to having a look. Full rehabilitation can only be achieved when all seven pathways have been integrated and addressed. The goal is long-term, fulfilling employment, which provides the stable platform for relationships, family, financial security and self-esteem – keys to well-being.

The final pillar is support. Unsurprisingly, in the context of this book, this is best delivered through mentoring. For those who may never had a trusted relationship in their lives, the power of a mentor walking alongside them as they face the many challenges of turning their lives around is priceless. In *Believe* we used ex-offenders as mentors since only they can truly step into the shoes of the traveller about to embark upon the journey they have already completed. They know what it feels like to be constantly rejected by those whose attitudes are crucial to success. The mentor is able to view the individual's transition holistically, understanding that their needs are manifold and complex. As I discovered, there is no point in helping someone find a job if their basic survival and safety needs (particularly accommodation) are not met – one of the reasons why I took the work developed by *Believe* to a large Bristol homelessness charity. The spirit of *Believe* has been subsumed into a new charity – Bristol Foundation Housing. This charity is pioneering an integrated resettlement pathway, creating a safe environment in which the needs of the individual can be addressed, planned for and supported.

My vision is that Christians will *be* the change in our prison system. Today there are 88,000 individuals in prison. A tiny percentage is too dangerous to be released, although we should all believe in the power of redemption even for these. I often wonder if there are 88,000 Christians out there who would be prepared to take just one offender under their wing and offer the relationship which might transform their lives. Just imagine individual churches adopting their local prison and providing those four pillars of rehabilitation. Imagine them going even further and reaching into the most disenfranchised parts of our society, working with those young people on the edge of crime, offering a way out. So many churches have become separated from the communities they inhabit, either dying for lack of support or becoming exclusive to their members in a way that makes them inaccessible. Separation leads to ignorance, which leads to fear, which leads to hatred, which leads to conflict.

How often have I seen good work unravelled by judgmental treatment – including, it has to be said, from some who would call themselves Christians. This is where the theory of discipleship is really tested. Are you prepared to welcome an ex-offender into your church? Would you even be prepared to invite one into your home? It is too easy to fall back on fear as a justification for rejecting the very people that Christ would have been the first to embrace. How can we expect the secular world to forgive if we, as Christians, are unable to be expressions of that forgiveness?

If we truly reached out and loved the unlovely as Christ did, what transformation we could bring. 88,000 souls. It doesn't seem a lot. Yet a whole industry depends upon them. It is worth approximately £12 billion per year. Look at the jobs it supports: police officers, solicitors, barristers, judges, prison and probation officers, social workers, charity workers. Is it really surprising that we don't really want to tackle it? But now is a time to be radical. I know that there are some who aspire to set up prisons on Christian lines. I share that aspiration. The Kainos Project has had some success in setting up wings in some prisons. So there is a blank canvas of opportunity within our criminal justice system for Christians to demonstrate their relevance. There are many other ways for individuals to become involved, and I leave it to those who have been called into this tough area to articulate them.

There are those who will be saying already, 'This is not my thing, or 'This is too big. How can I make a difference?' or 'I'm not a leader'. I can only offer my experience, but the point is that leadership starts within each of us, and, as has been said can be expressed in big and small ways. Mother Theresa put it this way:

'The biggest disease today is not tuberculosis or leprosy, but rather the feeling of being unwanted. The most terrible poverty is loneliness and the feeling of being unloved.'

So let me offer an alternative, which may be equally powerful in its impact, and is accessible to everyone. Between physical prison and the prison of ourselves, lies another prison which has been growing inexorably in our increasingly fragmented society. It is the prison of loneliness. One in six Britons now lives alone, isolated from the relationship through which humanity flourishes. Isolation breeds ignorance, which as we have seen breeds fear, thus creating further isolation. Churches have ceased to be the physical space in heart of the community, where most people came together in relationship to worship. Churches are increasingly seen as exclusive. So maybe the church could express itself by encouraging its members to step into the community to seek out and get alongside the lonely; not to proseltyse or evangelise, simply to offer friendship: to be an expression of compassion and kindness. Friendship and camaraderie are crucial to morale; and anyone can provide them.

The woodsmoke rose gently from the log fire heating the blackened kettle outside a newly rebuilt barn just outside Salisbury. Tea was brewed to accompany the fresh farmhouse fruit cake baked by our hosts at Riverbourne Farm. The first Pathfinder Experience commissioned by Help for Heroes was underway. I have been working with them to design a transitional reintegration process for recently 'retired' wounded, injured and sick veterans supported by a new mentoring programme. Creating a safe environment, cut off from the busyness of life, is one of the keys to success, so we spend a day on the farm with the opportunity both of working in teams again and having the time for reflection. Another key ingredient is service to the community. Thus we are able to combine all elements in rebuilding a barn that will house the animals that provide therapeutic support for young people with special needs.

Those participating were all ex-soldiers suffering from either the wounds acquired in combat in Afghanistan, or injuries acquired during service or the Post Traumatic Stress Disorder (PTSD) that often accompanies both. On first meeting them there was a natural anxiety about participating in the programme, but this was soon put to one side as they refreshed the bonds that exist between servicemen. The challenges that many of them face are not dissimilar from those coming out of prison although, of course, the context is entirely different. The vast majority are young men moving from a highly institutionalised environment where their basic needs are met and where there is somebody else managing most aspects of their day to day lives. The challenge is managing their transition to independent living with all that entails: perfect freedom to live their lives as they choose, balanced by the responsibility that goes with it. As someone who has made that transition I know how difficult it can be. It is not just the weight of responsibility but all the practical things that needed to be addressed from finding somewhere to live to getting a job. I was very grateful to be introduced to Gene Gitelson, a distinguished Vietnam War veteran who had set up a similar programme thirty years ago. It is just another of those things that happens on the *Disciple's Journey*, when the right person just shows up at the right time. He helped me to understand the real needs of combat veterans.

It is very easy for individuals to become isolated and lonely very quickly and feel forgotten about. This creates uncertainty and fear for the future. The key to breaking out of this is to discover a new vision for their lives when they are in transition; without it they are lost. They are leaving a highly institutionalized culture so the civilian world needs to reach into the military to start the preparation as soon as possible, stressing the importance of translating skills and language to maximise their chances of getting the right job for them. They need to believe that they still have value to society. A rite of passage back into 'civvie street' is essential in a way that honours their service. Wounded servicemen do not want to be treated as victims; they are incredible people with great leadership skills that need to be drawn out and translated. Mentoring is critical in providing an anchor of trust and a single point of contact through the challenges of transition. An integrated and holistic approach is essential to underpin the transition process, run in a collaborative environment devoid of silos and service rivalries.

The thing that strikes you most when you meet these young people is their humility. Whatever their condition, they are very clear that they don't want to be treated as victims. One, Jonny, a young Marine who stood on an IED in Afghanistan, had lost his right arm and his left leg. His left arm had been rebuilt, leaving him with a hand that had four stubs for fingers. The only working digit he had on his body was his left thumb. He had been a great sportsman and a top class rugby player. Instead of wallowing in the misery of not being able to play his favourite sports again, he took up one that he hadn't tried: golf, and within nine months was playing off a 26 handicap. But the most remarkable thing was his description of his rehabilitation at Headley Court. He told the group that as he lay in his bed waiting for the prosthetics that would restore some degree of normality to his life, he looked across at those in the other beds in his ward. *I thought, how lucky I am that I have only lost two limbs. Some of these guys have to face the rest of their lives having lost three.* No self pity, no sense of entitlement. Just the grace to accept that he was more fortunate than others.

What a lesson to us all. Furthermore, soldiers deal with some of these tough realities through a wonderful black humour. Andy has been a passionate Liverpool supporter all his life. Such is his commitment to his club that he had the opening line from their anthem 'You'll never walk alone' tattooed down his leg. It was the leg that was amputated below the knee after stepping on an IED. He proudly shows off his tattoo which now says 'You'll never walk' and lives his life in contradiction to that statement, running marathons and completing an array of physical challenges!

The key to all the transit on programmes I create is to quickly get participants into a safe place where they can be authentic, telling their story, often for the first time beginning the process of releasing themselves from the past. As we have seen in the *Disciple's Journey* it is the inability to face up to what has happened and slowly release ourselves from it that prevents us opening up a new future. So this is a key step, and for many it is the first time that they have been able to tell their story. The reality is that when you are on operations, whatever happens, the show has to go on. I remember talking to a young 21-year old who had witnessed his three best friends being blown up in Afghanistan. When he returned from this fateful patrol, his sergeant told him to clean up, get some food and get his head down. They were out on patrol again in six hours time. This is how it is and how it has to be. There is no time to dwell. But at some time there has to be a release from this. The Pathfinder programme is designed to provide this safe space with kindred spirits in a highly trusted environment.

It is hard to imagine, as you read this lying in your bed or sitting in the comfort of your favourite armchair, the challenge these young people face. One moment they are part of a high perfoming team, working with the best mates they will ever have, for whom the fear of death is trumped by the love they have for each other, at the peak of their physical fitness, with the security of a career ahead of them, all their survival needs catered for, confident and optimistic. In the next moment, with the next step, all of this is ripped away from them. Just imagine what that is like. Quite apart from their physical injuries, their sense of identity, their self-esteem, their future seems to have been blown away in that one step. By the time they reach us they have been through clinical treatment, rehabilitation and resettlement and are facing up to life without all that they had taken for granted (a great reminder to us all to be constantly grateful for what we have, while we still have it). So the first task, beyond coming to terms with the past, is to help each one of them answer the question 'Who am I?'

It is then possible to start planning for the future, not just the practical needs but the aspirational ones too. One soldier I was talking to told me that his biggest dread was ending up in a job he hated. When you have had the privilege of serving and working in closely knit teams working together for a cause greater than the individual, the prospect of ending up stacking supermarket shelves or working as a security guard is frightening. It might fulfil the statistician's need to fill the 'Employed' box on their resettlement plan, but it will quickly destroy the soul of the poor individual. So it is important to help them find a new vision for their lives and start putting this into a plan. It is hard and needs encouragement and accountability. Hence, again, the need for a mentor.

When they realised that their mentors were ex-servicemen too they relaxed in the knowledge that common language and experience would make relationship building easy. And relationship is the key to the programme, which is designed to bring strangers to a high level of rapport, thus creating a deep level of trust. A trusted, consistent relationship allows real conversations to take place, so that real need can be expressed. The programme is based largely on experiential learning. The mentors get to understand what mentoring is and have a chance to experience what it is like to be mentored and to mentor. Authenticity again is the key, since we can only mentor effectively if we are being real.

On the final evening a barbecue is combined with singing and story telling as the bonds between all those participating deepens. It is an unforgettable experience. By the end everyone talked about transformation and a renewed energy for life fired up by an inner motivation based on new purpose and hope. It won't be easy for them. For those with PTSD it is the silent disease since it is not apparent on the outside, unlike a lost limb. Those who suffer from it struggle alone for years to find work and acceptance. Pathfinder is designed to take the loneliness out of the struggle as they look forward to a new future.

I have a clear vision for some of these ex-servicemen. The taxpayer has already made a significant investment in recruiting, training and maintaining our Armed Services. As a result of recent conflict thousands are leaving with mental and physical injury, unable to continue a career they loved. Our ex-servicemen are a unique resource, apparently lost to the nation. Yet they provide an untapped capability, which can provide the street cred, respect, leadership, skills and camaraderie to provide outstanding role models, trainers and mentors. The interesting thing about people who have a service background is that when you put them together they just get on with whatever needs to be done.

The vision for *Serve On* is to create a new national mentoring service. As a social enterprise it will build a sustainable platform to transform lives. Using the untapped leadership skills and unique experience of ex-servicemen as mentors, *Serve On* will release a spirit of responsibility and leadership among our young and most marginalised citizens, including the long-term unemployed, ex-offenders and gangs, empowering them to be active citizens and a force for good within their communities. During times of austerity a trusted human relationship can fill the gap left by an expensive professional. Why spend millions of public money on vouchers for parenting classes when you could mobilise the millions of older women to become mentors to young and single mothers? Both would benefit hugely. The young mum receives wisdom and experience; the older woman finds new purpose to her life at a stage when she feels discarded. There is no aspect of human life that would not benefit from a mentor. But we need to embark on a journey from selfishness towards the common good. It is the balance I have described before between confidence – establishing our gift to the world, and, as we shall see, sacrifice – to make whole by using our gift for the common good. In a world that has abandoned the spiritual in pursuit of the markets, we have overlooked the needs of the civil society within which we live, and – more importantly – how we can become active citizens within it.

There are some 24,000 men and women who leave the armed services in the UK every year. There are 1.2 million young people below the age of 25 who are unemployed, up to 80% levels of re-offending for young offenders, and a gang culture that is destroying some of our most deprived communities. All currently lack role models and the personal leadership which encourages responsibility. *Serve On* is designed to create an army of mentors resulting in the positive transformation of individuals in service of a better society.

Serve On will retrain ex-servicemen as transformational mentors, using an innovative mentoring training methodology similar to that used in the *Disciple's Journey*. Working in teams, the ex-servicemen will then lead projects initiated by young people, which will make a difference to their community here or overseas while helping them to discover something in themselves which will lead to employment or entrepreneurship. They will in turn inspire others to leadership, creating a cascade of mentors and role models to empower young people to take responsibility for their lives so as to realise their full potential and maximise their chances of finding a rewarding future. It will link young people to the opportunities to find themselves through service to others, thereby changing their lives. Working in teams, each individual will have the opportunity to initiate change in their community and will themselves be given the skills to recruit another team, thus providing a beneficial cascade. An unlimited number of innovative and creative initiatives, working in collaboration with others, will create the on-going expansion and sustainability of *Serve On* as a social enterprise delivering tangible value to a range of stakeholders within society.

Ultimately, *Serve On* seeks to be international. Soldiers have a great track record in disaster relief and post conflict rebuilding. I have a dream of 'recycling' men of war to men of peace rebuilding communities around the world providing the regeneration that will begin to alleviate poverty.

Based on the successful US model, AmeriCorps, *Serve On* has the objective of strengthening communities and developing leaders through direct, team-based national and international community service. It brings together some of themes from my own *Disciple's Journey* and will encompass the work of a number of other projects I am involved in, including the Pathfinder programme I have developed with Help for Heroes, Bristol Foundation Housing the homelessness charity I chair, Bristol Together, founded by another modern day disciple, Paul Harrod, an award winning social enterprise that trains teams of ex-offenders to rebuild residential properties, Urban Pursuit, which provides alternative adventure training based provision for those struggling at school, and Friska, a great new healthy fast food business. All of these reflect passions of mine that have developed through hearing the *wail of hopeless misery* as so eloquently described by William Booth, quoted at the beginning of this chapter.

The concept of service to others, altruism if you like, is something that I believe strongly is at the heart of leadership and individual well-being. There is now more scientific evidence for this through the work of Prof David Sloan Wilson. Wilson's latest book is *The Neighborhood Project: Using Evolution to Improve My City, One Block at a Time*. He argues that *selfishness beats altruism within groups. Altruistic groups beat selfish groups. Everything else is commentary.* Thus within a group if everyone is motivated by selfish ends and is trying to pursue their own agenda, the group and its objectives will fail. Altruism is trumped by individual self-interest every time. However, an altruistic group will be more successful in achieving its objectives than a selfish group. It is this concept that, rolled out, could genuinely make a difference to our most disadvantaged communities and the individuals who live in them. *Serve On* aims to empower teams (groups) to subsume their individual self-interest in creating something that is altruistic in its ends to the communities they live in, and by so doing actually receive the gift of self-knowledge, the foundation for their future lives.

The *Disciple's Journey* is an inspiration to Christians to serve on too. True leadership is in service to the common good and releases the best in everyone. Imagine if 98% of Christians were envisioned and equipped to transform social justice across the world. Imagine making Christ relevant in a world that, despite its financial and intellectual wealth, still witnesses human suffering through war, hunger, poverty and disease every day. Imagine yourself being a leader in this world.

This is no time to 'think small' concerning your potential to be a catalyst for beneficial change. I have already told the story of one disciple who took up the challenge of faith. Here is another, which I hope gives an illustration of how the vision might unfold. Seb was sent to a Christian school. As a pupil he did everything to resist and reject the Christian message that underpinned the teaching. Like a contemporary Saul of Tarsus he did all he could to persuade others that it was rubbish. Then he had his Damascene moment. He came to faith as he left school and found a heart for marginalised young people. As a rebel himself, he understood them. When I met him he was searching. At the time, I was mentoring a youth leader at a church in Bath who was trying to find a new way of engaging the young people on the local 'sink' estate. I introduced him to Seb. I had been encouraging him to move away from the model whereby well meaning churches try to do stuff for young people without really asking them first. As I have written before, starting where individuals are, rather than where you want them to be, is so important when working with young people. Seb joined the youth team and began to search out the natural leaders in the group of young people. Young people love to be trusted, and when you do they can achieve anything. The Disney Institute polled a group of 8 – 15 year olds about what the biggest obstacle to making a difference in your community was. The most common answer by far was the fact that adults didn't take them seriously. He created an environment within which strong relationships of trust were established. He then encouraged them to come up with the ideas and take a lead, so that they too could recruit teams of young people that could make a difference to their community, creating the cascade of leadership I have mentioned before. Having unleashed this leadership, the group are now planning a trip to Malawi to work on a number of projects there which will empower young people there to take responsibility for their lives. Imagine churches engaging with young people in their parishes in this way. Imagine the impact.

It is time to get on the right side of history. So the church needs new leadership and it has it. Within two days a new Pope and a new Archbishop of Canterbury were enthroned. Both have signalled a passion for social justice, a passion I hope shines out of this book. In his first sermon Pope Francis says this, "Life is a journey. When we stop, things go wrong. We must build a church from living stones, stones anointed by the Holy Spirit. With every movement, let us build". This is the cue to build, not a physical building, but a living church based on social justice, where we begin the task of creating the kingdom. We are like an army given new orders, and as good followers, we must respond and step into step into our individual Disciple's Journey to create the leadership that will transform our world.

It was unusual for me to be alone at home on a Saturday night, so I decided to go and listen to a vicar from the Somerset levels, called Keith Powell, who was setting out a vision which he called 'The Battle for Britain'. I had never met him and he didn't know me. Later we were to compare notes. As he spoke, often in militaristic terms, I felt very drawn to him. I was looking for a sign of confirmation that would give me the opportunity to connect with him afterwards. Meanwhile, as he was speaking, an internal voice was insisting, *Tell the story about the tank*. It didn't make any sense so he ignored it. But it persisted. He was about to finish when the voice screamed from within: *Tell the story about the tank*. So he did. *I don't know why I am telling this story, but maybe it is for someone here. I was talking to a group in a parish on the edge of Salisbury Plain. When I had finished a young boy came up to me and said, "When you were talking I had a picture of an army spread out either side of Salisbury Plain advancing north east away from the south west. In the centre was a leading the army was a tank covered in the blood of Christ."* As he spoke, I realised he was speaking to me. One of my last roles in the Army had been commanding a squadron of tanks. You might say: so what? But this book, which had been lying dormant, was the fruit of that inspiration. And I find myself working with soldiers again for the first time in twenty years … on the edge of Salisbury Plain. Coincidence? Or is this just the way that God calls his disciples to service in the kingdom? Throwing down the gauntlet of life. The disciples took up the challenge when asked to; so what is stopping you? The world is asking....

Be who God meant you to be and you will set the world on fire. *St. Catherine of Siena*

To be or not to be? Only you can answer.

ACKNOWLEDGEMENTS

In acknowledging the life that has gone into creating the story that underpins this book, I have to acknowledge the part played by my wife, Cerys and my four daughters Fionnoula, Mathilda, Georgia and Lily. They have had to make many sacrifices along the way as I have pursued my own Disciple's Journey. It is hardest for those who sit in the wake of the Disciple, since it is not their journey. Yet they bear the brunt of the reality of it. It would not have been possible without them since they have provided the unconditional love and support which have kept me going when every fibre of my being wanted to give up. Cerys particularly has endured the many early starts to work in a hospital to keep our heads above water during those many periods when there was no income and has through her astute management kept us afloat. I must also thank my wider family, especially my mother, who has probably never really understood what I have been up to but have provided support in so many different ways.

It is tough opening your heart to the world and the temptation is to hold it back. As I have written in the book, I realise even more that we only understand life by looking backwards. In identifying the trail that finally inspired me to translate my experiences, diaries and thoughts along the way into this book, there are numerous links who played their part, too long a list to name them individually, but they will all know who they are. The final commission to do so came from the School of Formation at the Diocese of Bath & Wells, to whom I am eternally grateful. It is for the Disciple to discern the path and respond when required.

Since the heart of the book is about mentoring it would be remiss not to mention the many mentors along the way who have all played significant parts. Towering above some great men is Jeremy Gilmer, who caught my initial vision for *Believe* and steadfastly supported me as we brought the dream to reality. His unstinting support at every stage has laid the foundation for this entire story. He kept me going emotionally and financially, at great personal sacrifice. Without him this book would not have been written. It was through him, when all seemed lost, that the opportunity to lead the founding of the Mowgli Foundation came about. From this I was able to explore a completely different perspective of the world. This gave me the opportunity of launching the concept of mentoring into the Arab culture, for which we recently proudly received the Mohammed Bin Rashid award for Best Mentor Network in the Arab world. Through this learning, I have been able to come full circle and create an innovative transitional support programme for service veterans to help them rebuild their lives, in conjunction with Help for Heroes.

Finally, I want to thank the young Indian man who was sitting next to me in the departure lounge of Dubai airport, while I was making a start on the book. He was clearly reading over my shoulder as I was writing. When I got up to catch my plane he said: "That is really inspiring. I hope you are going to write a book." With affirmation like that, how could I not!

I must, of course, conclude by saying that all the views expressed within the book are mine alone and should not be attributed to those who have assisted in its production.

Simon Edwards
Bath
March 2013